ENDORSEMENTS

God wants us to hear His voice for ourselves. Dr. Hakeem Collins has been called by God to make hearing God's voice easy!

SID ROTH
Host, *It's Supernatural!*

As you often hear me say, "God is speaking way more than we're listening." Over the years of equipping thousands of people in the prophetic, I've realized sometimes believers just don't pick up on the way God is speaking or we get too comfortable hearing Him one way. In *101 Prophetic Ways God Speaks*, Hakeem Collins demystifies the way the Holy Spirit communicates with us. Whether you need to make major life decisions or just want to engage with the still small voice of God at a deeper level, *101 Prophetic Ways God Speaks* will give you the pieces of the puzzle you may be missing to see the big picture. Written by a veteran in the modern prophetic movement, I highly recommend this book!

JENNIFER LECLAIRE
Author, *The Making of a Prophet*
Senior Leader, Awakening House of Prayer

Our Heavenly Father desires and has purposed that we all know and hear His voice. He is a Father whose intent is to relate to each of us as His sons and daughters. Dr. Hakeem Collins has written a vital, in-depth message in which he shares and equips regarding the different ways we can hear the voice of God. This book will empower you into a deeper personal relationship with our Father and bring you into a pure anointing to hear and prophesy. You will be equipped on how to understand and grow even when the Lord speaks to you in riddles. I love the integrity and purity of this message along with the practical revelation that it brings. *101 Prophetic Ways God Speaks: Hearing God is Easier Than You Think* is a now message to take you into a deeper journey of discovery of how your Heavenly Father is speaking to empower you in your purpose, calling, destiny and life!

REBECCA GREENWOOD
President and Co-Founder
Christian Harvest International
Strategic Prayer Apostolic Network
Author of *Glory Warfare, Authority to Tread, Defeating Strongholds of the Mind, Let Our Children Go*

Dr. Hakeem Collins' breakthrough book: *101 Prophetic Ways God Speaks* has opened the floodgates of revelation in scriptures to bring to us a myriad of divine communication to humanity. Many are not quite aware that hearing God is easier than we think. This exhaustive manuscript unpacks that purpose. My brother has literally pushed the prophetic to the limits in unlocking, uncapping and uncovering as a prophet the multiplicity of hearing the voice of God and helping all believers to discern and distinguish Him speaking in their everyday life. Oftentimes, we view the voice of God speaking to us in just visions, dreams and inspired utterances.

Dr. Collins has uniquely written with practical, experiential and revelatory insight of scriptures in short, easy-to-read chapters on how you can access divine intelligence and position yourself to hear God's voice for yourself and others. You will be blown away as I was, reading 101 different channels, mediums and methods in this phenomenal book. God in Genesis sets the precedence and foundation by which God would communicate prophetically. Adam declared that he heard the "sound" of the Lord walking in the midst of the garden (Genesis 3:8). This sound is literally translated as the "voice" of the Lord. The sound that Adam heard was God's voice and presence all around him which Dr. Hakeem has eloquently done in *101 Prophetic Ways God Speaks* in helping every reader of this book interpret the sound of the Lord as His voice speaking in their midst. He has set a new precedence of hearing the voice of God. I emphatically endorse this book to all believers who desires to learn the voice of God unlimited.

Dr. Naim Collins
Naim Collins Ministries
The League of the Prophets
Author of *Realms of the Prophetic*
naimcollinsministries.com

When Samuel was a boy, God spoke clearly to him, but he did not realize that it was the Lord until he was instructed by Eli (1 Samuel 3:1-14). In the same way, God is always speaking, but we must learn to recognize His voice. In *101 Prophetic Ways God Speaks*, Hakeem Collins has given us a powerful and practical manual for how to tune in to the many ways that God communicates with His people. Read this book and begin to recognize the voice of God in a greater way!

Jake Kail
Lead Pastor, Threshold Church
Author, *Keys for Deliverance*

Dr. Hakeem Collins has done it again! He has blessed us with another prophetic jewel, filled with revelation, wisdom, knowledge and experience. He is truly a leading prophetic voice for his generation! In *101 Prophetic Ways God Speaks*,

Dr. Collins lets the reader know that hearing the voice of the Lord is much easier than they thought. He lavishly makes use of Scripture to support and validate his many points in reference to God speaking. He challenges us with a statement and a question: God is trying to get your attention. Are you listening?

In this hour, it's both paramount and prudent to know that God still speaks today. He is relational. The Lord longs to express Himself to His people in a myriad of ways. The problem is that some aren't paying attention to Him. Years ago, the Lord told me that He is talking to His people, but they are not listening! He added that they're too busy talking! Collins breaks down this dilemma in this book by providing real-life scenarios that are married to divine revelation. This is done to further your capacity to hear the Lord and act on His instructions.

I love how Hakeem emphasizes the use of the gift of discernment. I agree that it's one of the most neglected gifts in a believer's arsenal. Topics such as seeing God as a Father, being relational and not religious, the "still small voice" and many others will equip the reader with what is required to make the voice of God easier to comprehend! I highly recommend that you add this great work to your literary library. It's a welcome addition to the other books that Dr. Collins has written on the prophetic!

Dr. John Veal
Author of *Supernaturally Prophetic: A Practical Guide for Prophets, Prophetic People,* and *Supernaturally Delivered: A Practical Guide to Deliverance and Spiritual Warfare*
Johnveal.org

101 Prophetic Ways God Speaks by Dr. Hakeem Collins is written by an emerging prophetic voice in his generation that is called of God to teach, equip and activate *all* believers into hearing and recognizing the many languages of God for themselves. When we hear God's voice and respond to what He says, we will step into new dimensions of anointing, blessing, and destiny! Hearing God is not complicated! It is easier than we think. Collins has dedicated his life in assisting people in launching out into deeper realms of the things of the Spirit. He has served under my ministry for several years when I pastored a church in Wilmington, Delaware and I know the fruit of his prophetic ministry. I am so godly proud of what God is doing in his life and ministry and to call him and his twin brother spiritual sons of mine in the faith. This book will help you—the reader to discover *101* creative methods, ways and channels God talks to His children today.

God still speaks! We often think the process of hearing God's voice is more complex than it simply is. We may be straining to hear Him speak in one or two specific ways, when in fact, He is always communicating in unusual ways that we must learn to decipher. As you discover the plethora of different ways God communicates, you can reposition yourself to listen closely to His voice with fresh, revelatory clarity! I recommend this book for *all* believers ready to hear God's voice here and now.

BISHOP GREG M. DAVIS
National Television/Radio Host, *The Word Network* and *Greg Davis Show Live!*
Lead Pastor of Celebration Church of Detroit
www.gregdavisshow.com

Sometimes prophecy can seem hard to grasp and very subjective. However, in this book, seasoned prophet, Dr. Hakeem Collins gives you powerful, yet bite-sized strategies for accessing the *101 Prophetic Ways God Speaks.* You will truly love how he condenses truth in each chapter so you can digest the prophetic systematically and understand the language of God. If you have ever wondered how to get started with hearing the voice of God and drawing closer to His heart, look no further, as this book is a practical approach to daily connection with Him along with the tools to step out in faith to prophesy.

DR. CANDICE SMITHYMAN
Host, *Glory Road TV* Show and Founder, Dream Mentors
Transformational Life Coaching Institute

Dr. Hakeem Collins is a prolific voice that the Lord is using profoundly in this generation to impact the nations of the world. *101 Prophetic Ways God Speaks: Hearing God is Easier Than You Think* is a masterful work that de-mystifies the prophetic and fashions it in the way the Lord intended. Powerful, provocative, and purposeful—the reader will gain a clear understanding of how God speaks, why God speaks, and what to do with what God has spoken.

APOSTLE RANDALL C. FURLOW
Senior Pastor, Founder and CEO of New Life Covenant Church,
The Ekklesia Global Network and R.C Furlow Global
www.rcfurlowglobal.com

As one of the foundational prophetic mentors and fathers of Prophet Hakeem Collins, I count it an honor and a privilege to echo the power of the contents of this book. It fully and accurately gives the different ways that Yah speaks prophetically. Prophet Hakeem Collins has pinpointed and shares in detail how to not only hear but also how to recognize how Yah speaks prophetically. He was anointed to write this book, so sit in your favorite chair with the right amount light, and your glasses if necessary, and a nice cup of tea and allow the revelation to unfold as you read. I would admonish you to carry this book with you wherever you go, so you can have access to the prophetic treasures that lie between the pages of this book. It's not only a great message but it's a timely and revelatory message. Let The Most High Yah speak to you as you read and partake of this prophetic feast. And buy an extra copy of this *101 Prophetic Ways God Speaks* to give to someone else who will be blessed by the essence that flows out of this Eden.

APOSTLE RAYMOND P. STANSBURY
Prophetic House of Truth Outreach (P.H.O.T.O.)
Natsarim Hebraic Assembly,
New Castle, Delaware USA

It is a very rare and almost once-in-a-lifetime encounter to witness the limitless heavenly downloads from an apostolic prophet in the likes of Dr. Hakeem Collins. Whether you consider yourself as one who can accurately discern the voice of the Lord or a novice, *101 Prophetic Ways God Speaks* will confirm the inklings you always had but were afraid to ask. This literary work will clearly and systematically show you how the Lord speaks, with biblical references to back it, and provide a plethora of personal divine encounters to bring you into a new dimension of understanding heavenly communication. This one leaves you running to get back in God's presence to hear what He will say next!

APOSTLE CHRIS and PROPHETESS KARYN WATSON
Lead Pastors of Living Waters Christian Center
Suffolk, Virginia, USA

I only wish this very complete work *101 Prophetic Ways God Speaks* would have been available to me in 1988 when God began to speak prophetically to me. It took me many years to learn about all these different ways God speaks. Now, armed with this book, you can quickly see the fascinating categories of ways God Speaks. Plus each category is complete with examples and stories to illustrate how God's voice is heard on the earth today. This book is truly "a keeper." You might even want to go through this book over many weeks in a home group. Buy this book and while you're at it, get one for a friend! Good job Dr. Hakeem Collins!

STEVE SHULTZ,
Founder, *The Elijah List* and Elijah Streams TV

In this new book, respected prophet and apostolic leader Hakeem Collins makes operating in the prophetic accessible for every believer, demonstrating how they can hear and discern the supernatural voice of God and apply His direction to every area of life.

SHAUN TABATT,
Host of *The Shaun Tabatt Show*

101 PROPHETIC WAYS

GOD
SPEAKS

DESTINY IMAGE BOOKS BY DR. HAKEEM COLLINS

Command Your Healing

Prophetic Breakthrough

Heaven Declares

101 PROPHETIC WAYS

GOD
SPEAKS

*Hearing God Is Easier
Than You Think*

HAKEEM COLLINS

DESTINY IMAGE® PUBLISHERS, INC.

P.O. Box 310, Shippensburg, PA 17257-0310

"Promoting Inspired Lives."

This book and all other Destiny Image and Destiny Image Fiction books are available at Christian bookstores and distributors worldwide.

Cover design by Eileen Rockwell
Interior design by Terry Clifton

For more information on foreign distributors, call 717-532-3040.

Reach us on the Internet: www.destinyimage.com.

ISBN 13 TP: 978-0-7684-5066-8
ISBN 13 eBook: 978-0-7684-5067-5
ISBN 13 HC: 978-0-7684-5069-9

For Worldwide Distribution, Printed in the U.S.A.

3 4 5 6 7 8 / 23 22 21 20

CONTENTS

FOREWORD

We each start somewhere. I remember in my early development being marked by the words of Jesus as recorded in John 10:27. Jesus stated, *"My sheep hear my voice, I know them and they follow me."* I believed the Bible was God's Word and was learning to pray the Word back to God.

In that pivotal season of my life, while in a time of dedication and consecration, I turned the direction and control of my life over to the Lord Jesus Christ. I took these words of Jesus and prayed something like this. "I know that I am Your sheep and therefore I accept by faith that I do hear Your voice. I have no problem with the middle part of the verse because I know You know me better than I know myself. But it is the last phrase that I need help with. If I am going to follow You, then I need to do more than merely hear Your voice. I need to discern Your voice from the voice of the world, the devil and my flesh. Therefore, I enroll today into Your School of the Holy Spirit in Jesus' name! Amen!"

Since that time, the Holy Spirit has been raising up a new generation of hungry, consecrated believers who have also signed up to take classes in the School of the Holy Spirit. We are truly living in the "Joining of the Generations" and the "Days of Convergence." Not only are there introductory classes being offered in the prophetic today, but we now have advanced classes being taught by next-generation leaders. Hakeem Collins is one of those equippers the Holy Spirit is raising up for such a time as this.

As you take a perusal of the *101 Prophetic Ways that God Speaks*, you will find an encyclopedia of both information and revelation right at your fingertips.

Dreams, visions, angelic encounters, divine knowings, impressions, discernment, the gifts of the Spirit, the illumination of the Word of God and so much more. If you are looking for a tool that will lift the lid off of your box, then this is it!

It is my honor to commend to you the writings, the prophetic gifting and the life and ministry of Hakeem Collins. Well done! Well done!

In Christ Jesus,

James W. Goll
Founder of God Encounters Ministries
Author, Speaker, Communications Trainer and Recording Artist

INTRODUCTION

With the spirit realm aflush with paganism, upgraded new ageism, this era is saturated with revived deities and their ancient witchery-laced arts and rituals. Of the many tools emerging to combat them in the name of Jesus Christ and His brand of Christianity, a book like *101 Prophetic Ways God Speaks* is priceless. Such works throw up a powerful defense against the inrush of archaic spirituality and demonics storming Christianity's gates today. Other reasons for such a text are the principles essential to prophetic defense and spiritual safeguards. These run throughout every section. Instructions are balanced and content engaging. Materials open with one of the most critical faculties all Christians need: the power of discernment. It sows solid foundations in readers that pave the way for divine revelation, something all divine communicants can appreciate. Introductory treatments deliver rich discussion on how God reveals secrets. The journey of *101 Prophetic Ways God Speaks* takes off from here.

Next is the Holy Spirit, divine revelation's energy source. He is how we get to our prophetic "ear to hear" destination. His quickening power is explained picturing Him as engineer, conductor, and communicator in one. Learning how God speaks demands insightful knowledge of how His Spirit conveys, translates, interprets and relays His thoughts to us. Discussions draw on one or a combination of the 101 Prophetic Ways He does so as later detailed in this book. The Holy Spirit's main personas follow to assure no other spirit or power takes credit for God's disclosures, or takes advantage of His seekers' quest for His truth.

Compelling, capacitating, and clarifying, *101 Prophetic Ways'* teachings move from prophetic theory to God's spiritual communication technologies.

It uses language that mechanically depicts prophecy's medias, mediums, and instrumentality. Robust foundations clarify and classify divine encounters, tying them to accompanying effects and emotions. The greatest and most recurring of them being God's love. The journey to hearing God fully, deftly walks readers through the 101 Ways to doing so by skillfully elaborating on each way. Prophetic academics ground thoughts and concepts so scholars and prophesiers recognize the most common ways the Lord speaks to them. Intelligently described and articulately expressed, the text supplies divine communicants with safe building materials to base their own teachings and readiness programs on. Explanations though succinct are insightful, examples plentiful and practical. Outstandingly, the author Dr. Hakeem Collins attaches vital wisdoms and resources to each topic, topping all that went before with final touches avid learners crave: Sources, resources, recommendations and direction.

101 Prophetic Ways God Speaks completes its journey on a welcome educational note. Item by item discussion of the 101 prophetic ways God speaks entices readers to continue learning by directing and urging them to not stop at the end of the book. Supportive resources and prophetic nuances enable what was learned to be used right away. To this end, a series of know-how, how to, "what next?" and "where to find it" wrap up the work. Located in the back of the book are brief talks about symbols, colors, numbers, typology, and parables to aid ongoing exploration of the book's substance.

With paganism's hard push to stamp out or obscure true Christianity bearing down on us, studious texts such as this provide the rod that corrects, the staff that guides, and standards to verify or disprove unscriptural prophets and prophetics. The three bond together to cohere the functions and wisdoms that return divine communicants to Christ and His ecclesia. And, His scepter of rulership to His faithful divine communicants. The book has the power to fundamentally equip and enlighten its readers and motivate them to return prophets to their kingdom role and thereby modern governments to Jesus Christ's shoulders. What Isaiah's vision declares is the Almighty's will for His servants on earth.

PAULA A. PRICE, PH.D
Bestselling Author of *The Prophet's Dictionary*
Tulsa, OK

1

POWER OF DISCERNMENT

I am your servant; give me discernment that
I may understand your statutes.
—PSALM 119:125

One powerful way of hearing and recognizing the voice of God is the ability to "discern" His voice. We must know unequivocally His voice, ways, and nature by the Spirit, through faith, and in His written Word. It is equally important as children of God to listen, obey, and respond to His instructions. The Holy Spirit will help us to precisely distinguish, decipher, and discern the Father's voice, the voice of the enemy, and our own voice.

What is discernment? The word *discern* and its derivatives are translations of the Greek word *anakrino* in the New Testament. It means "to distinguish, to separate out by diligent search, to examine" (Strong's G350). Discernment is the ability to properly discriminate or make determinations. It is closely related to wisdom. We are admonished and encouraged in the Word of God itself to discern the thoughts and intentions of one's heart (see Heb. 4:12).

God can speak to us prophetically through Spirit-filled discernment. I call them several things: "checker," "knower," "flagger," or "distinguisher." I believe every person, whether a believer or unbeliever, has an inner knowing of what is right from wrong. There is an innate gift and ability to know something is not right or accurate. We must trust the inner knower that can be quickened by the Holy Spirit at conversion. Also, the gift of discerning of spirits is activated at the same time. I will cover the gift of discerning of spirits later in this book.

The power of discernment is a great weapon given by the Holy Spirit for the believer to possess. The Holy Spirit will equip us to know the mind, will, ways, plans, intentions, and thoughts of God. The power of discernment is supernatural in itself. As Spirit-filled believers we possess a discerning mind through the Holy Spirit that demonstrates wisdom and insight that goes beyond what is naturally seen or heard. For example, when studying God's Word it must be "spiritually discerned." To the finite human mind without the Spirit of God, the things of God are considered "foolishness" (1 Cor. 2:14).

The Spirit, then, gives us spiritual discernment or ability to discern by comprehending spiritual things or matters. I am reminded of King Solomon in his day noted for his power of discernment in making wise decisions, administrating justice, and having moral judgments (1 Kings 3:9,11). Today, Christian believers are to follow in those same footsteps to be discerning. Moreover, the apostle Paul prayed for believers *"to discern what is best…for the day of Christ"* (Phil. 1:10).

King Solomon in a dream acquired wisdom and a discerning heart to fulfill the call on his life. Solomon was wise enough to seek discernment and godly wisdom (Prov. 1:2; 1 Kings 3:9-12), to explore the handiwork of God (Eccles. 1:13), and to search out the meaning of life (Eccles. 12:13). Likewise, as Christian believers we must possess the power of discernment in hearing God's voice daily while asking and seeking the *"wisdom that comes from heaven"* (James 3:17). We must study the Word of God, which declares it is *"able to make you wise for salvation through faith in Christ Jesus"* (2 Tim. 3:15).

I believe that a Spirit-filled believer can be a discerning person by default due to the fact that they will acknowledge the worth of God's Word: *"All the words of my mouth are just; none of them is crooked or perverse. To the discerning all of them are right; they are upright to those who have found knowledge"* (Prov. 8:8-9). One of the main objectives and goals should be our pursuit as believers to continue seeking and desiring to walk righteously before the Lord: *"Who is wise? He will realize these things. Who is discerning? He will understand them. The ways of the Lord are right; the righteous walk in them, but the rebellious stumble in them"* (Hos. 14:9 NIV).

The voice of God must be also spiritually discerned. The power of discernment is crucial and necessary in this day and age. God is a Spirit and a speaking being—His words must be spiritually discerned and obeyed.

This is what we speak, not in words taught us by human wisdom, but in words taught by the Spirit, expressing spiritual realities with Spirit-taught words. The person without the Spirit does not accept the things that come from the Spirit of God but considers them foolishness, and cannot understand them because they are discerned only through the Spirit. The person with the Spirit makes judgments about all things, but such a person is not subject to merely human judgments (2 Corinthians 2:13-15).

The Bible goes on to say that a carnal mind cannot comprehend or discern spiritual things. It will take a spiritual mind to understand spiritual things and the language of God. Jesus discerned that satan was misquoting the Word of God in the wilderness concerning angels that would rescue Him if He tripped over a stone or committed suicide. Jesus knew the Word of God because He is the Word of God made flesh. He instantly discerned what was not accurate concerning the Word while discerning the agenda behind satan's temptation. Jesus discerned the motive, heart, and evil intentions of satan, who questioned His relationship and Sonship with the heavenly Father. The power of discernment is one of the ways that God uses to assist His people in recognizing His voice.

A biblical example of the character of a person who learned how to recognize the voice of God is the young prophet/priest Samuel. He couldn't discern or recognize the voice of God at first, but he was later called to the prophetic office. At first, Samuel only recognized the familiar voice of Eli his guardian, the current authority in his life.

Oftentimes our gut feeling is a physical and outward manifestation and confirmation that the Lord is getting our attention. Trust the Holy Spirit's indicators—the "bells and whistles" that are going off in your spirit when you hear, feel, or sense something that is not in alignment or agreement with the Spirit of God.

2

DIVINE REVELATION

These are the things God has revealed to us by his Spirit. The
Spirit searches all things, even the deep things of God.
—1 CORINTHIANS 2:10

God speaks through *divine revelation*. Throughout the Old Testament He talks to His holy prophets—and, in the New Testament, apostles—through divine revelation. Jesus said that He speaks what He hears the Father says and does what He sees the Father doing (John 12:49). Furthermore, He said that His meat or nourishment is to do the will of the Father who sent Him (John 4:34). Jesus received His instructions by a prophetic revelation from the Father Himself through prayer.

Have you ever been pondering on something for some time and later the light bulb comes on? You finally received a revelation to a problem or solution you've been waiting for. Today, God speaks to us through the Holy Spirit to make known His secrets and will.

> *For the Lord God does nothing without revealing his secret to his*
> *servants the prophets* (Amos 3:7 ESV).

God has secrets and will reveal them to His prophets. God utilized divine revelation to speak to His prophets and apostles. However, today they are readily available to you by way of the *Holy Spirit*. He downloads them through the Holy Spirit by disclosing His heart, mind, and will to you, concerning you personally. God desires to share His plan, blueprint, and secrets with those who are His.

Moreover, God uses divine revelation to reveal something to us that has not been revealed before. He speaks prophetically to us through revelation, whether we study the Word of God, prepare for a message, worship, fast, or read a book. When I say divine revelation, I am speaking about anything that pertains to God. There is a revelatory realm that we all can tap into by the Holy Spirit, but it will take time and patience to understand.

What is revelation? *The Oxford English Dictionary* defines revelation as "the divine or supernatural disclosure to humans of something relating to human existence." If we are to know God, it is essential that the Lord reveal Himself to us. Revelation must come from God's initiative. On our own, we cannot know God. I believe that there are two primary forms of revelation. One form of revelation is God making Himself known to us through the Holy Spirit in a covenant relationship. We ask God to reveal Himself to us, and we wait for the revelation to manifest. The other form of divine revelation is God speaking to us prophetically.

When the Lord speaks to us prophetically through divine revelation, He is disclosing His thoughts, heart, mind, and will concerning our purpose and destiny. The things God reveals are not always confirmations; sometimes they are divine revelation. The Bible does not define prophecy as a confirmation. A prophecy is a divine revelation that God brings to our attention through the spoken word. That is why we need modern-day prophets who will reveal the will of God to us through the Holy Spirit. Revelation spoken by the Lord plainly reveals what's on His mind toward us. God's thoughts toward us are not of evil but to reveal our destiny and future (see Jer. 29:11). We should receive divine revelation from God rather than demonic revelation that breeds confusion, division, and deception.

I love it when the Lord speaks to me through divine revelation. Oftentimes, God speaks by shedding light on something specific. I may have been studying a subject for a long time. After processing what I have studied, all of a sudden God gives me a divine revelation that I didn't see before and I receive a clear understanding.

There was a time I was studying on the subject of the love of God. I enjoyed the teaching and received good information. At this time, there was a family member who treated me badly every time she saw me. Suddenly, the information I had been studying became my reality—she needed my help, and I was faced with a decision to demonstrate the love of God or deny her my assistance.

God gave me a revelation of how I must walk in His love regardless of how awful she treated me. So I helped her and loved on her. She couldn't believe that I was willing to help her after how harshly she treated me for many years. God imparted His love through revelation. I received the revelation of God's love through my study and through the voice of the Lord. I had to become one with the revelation that I received from God. I needed to obediently walk by faith and love.

The Lord speaks to us by revelation that becomes our realization. We cannot teach and study His love until we can identify with it personally. In other words, I can study and learn about love, but the revelation comes when I realize I need love or when I express love. Then it becomes my personal reality.

God uses revelation to shape our reality. We have to practice what we preach, teach, and prophesy. The only way we can see the Father, as the disciples asked Jesus, is through the lens of revelation. Jesus was sent by the Father to be that revelation and was there in the beginning with the Father. To see Jesus is to see the Father.

3

Quickening Power of His Spirit

It is the spirit that quickeneth; the flesh profiteth nothing: the words that I speak unto you, they are spirit, and they are life.
—John 6:63 KJV

An interesting way that the Holy Spirit communicates to us is through the quickening power of His Spirit. A quickening from the Holy Spirit is when He will "jump" something at you. For example, the Holy Spirit will highlight a Bible verse to you that you didn't notice before. The Holy Spirit does this so that you can examine what God is communicating and gain a full understanding and answer to your situation.

Oftentimes, the Lord will quicken a verse to me that will help solve a specific problem or issue I am having. There may be times you are listening to a minister preach or teach something that will get your undivided attention. This happens often when you hear a prophetic word that quickens in your spirit.

For example, I would be driving down the road in my car listening to a pastor teach on the radio when all of a sudden something they spoke jumped right out at me. I received a quickening or witness by the Holy Spirit that God was speaking through them. This is one way the Holy Spirit brings you specific knowledge, confirmation, and affirmation.

This type of Holy Spirit quickening can happen anywhere—at the grocery store, mall, local bookstore, worship service, or prayer service. For instance, you could be in the bookstore when all of a sudden a book title and cover get your attention. Or you may overhear a prayer that really touches you deeply concerning something you have been waiting on God for. Or a song sung in worship could resonate with you and bring you to tears.

When these types of things occur, the Holy Spirit is quickening and selecting that song or book for you personally. As you hear God's voice through His quickening power by His Spirit, obey His leading by purchasing that song or book or sealing that prayer you overheard in Jesus's name with an amen! We have to keep in mind that the Holy Spirit's quickening power may be leading you to imperative, life-changing, and inspiring information found in that book that jumped out at you. I cannot tell you how often the Lord has personally picked what clothes I should wear for a job interview. Later I'm offered a job because of my obedience to follow the leading of God's quickening Spirit. We are not to go searching for or trying to make these quickenings happen. Allow the Holy Spirit to initiate them organically and naturally.

John 6:63 simply declares that the spirit gives life and that the flesh profits nothing. Jesus later goes on to say that the words that He speaks are spirit and they are life. These are two components of the Word of God—they have potency and ability to give life and they are emphatically and solely spiritual.

All the words of the Lord, regardless of what form we hear them in, are quickened by His Holy Spirit. There is an inner witness that awakens our spirit and confirms that what is spoken, heard, sensed, and discerned is the nature and expression of God.

God's Word has resurrection power! A believer can feel it tangibly when His Word is spoken, read, heard, or imparted through the laying on of hands. Only God's Spirit can awaken and bring life. There are times I can discern a true prophetic word spoken or released with power because I will feel God's glory, weight, presence, and power confirming it. When there is a quickening of God's Spirit, I oftentimes will shake, jerk, or feel a cool tingling in my belly like a gushing of water being released.

It's like the Holy Spirit's chills that come on me when there is a quickening of God's Spirit confirming what He is speaking. There are also times I can tangibly feel an overwhelming heat, electricity, or power surge shooting through my body. I cannot fathom or understand, it but my natural senses are superimposed upon and I cannot control what I feel physically. The power of the quickening of the Holy Spirit is real and raw.

When God speaks, something is awakened by the Spirit of God that becomes an instantaneous currency and movement. Something is revived when the quickening power of God is released and spoken. I am reminded of Elizabeth when Mary's greeting caused her baby to leap, move, and jump within her womb (see Luke 1:41-43). There was a quickening response that caused John the Baptist within his mother to bear witness to the voice of Mary, Jesus's earthly mother. The voice of Mary became the ultrasound that caused John to respond to confirm the supernatural working of God.

Jesus and John both bore witness in their mother's wombs. John was filled with the Spirit in the womb, and Jesus was conceived miraculously by the Holy Spirit. When I hear something new by revelation or when something confirms God's Word, instantly my inner man and spirit bears witness with what is spoken or done.

4

THE HOLY SPIRIT

*On my account you will be brought before governors and
kings as witnesses to them and to the Gentiles. But when they
arrest you, do not worry about what to say or how to say it. At
that time you will be given what to say, for it will not be you
speaking, but the Spirit of your Father speaking through you.*
—MATTHEW 10:18-20

We must have the Holy Spirit operating in our lives in order for us to properly, accurately, and precisely know the nature, ways, and voice of God. To hear the voice of God, we must receive the baptism of the Holy Spirit. In order to speak for God we must be immersed in the Holy Spirit. You can be saved but still need the Holy Spirit to hear and demonstrate God's power!

The Holy Spirit possesses a speaking nature to communicate through the believer. God is a speaking Spirit, and through the Spirit we understand spiritual things and the nature of God. Moreover, the Holy Spirit is the most important Person to aid us in our spiritual walk, journey, calling, ministry, and life. Briefly, we will understand the role, function, and nature of the Holy Spirit—the Person speaking and working in us and through us daily. As we embrace and appreciate the role and function of the Holy Spirit, we can grow in hearing the voice of God.

The Holy Spirit loves to share and interpret the will of the Father to us and allow us to explore the endless possibilities available to us as heirs of Christ. The Holy Spirit is a prophetic Spirit. I want to focus on the Person of the Holy

Spirit so that we can tune in prophetically to what God is saying and doing in and through Him. The Holy Spirit speaks to us daily from Heaven and reveals what's on the Father's heart in the realm in the earth.

The Holy Spirit can communicate with us and help us just as a person would when we ask. We must understand that the Holy Spirit is the third Person of the Trinity, equal with the Father and Son in essence but not in functionality. One of the major aspects of God's nature is that He is a Person. We know that Jesus is a Person who actually lived, died, raised from the dead, and ascended to sit at the right hand of the Father. It follows that the Holy Spirit is a Person too.

In addition, in the Word of God we see that the apostle Paul noted the intellectual attribute and ability of the Holy Spirit: *"For what man knoweth the things of a man, save the spirit of man which is in him? even so the things of God knoweth no man, but the Spirit of God"* (1 Cor. 2:11 KJV). The rational capacity and function of the Holy Spirit was expanded and extended.

One of the fascinating and interesting characteristics of the Holy Spirit is that He has real feelings and emotions as we do. When someone is offended or grieved you will know it because they will communicate and express it emotionally. I believe that one of the problems associated with emotions is the possibility of being grieved by someone you love. The Holy Spirit is a Person because He demonstrates a personality—He demonstrates a personality *because He is a Person*. Consider the list below of the things the Holy Spirit does that only a person can do.

The Acts of the Person of the Holy Spirit

1. He as a Person teaches (John 14:26)

2. He as a Person testifies (John 15:26)

3. He as a Person guides (Rom. 8:14)

4. He as a Person speaks (1 Cor. 2:13)

5. He as a Person enlightens (John 16:13)

6. He as a Person strives (Gen. 6:3)

7. He as a Person commands (Acts 8:28)

8   He as a Person intercedes (Rom. 8:26)

9.   He as a Person sends workers (Acts 13:4)

10. He as a Person calls (Rev. 22:17)

11. He as a Person comforts (John 16:7)

12. He as a Person works (1 Cor. 12:11)

13. He as a Person anoints (Luke 4:18)

14. He as a Person reveals (John 14:26; 1 Cor. 2:10; Rom. 8:16)

15. He as a Person prophesies (Acts 2:4; 1 Cor. 12:8)

16. He as a Person bears witness (Rom. 8:16)

17. He as a Person ordains (Acts 13:2)

18. He as a Person assists (John 14:16-18; 16:7)

As we recognize and embrace the Person and actions of the Holy Spirit, we can tune in more frequently to what God is doing and saying to us daily. We can see Him around us, involved in our daily affairs. As a Person, the Holy Spirit can relate to us intimately. As we address the Holy Spirit as a Person in our lives He will manifest Himself as such, working through us and with us. If we realize the Holy Spirit is a Person speaking to us then it is easier to hear the voice of God daily.

The Holy Spirit is sent to comfort, advise, encourage, and lead believers. The Greek word translated "Comforter" or "Counselor" is *parakletos* (John 14:16,26; 15:26; 16:7). This form of the word is passive and means "one called to the side of another" (Strong's #G3875). The word carries a secondary notion concerning the purpose of coming alongside—to counsel or support the one who needs it.

There was a time when Jesus announced to His disciples that He would be leaving them soon. He then gave them an encouraging statement: *"And I will ask the Father, and He will give you another Counselor to be with you forever. He is the Spirit of truth"* (John 14:16-17 HCSB). God can speak to us through the Holy Spirit—a Person who sends and relays a message to His children.

5

STILL SMALL VOICE

*And after the earthquake a fire; but the Lord was not
in the fire: and after the fire a still small voice.*
—1 Kings 19:12 KJV

Hearing the still small voice of God is another supernatural way God
speaks to His people. Whether you recognize it or not, the Lord speaks
to us frequently through the Holy Spirit. This type of communication is a soft
and gentle voice of God, which comes as we wait on the Father in prayer, worship, or meditate in His Word.

The Lord speaks in this way to give personal directives, guidance, or
encouragement. It is a highly subjective way of hearing God's voice because it's
quiet and internal. The still small voice must be judged in light of the desires
of our hearts.

Communicating with the Lord should be a habit for every believer. We
serve a speaking and living God who enjoys communicating with His people,
and the Lord often speaks to us within our spirit. This type of communication
is identified as a "still small voice" in the Book of First Kings. In this account,
the voice of the Lord passes by Elijah as a gentle blowing or whisper speaking
in a different and unfamiliar way to the prophet:

> *"Go out, and stand on the mountain before the Lord." And behold,
> the Lord passed by, and a great and strong wind tore into the
> mountains and broke the rocks in pieces before the Lord, but the*

Lord was not in the wind; and after the wind an earthquake, but the Lord was not in the earthquake; and after the earthquake a fire, but the Lord was not in the fire; and after the fire a still small voice (1 Kings 19:11-12 NKJV).

With all of the various ways God can speak to His people, He often speaks within our spirit as an inner voice. This can start as a passing thought, word, concept, idea, or impression. Oftentimes, we are not aware of this inner voice speaking and can dismiss or skip over His voice, not understanding this is actually the Lord speaking.

Imagine a married couple whispering sweet things into each other's ears. There is no need for them to be shouting at each other because they are so close and what they are sharing is private. This is a perfect illustration of how the Lord's still small voice is expressed. When we come into intimate covenant relationship with the Lord, we will be awakened to direct supernatural encounters and secrets of God. God will awaken our ears to His love melodies.

God is always speaking! Unless we learn to distinguish His thoughts from our own, we will continue to group all thoughts together, thinking they are our own concepts, ideas, thoughts, and impressions.

There is only one place in Scripture where God is said to have spoken in a "still small voice," and it was to Elijah after his dramatic victory over the prophets of Baal (1 Kings 18:20-40; 19:12). However, other Scripture references reveal that God whispers, blows in the wind, or speaks through a sound of His voice. Elijah the prophet was informed that Jezebel, the wife of Ahab, king of Israel, was seeking to kill him.

Elijah ran for his life and entered the wilderness, collapsing in exhaustion. God sent an angel with food and water to strengthen him, instructing him to rest, and later sent him to Horeb. There, Elijah verbally expressed his complaint to the Lord that Jezebel killed all of the prophets and he alone had survived. God instructed him to stand on the mountain in His presence. Then the Lord sent a mighty wind that broke the rocks in pieces, an earthquake, and a fire, but His voice was not found in any of them.

After all that, the Lord spoke to Elijah in a subtle manner—the "still small voice" or "gentle whisper." This was to illustrate that the work of God need not always be accompanied by dramatic revelations and divine manifestations. In other words, God is not restrained to one method of communication that we are accustomed to. He can also speak in ways that we are not familiar with.

We cannot put God in a box. God can communicate more than just audibly and visually but supernaturally and naturally if we pay close attention. He can speak many languages and dialects and use many ways, methods, and manners fluently as well as give the interpretation, understanding, and translation of that which is spoken. I believe that "divine silence" does not necessarily mean "divine inactivity." God can speak to us even when He is silent, triggering us to pursue Him to get a response.

We can see elsewhere in Scripture that He is said to communicate through a whirlwind (Job 38:1), to proclaim His presence by an earthquake (Exod. 19:18), and to speak in a thunder-like voice (1 Sam. 2:10; Job 37:2; Ps. 104:7; John 12:29). Furthermore, Psalm 77:18 compares His voice to both thunder and a whirlwind. And we're told that lightning and thunder proceed from the throne room of Heaven according to Revelation 4:5.

The contrast between the Lord speaking through thunder and through a still small voice illustrates the difference between the two dispensations of law and grace. The law is a voice of terrible words and was given amidst a tempest of wind, thunder, and lightning, attended by an earthquake (Heb. 12:18-24). The still small voice, however, represents His grace.

6

FIRST PERSON

*With him I speak mouth to mouth, clearly, and not in
riddles, and he beholds the form of the Lord. Why then were
you not afraid to speak against my servant Moses?*
—NUMBERS 12:8 ESV

When the Lord communicates He will often speak directly to us in first person. The *Merriam-Webster Dictionary* defines first person as *"reference of a linguistic form to the speaker or writer of the utterance in which it occurs."* In first person, God identifies Himself with the word "I," and you are the person He is speaking to directly. First person makes His speech very personable and intimate.

I love this way that God speaks because it doesn't come through any other person, third-party source, or someone like a prophet communicating a message from God. God makes Himself known to His children directly and plainly. There are times when I speak in first person when I am prophesying over someone or releasing a corporate prophetic word over whole congregations. There is something powerful when that is done because the prophet is speaking as God is speaking directly. I am honored when God speaks to me personally.

The Bible says that God spoke to Moses mouth to mouth—basically, in first person (Exod. 33:11). When Moses was sent to Pharaoh to deliver God's people out of bondage, Moses asked God what to say if Pharaoh asked who sent him. God replied in first person, telling Moses to tell Pharaoh, "I AM that

I AM sent you." The message was spoken in first person even through Moses was sent as a prophet on an ambassadorial assignment to bring liberation.

When the Lord speaks in first person, it is what the Scripture describes as mouth to mouth. Numbers 12:8 says, *"With him I speak mouth to mouth, clearly, and not in riddles, and he beholds the form of the Lord. Why then were you not afraid to speak against my servant Moses?"* (ESV). We clearly see that God spoke to Moses His servant mouth to mouth and not in riddles or dark sayings. Moses was a friend of God. He spoke to him in a direct language he could understand.

I remember a time when I was worshiping and praying and thinking on the love of God, tears rolling down my face because of the Lord blessing me to see my thirtieth birthday. Where I am from, most young black males don't make it to see their thirtieth birthday. As I was in tears, I heard the Lord say to me in a direct voice, *"I love you, Hakeem"* and *"I will never leave you and never forsake you if you continue to obey Me."* You can see that God spoke to me clearly in a still small voice, identifying that He personally loved me and will never leave me as I obey Him. He revealed Himself to me in first person. He said *I* love you. God wants to speak to us personally and directly daily.

Prophets have been given divine authority by the Holy Spirit to speak for God as His mouthpiece. For that reason, there have been times I would release corporate or personally prophetic words in first person. If I was prophesying about prosperity in a person's life, then I would say, for example:

> *"Son (or daughter), I, the Lord your God, have come to break you free from the spirit of poverty, and I desire for you to prosper in Me as your soul shall prosper. And know that I am with you, My child, and, I will give you the power to get wealth. For I will not have you ignorant of the enemy's devices but give you a way of escape, saith your God. For this is the season that I am breaking lack, poverty, bondage, spiritual limitation, and I am causing you to prosper on every side. As I gave Abraham the Promised Land as his portion, surely I your God will do the same for you as heir of My Son Jesus Christ and the land as your possession, says the Spirit of God."*

Clearly, there was nowhere in the prophecy that I referred to myself, saying, "Hakeem will do this or that." Nowhere in the prophecy were my name or identity mentioned. I spoke as a prophet in first person, as if God Himself was speaking. Of course, I am not God! However, I am an ambassadorial prophetic voice of God to speak the oracles of Him who sent me.

There is an anointing when prophets speak in first person. Some say that I have no right or authority to speak like God. Read what this passage of Scripture says with regard to those who have the gift of speaking:

> *Do you have the gift of speaking? Then speak as though God himself were speaking through you. Do you have the gift of helping others? Do it with all the strength and energy that God supplies. Then everything you do will bring glory to God through Jesus Christ. All glory and power to him forever and ever! Amen* (1 Peter 4:11 NLT).

Do you see? Speak as though God Himself were speaking! This applies to those called as prophets and those called to speak prophetically. Therefore, scripturally we can speak as oracles of God—His divine communicators. We give language to what God wants to articulate.

7

DARK SPEECHES
AND RIDDLES

With him I speak face to face, clearly and not in riddles;
he sees the form of the Lord. Why then were you not
afraid to speak against my servant Moses?
—NUMBERS 12:8

God spoke with Moses face to face, clearly and directly and not in riddles. But there are times when the Lord will say something in riddles or dark sayings so that the hearer will seek out the true meaning of what He is saying.

> *So was fulfilled what was spoken through the prophet: "I will open*
> *my mouth in parables; I will utter things hidden since the creation*
> *of the world"* (Matthew 13:35).

What is a riddle? "A riddle is a statement or question or phrase having a double or veiled meaning, put forth as a puzzle to be solved. Riddles are of two types: enigmas, which are problems generally expressed in metaphorical or allegorical language that require ingenuity and careful thinking for their solution, and conundra, which are questions relying for their effects on punning in either the question or the answer."[1]

God doesn't want to confuse us when He speaks to us. However, He looks to be sought after. Oftentimes, He does this to increase our appetite for Him, so that we will seek to understand His mysteries. We are not to try to fully explain God but to have faith and believe in Him (Heb. 11:6). We should pursue Him to understand His ways and listen, obey, and respond to His voice.

God speaks at times in dark sayings to challenge His people to seek out the truth. There are things God would hide from the prophets on purpose. Deuteronomy 29:29 says, *"The secret things belong to the Lord our God, but the things that are revealed belong to us and to our children forever, that we may do all the words of this law"* (ESV). The Lord reserves the secret things to Himself, but the things that are revealed belong to us—the believers by the Spirit. God has secrets that He will disclose to us in part.

> *For now we see only a reflection as in a mirror; then we shall see face to face. Now I know in part; then I shall know fully, even as I am fully known* (1 Corinthians 13:12 NIV).

This verse shows us what it looks like when a riddle is given. Things are not clear but darkly stated and need more understanding. The King James Version calls it "dark speech." Understanding this strange way God speaks at times is not an instant process. Riddles or dark sayings need a divine understanding through the Holy Spirit to dissect God's allegorical language.

> *These things God has revealed to us through the Spirit. For the Spirit searches everything, even the depths of God* (1 Corinthians 2:10 ESV).

The Spirit of God searches and investigates everything and even the depths of God. It is imperative in this hour that we access the Spirit of God to discern what He is saying in riddles and dark sayings. Christian believers must do their due diligence when it comes to the mysteries of God. When I am in prayer, there are times God gives me bits and pieces of things but not the full revelation or understanding. It takes me some time to dig it out through studying until it makes sense.

The Lord gives me clues and hints concerning things I am researching. Like a forensic detective, over time I am able to solve the case. We have been given keys to the Kingdom of God, but we must learn how to access it by the Holy Spirit. Matthew 13:11 clearly says, *"The knowledge of the secrets of the kingdom of heaven has been given to you, but not to them."*

As children of God, we are given the knowledge of the mysteries of the kingdom of Heaven. It is our spiritual inheritance! When God speaks to us in riddles and dark sayings it's not that He doesn't want to us to know things; it's really the opposite—He does! Are we open and willing to search it out like treasure in the sea? Unraveling and understanding riddles and dark speeches will take the quickening response of the Holy Spirit to make sense of dark sayings of the Lord.

Let me give you a prime example of a riddle or dark speech. There was a time I was ministering to a woman and the Lord spoke to me and said, "Kathy, Philadelphia's Liberty Bell." I heard the Spirit of God speaking this to me in my spirit about her life and current spiritual relationship with God. I said to myself, *The Liberty Bell? What does that have to do with Kathy?* And the Lord revealed to me that Kathy had turned her back on the church and stopped putting her trust in God. When I heard the Lord speak this to me He began to pull back the layers and unveil the beauty of His Word.

God was basically using the Philadelphia's Liberty Bell as a prophetic dark speech or riddle for me to get the understanding as I ministered to her. Knowing the background of the Liberty Bell, I was able to speak prophetically. God was saying that he was going to summon Kathy back to Him after she had become independent and not interdependent.

Religious bondage had turned Kathy away from the church, but by His Spirit God was going to bring her back to her homeland—which is actually Philadelphia, her birthplace and home—and set her in a place where the Spirit of the Lord dwells, which is a place of liberty. She had many cracked and broken promises in her life through bad relationships, but God was going to preserve her and restore back her honor and integrity and make her a symbol of freedom like the Liberty Bell.

NOTE

1. Wikipedia, s.v. "Riddle," accessed April 14, 2019, https://en.wikipedia .org/wiki/Riddle.

8

PERCEIVING THOUGHTS

The Pharisees and the teachers of the law began thinking to themselves, "Who is this fellow who speaks blasphemy? Who can forgive sins but God alone?" Jesus knew what they were thinking and asked, "Why are you thinking these things in your hearts? Which is easier: to say, Your sins are forgiven, or to say, Get up and walk?"
—LUKE 5:21-23

One of the ways that God will speak to us prophetically is through *perceiving thoughts*. God will give you a supernatural ability to know what's on a person's heart or mind. I don't believe its "mind reading" per se because we don't walk around knowing what is on everyone's mind; we simply perceive their thoughts. Our thoughts, ideas, concepts, and feelings are usually confidential or private. Someone who knows everything on a person's mind would be omniscient—like God.

As a prophetic minister, I don't know everything someone is thinking, and to be honest I don't want to know. I believe that God at times will give us accurate insight and understanding into something specific on a person's heart. God has revealed motives and people's agendas against me even though they didn't know what was revealed to me.

Jesus was able to perceive what was in the hearts of His disciples and even the religious leaders of His day. He perceived their thoughts or what was in their hearts through their actions, conversations, and religious paradigms. He was able to perceive their purpose for challenging His decisions. He was able to perceive that their hearts were evil or wicked.

> *And behold, some people brought to him a paralytic, lying on a bed. And when Jesus saw their faith, he said to the paralytic, "Take heart, my son; your sins are forgiven." And behold, some of the scribes said to themselves, "This man is blaspheming." But Jesus, knowing their thoughts, said, "Why do you think evil in your hearts?"* (Matthew 9:2-4 ESV)

In this story, Jesus sharply addresses the scribes who saw His forgiveness of a man's sin as an act of blasphemy. He already knew their thoughts.

> *"For I know the plans I have for you," says the Lord. "They are plans for good and not for disaster, to give you a future and a hope"* (Jeremiah 29:11 NLT).

> *And knowing their thoughts Jesus said to them, "Any kingdom divided against itself is laid waste; and any city or house divided against itself will not stand"* (Matthew 12:25 NASB).

> *Immediately Jesus, aware in His spirit that they were reasoning that way within themselves, said to them, "Why are you reasoning about these things in your hearts?"* (Mark 2:8 NASB)

> *But He knew what they were thinking, and He said to the man with the withered hand, "Get up and come forward!" And he got up and came forward* (Luke 6:8 NASB).

> *But He knew their thoughts and said to them, "Any kingdom divided against itself is laid waste; and a house divided against itself falls"* (Luke 11:17 NASB).

All the above Scriptures give us an understanding that to perceive a person's thoughts is only to know what they are thinking at the time and not what they are thinking all the time. There is a difference. We don't know what people are thinking all the time and every time. Only God knows that and has access to that because He is omniscient, but we can perceive at times things that God discloses through the Holy Spirit. The Bible says we know in part and prophesy in part (1 Cor. 13:9).

When I am ministering in the prophetic gift to someone, I often will reveal to them something they said in prayer to God. I get a response of tears, screaming, or a surprised expression on their face. Why? Because I revealed something that was on their mind and I said exactly what they were thinking in their heart.

The word "perceive" in the Greek is the word *epiginōskō,* which means "to know upon some mark, i.e. recognize; by implication, to become fully acquainted with, to acknowledge: to know well, or perceive" (Strong's #G1921). Sometimes this can come naturally when you are better acquainted with someone—a friend, spouse, co-worker, employer, or anyone in a covenant relationship. Knowing someone personally will help you to understand how they think or conduct themselves. I know what my mother would say in a situation because I know what's on her heart about it. I can even speak for my mother concerning specific things because I know how she thinks. This is *natural* perception.

God wants us to know His mind and thoughts through His Word and Holy Spirit—this is *supernatural* perception. Our ideas and principles, words and mental pictures will grow more like His with increasing awareness, clarity, unfolding, intensity, conviction, or volume in our mind. Have you ever said something to someone and they said, "You read my mind"? You were thinking what they were thinking. Now imagine if you could do that with God! If His thoughts were in your mind and came out of your mouth!

9

AUDIBLE VOICE
OF ANOTHER

Now Samuel did not yet know the Lord, nor had the word of the Lord yet been revealed to him. So the Lord called Samuel again for the third time. And he arose and went to Eli and said, "Here I am, for you called me." Then Eli discerned that the Lord was calling the boy. And Eli said to Samuel, Go lie down, and it shall be if He calls you, that you shall say, "Speak, Lord, for Your servant is listening." So Samuel went and lay down in his place.
—1 SAMUEL 3:7-9 NASB

God has unique ways of speaking to His people in unusual circumstances. Oftentimes believers are looking for confirmation of what God has spoken to them personally. In other words, we can ask the Lord to confirm something He spoke through a prophecy, dream, vision, or burden. Also, we can ask the Lord for a sign concerning something personal—our purpose, calling, and destiny. God loves to speak and answer our petitions and supplications.

Then the Lord spoke again to Ahaz, saying, "Ask a sign for yourself from the Lord your God; make it deep as Sheol or high as heaven." But Ahaz said, "I will not ask, nor will I test the Lord!" (Isaiah 7:10-12 NASB)

We see that the Lord spoke to Ahaz, telling him to ask Him for sign or confirmation. Ahaz decided not to ask or test the Lord. Ahaz was confident in his God and didn't need to ask for a sign. There will be times when you may want to hear God speak through outside, audible voices of confirmation. Sometimes other people can confirm something you were praying about or believing God for. I receive confirmation through conversations with people as God speaks through that individual.

For example, God allowed me to resign from my job to pursue full-time ministry. However, I was a little reluctant to do so because of fear and not knowing where my main source of income would come from. I knew that it was my last year at the bank but didn't know the timing of the Lord to make the decision to resign. As I was on my lunch break, I was watching the news and heard the news anchor say, "For many Americans, this will be the year to leave that job you dread and go with your passion and dream."

Oddly, at the same time the news anchor was talking, I heard the Lord's voice through her and it was loud and clear as if God said it personally. I was listening to the woman on the news, but at the same time God was speaking too in a still small voice in my spirit. I felt the quickening witness of God. My desire was to leave seven years of banking and fulfill the passion, dream, and call of the Lord. Her voice and words were prophetic, and it was like God spoke through her to me in my spirit. That is what I call an outside, audible voice of God.

Moreover, I always hear prophetic confirmations and signs through everyday, regular people or other believers. I recall a time I was trying to get a new car and I didn't want another car payment. Wrestling with that decision, I was in a restaurant and I overheard the couple sitting next to me. The whole time, their conversation was about establishing a great credit report and what it takes. In their conversation was like the Lord was speaking to me simultaneously.

In addition, several trusted prophetic voices to whom I am accountable said, "Hakeem, while I was praying for you I saw you with a new vehicle, and God is going to give you favor when you go get this Mercedes Benz." Furthermore, these were the same prophetic voices who saw me going into full-time ministry and resigning from my job. The Bible establishes His Word out of the mouth of two or three people.

> *This is the third time I am coming to visit you (and as the Scriptures say, "The facts of every case must be established by the testimony of two or three witnesses")* (2 Corinthians 13:1 NLT).

It took audible voices of others to confirm what God revealed to me so that I would obey what God was saying. I wanted to be obedient to God but was afraid initially when I heard the Lord say to leave my job and later get a new car. Often, God will encourage us and bring others to speak what we heard. There are also times God will not send confirmation; His revelation will be new and directly for you, as it was with Noah building the ark, Abraham leaving his father's house, and other biblical examples.

In my case, God was affirming the faith required to get a new car. The conversation I overheard actually blessed me because they not only talked about credit but they talked about the whole process of getting a new car and the strategies to improve credit. I was taking mental notes—it seemed like all I could hear was their conversation and I couldn't focus on what I was doing or my food. God was speaking to me while at the same time speaking through others as voices of confirmation.

A month later I applied the principles they shared and I got a new Mercedes Benz C300. In addition, I was able to trade in my car and receive a low monthly payment and the car dealership gave me a credit card with a $2,500 credit limit. In six months, my FICO credit score went from 620 to 712.

God can speak in different ways if we are open to listening first and responding by faith and in obedience next. God will speak through others and also to bring confirmation when we are not sure. I am not talking about fleecing Him for a sign or negotiating with Him. I am talking about receiving confirmation or clarity of what He already spoke.

The Bible records many instances in which God used one individual to deliver His message to another individual. (See 1 Samuel 13:13-14; 15:23; 2 Samuel 12:7-15; and Acts 9:10-18; 10:1-33.) God may speak to you through another individual—a friend, parent, pastor, even a stranger. You would be wise to confirm what you hear God saying by seeking affirmation of that direction through wise, godly people.

One of the best places to find individuals who can give you godly counsel is your local church. Even if your fellow church members do not directly give you counsel, God can use their words to reveal or confirm His will as the Holy Spirit works in your lives. Also, as a member of a local church you can observe what God is saying to the entire church. God often will direct you personally through the input of others who are regularly in Christian fellowship with you.

10

Audible Voice of God

And your ears shall hear a word behind you, saying, "This is the way, walk in it," when you turn to the right or when you turn to the left.
—Isaiah 30:21 ESV

One powerful way that God spoke many times in the Old Testament was through an audible voice. The Lord would speak to His prophets, kings, priests, and leaders in such a way that they didn't question who was talking. The Bible gives many different outward expressions of how He spoke audibly as you research throughout the Old Testament. Furthermore, there is no biblical account that proves that God stopped speaking in that way. If it's recorded hundreds of times that God spoke to people audibly than we must believe it as biblical fact and not a myth. The audible voice of God is more easily recognizable than the still small voice of God.

The Holy Spirit will help you hear God's voice whether God decides to speak audibly, visually, or inwardly through impressions. We were created to hear the audible voice of God. Adam and Eve heard the voice of God walking in the garden and hid themselves (Gen. 3:8). The Lord can speak today in an audible way just as He did with many others in the Bible and with the first family Adam and Eve. It wasn't clear how they heard God's voice but it sounded like Him walking, which indicates that His voice was audibly heard outwardly with their natural ears and not spiritual ears. Clearly, Adam held a conversation with God because God called Adam by name:

And they heard the voice of the Lord God walking in the garden in the cool of the day: and Adam and his wife hid themselves from the presence of the Lord God amongst the trees of the garden. And the Lord God called unto Adam, and said unto him, Where art thou? And he said, I heard thy voice in the garden, and I was afraid, because I was naked; and I hid myself (Genesis 3:8-10 KJV).

So God created man in his own image, in the image of God created he him; male and female created he them. And God blessed them, and God said unto them, Be fruitful, and multiply, and replenish the earth, and subdue it: and have dominion over the fish of the sea, and over the fowl of the air, and over every living thing that moveth upon the earth (Genesis 1:27-28 KJV).

Adam and Eve's first introduction to God was hearing His audible voice. I believe every Spirit-filled believer can sharpen their ability to hear the voice of God if they are open. The audible voice of God may not be as frequent as the still small voice of God and other means of communication; however, we must not rule it out. God does sovereignly still speak audibly and outwardly.

The Lord spoke to the first family audibly. If He spoke to Adam audibly, He can speak to you today in the same manner. God will make Himself known to you outwardly and audibly as He deems the season and time fitting. The Israelites heard the outward voice of the Lord and wanted Moses to speak to them instead of God. This is not a fairytale story; it's the Word of God interacting with real people just like you and me.

And he said, Hear now my words: If there be a prophet among you, I the Lord will make myself known unto him in a vision, and will speak unto him in a dream. My servant Moses is not so, who is faithful in all mine house. With him will I speak mouth to mouth, even apparently, and not in dark speeches; and the similitude of the Lord shall he behold: wherefore then were ye not afraid to speak against my servant Moses? (Numbers 12:6-8 KJV)

What is God saying here? He is basically saying that most people mainly hear His voice internally. This Scripture indicates that God speaks to prophets in visions and dreams—that is the Lord's general way of speaking to them.

However, Moses had a unique place in history, for God to decide to speak to him externally in an audible voice.

What makes Moses so different from other prophets? I believe it was based on the sovereignty of God and the individual He chose. Moses had a greater sphere of authority, so it would make sense for God to speak to him directly, clearly, and externally. I believe that it also depends on a person's assignment, mantle, calling, and sphere of responsibility.

In Scripture, God spoke to Moses face to face (mouth to mouth). Clearly, God is making a distinction between dark speeches, mouth-to-mouth encounters, and dreams and visions. All are ways God speaks, but all are distributed and expressed differently as God chooses. We must also take into consideration that there are different levels of hearing and receiving revelation from God. For example, God will speak to prophets by revealing secrets and divine plans to them according to Amos 3:7. However, as a Christian believer you still have access to know the plans, mind, and purposes of God for your life through the Holy Spirit.

Moses heard on another level. God spoke to him face to face, or other Bible translations say mouth to mouth. He heard the audible voice of God through a burning bush. There are prophetic expressions of God that were unique to Moses, but I believe God wants to establish a face to face or mouth-to-mouth encounter with all His children daily.

Hearing the audible voice of God was terrifying to the people in the days of Moses. The people wanted Moses to speak on the behalf of God. The voice of God is the sound of thunder! We can see this in Exodus 20:18-21:

> *All the people perceived the thunder and the lightning flashes and the sound of the trumpet and the mountain smoking; and when the people saw it, they trembled and stood at a distance. Then they said to Moses, "Speak to us yourself and we will listen; but let not God speak to us, or we will die." Moses said to the people, "Do not be afraid; for God has come in order to test you, and in order that the fear of Him may remain with you, so that you may not sin." So the people stood at a distance, while Moses approached the thick cloud where God was* (NASB).

One of the things that I wanted to know growing in the prophetic was—what does the audible voice of God sound like? Some would say that the voice of God sounds like your own voice, which I agree with when you are Holy Spirit baptized. Moreover, I know personally that the voice of the Lord sounds like the voice of a Father. When I heard the voice of the Lord audibly and not in a still small voice, I heard a thunder-like voice that frightened me. So I had to search the Scriptures for biblical support. This personal encounter that I experienced at the age of seven cannot be explained except through the Word of God.

Biblically, I found something that blessed my life forever after hearing the outward, audible voice of God. His voice is found in Job 37:2, which got my undivided attention. This passage of Scripture validates and confirms my personal encounter with God: *"Listen closely to the thunder of His voice, and the rumbling that goes out from His mouth"* (NASB).

The voice of God can be revealed expressively through mountains, water, trees, meadows, clouds, valleys, landscapes, and so much more. Biblically, God's voice is heard through thunder and clouds, upon the many waters, and lightning:

> *The Lord thundered from heaven; the voice of the Most High resounded* (2 Samuel 22:14 NLT).

> *Then there comes a roaring sound; God thunders with his majestic voice. He does not restrain the lightning when his rumbling voice is heard* (Job 37:4 CSB).

> *God thunders wondrously with his voice; he does great things that we cannot comprehend* (Job 37:5 ESV).

> *The voice of the Lord is over the waters; the God of glory thunders, the Lord thunders over the mighty waters* (Psalm 29:3).

During the time I heard the audible voice of God, it was not thundering or cloudy out but a beautiful afternoon while I was playing basketball with some neighborhood friends. God spoke from Heaven, but some people who stood nearby thought they were hearing thunder. I could only describe His voice as like thunder—most young people and small animals are scared of the rumbling thunder sound when it does rain. There's the possibility that this could happen today.

We must understand that this is a unique and high-level way God speaks to us. We may not all hear the voice of God like me when I was seven years old. However, we all can by faith know that the worlds were framed by what God spoke into being.

11

FAITH

*Now faith is the substance of things hoped
for, the evidence of things not seen.*
—HEBREWS 11:1 KJV

Faith is another unique way that God speaks. Faith is summoned and is developed when we have the capacity to hear God daily. The Bible says that faith comes by hearing and hearing by the Word of God. Hearing God's Word causes our faith to increase. We can hear God speak when we know by faith that He does speak and we can hear Him.

> *So then faith comes by hearing, and hearing by the word of God* (Romans 10:17 NKJV).

We can see that the apostle Paul in the above text is talking about saving faith, and the Word of God is the only thing that can produce this kind of faith. Faith can be heard, received, and confessed. As we confess with our mouth that Jesus Christ is Lord over our lives and believe in our heart that God raised Him from the dead, we are saved (see Rom. 10:8-9). According to *Strong's Concordance* (#G4102), the word *faith* in that verse is the Greek word *pistis*, which means "conviction of the truth of anything."

In other words, this means that when we as believers hear God's Word or receive His divine direction concerning any issue we are convinced beyond every doubt about the authenticity of the issue. When you hear the voice of God in a *rhema* way it will encourage you and build your faith in God's ability to empower you to overcome any wiles of the enemy. In addition, when you hear God's voice regarding an issue or a circumstance, it builds your faith and empowers you to run your race in God with certainty of victory.

Hebrews 11 talks about faith with regard to pleasing God, and without faith we cannot. In this entire chapter regarding faith we can see men and women of faith who heard God and obeyed. These heroes of faith heard the voice of God just as you can hear His voice today. These faith heroes were certainly able to run their own race and overcome fear obstacles because they heard from God on many occasions. As we grow in faith hearing the voice of God prophetically, we can develop the faith required through trained spiritual ears to please God by responding to God in faith. Having ears to hear is key to growing in faith.

Faith has to grow to the place that we can recognize, discern, understand, and respond to the voice of God's Word. Our faith becomes full grown in the spirit through the development of His Word spoken in our ear gates daily.

We need to develop faith that says, "I believe that God spoke to me and I have faith to believe that what He spoke I understand." Faith comes by hearing and believing what you hear from God. Our faith in something is connected to our belief system. For example, I am not going to have faith to believe in my favorite sports team if I didn't believe they would win. As we mature in the Word of God and trust in His Word, our ability to recognize, discern, and understand His ways will improve. As our faith increases, we are entrusted with greater responsibilities by the Lord.

When God spoke to me to resign from my job, I didn't know what was next for me. It wasn't easy for me to make that decision because I didn't know where my income was coming from. It wasn't that I didn't know His voice; it was the faith required to respond and obey what I heard the Lord say. I knew it was the voice of the Lord because of my understanding of His will and how He operates, so I knew He was telling me to leave my job. Knowing God's Word will give you the faith required to trust Him when it seems impossible. We are to walk by faith and not by what we see naturally. Faith is supernatural and hearing can be supernatural as well.

The Bible says, *"Now faith is the substance of things hoped for, the evidence of things not seen"* (Heb. 11:1 KJV). Oftentimes, believers block faith because they trust what they experience first and depend on their knowledge. God has given us two ears and one mouth. I believe we are to learn how to listen more and speak less. But when a person is speaking, we have two ears as a witness to confirm what we hear.

We have to learn the process of listening. We are speaking while God is speaking. Hearing is not speaking. To hear God is to listen and not speak. Moreover, authentic communication is established in the listening process. I believe that supernatural faith supersedes and transcends language barriers, knowledge, the mind, and our ideas and breaks through the heart with belief.

> *This is what the ancients were commended for. By faith we understand that the universe was formed at God's command, so that what is seen was not made out of what was visible. By faith Abel brought God a better offering than Cain did. By faith he was commended as righteous, when God spoke well of his offerings. And by faith Abel still speaks, even though he is dead* (Hebrews 11:2-4).

God spoke everything into being. What we see in the visible world was created by the invisible Word and spoken into being. Those in the hall of faith in Heaven understood by faith that God still speaks. God will always require faith in Him before He can use us prophetically. Faith without works is dead, and a deaf ear to faith is a disobedient believer. Faith coupled with action pleases God. God is speaking faith into us to believe what we hear Him say and respond accordingly.

12

JESUS—SON OF GOD

*Then a cloud appeared and covered them, and a voice came from
the cloud: "This is my Son, whom I love. Listen to him!"*
—MARK 9:7

God speaks to us through His Son Jesus Christ. The Holy Spirit is the
divine witness of the Father and the Son. There is an abiding connection
to Jesus through His Word and the Holy Spirit. When I am reading stories in
the Gospels concerning the ministry of Jesus while on earth, God begins to
take me into the stories and allows me to experience what Jesus experienced. I
often go through an emotional roller coaster of what He had to face from those
who were His very own.

When Jesus was on the earth, God spoke to us through Him, and
when Jesus returned to the Father, the Holy Spirit was sent to lead us into
all truth—to be our "communicator" from God. (Read Matthew 10:18-20;
John 14:26; 16:7-8,13; Romans 8:26; 1 Corinthians 2:9-16; Acts 8:29; 13:2.) If
you are a believer, the Holy Spirit dwells within you, but it is still necessary to
nurture your relationship with your heavenly Father in order to learn how to be
attentive to His voice. As you grow in faith and mature as a believer, you will
learn to hear God speak. Jesus said, *"My sheep hear my voice, and I know them,
and they follow me"* (John 10:27 ESV).

Through Jesus' earthly ministry I come away with life lessons and divine
principles to live by. The many miracles He performed increase my faith to
believe that I too can work them. The Bible says we can do greater works than

Jesus did (John 14:12). The words of Jesus are spirit life. They become a prophetic force of faith that causes us to do the impossible in the Holy Spirit.

Jesus would often speak in parables when He was speaking to the religious leaders of His day. Then He would explain them to the disciples because it was given to them to know the mysteries. Jesus's life in itself and what He had to give up for us speaks to us centuries later. Jesus is the Word who was with God in the beginning of time.

When God is speaking to us, the Son is speaking to us through the Holy Spirit. Jesus sent the Holy Spirit to us on purpose. Through the Holy Spirit we have the triune divine witness speaking and quickening us. Jesus said His sheep know His voice and they will not follow a stranger. God speaks to us through the life and ministry of His Son. His life, death, burial, and resurrection are the reason we are alive. We are sons of God and Jesus is the model Son who took the sin of the world on the Cross.

God's special plan was done in the New Testament. It's the Gospel—the good news of Jesus Christ. *"In the past God spoke to our ancestors through the prophets at many times and in various ways, but in these last days he has spoken to us by his Son, whom he appointed heir of all things, and through whom also he made the universe"* (Heb. 1:1-2). Through Jesus's own words in Scripture, we can hear God's heart and God's voice and know what God is truly like.

We must know that His words were not written for just a few, special individuals who could jump through the right spiritual hoops, but for all who are His (John 3:16). We all can hear the voice of the Father and see Him through the lens of the Spirit of Jesus. Christians in Africa, Germany, United Kingdom, China, Mexico, Brazil, in the Big Apple of New York City, or in the small state of Delaware can hear Jesus's voice by reading the same Bible.

In Scripture, we are sheep and Jesus is our Shepherd. Jesus says in John 10:27, *"My sheep hear My voice, and I know them, and they follow Me"* (NKJV). Why? They belong to Him, and they recognize Him by the sound of His voice. He's the one who will always lovingly lead them on the right path again and again. Jesus was very clear about the words that He spoke. We can hear the voice of the Father in Heaven through the life Jesus lived and His words. His words were not His own but the words of the Father who sent Him to us.

For I did not speak on my own, but the Father who sent me commanded me to say all that I have spoken, I know that his command leads to eternal life. So whatever I say is just what the Father has told me to say (John 12:49-50).

He didn't speak on His own even while here on earth. The words that Jesus prophetically spoke were from the Father in Heaven. We, too, are to hear and speak what the Holy Spirit has revealed to us. Jesus speaks to us through the Holy Spirit what the Father is saying. The Father and the Son are One. As we have the Holy Spirit living on the inside of us we become one with the Father and Son as well. The Father and Son are working on the inside of us through the ministry of the Holy Spirit.

As sons and coheirs with Christ we are seated in heavenly places with Christ Jesus. We have access to go before the throne of grace in prayer and make our request known unto the Lord. The veil has been torn and we can ascend in prayer to hear from God and speak to God. We are sons of God and adopted into the family of God because we are redeemed and restored back to our rightful place through Christ on the cross.

Jesus still speaks today to us through the Holy Spirit and His written Word, just has much as He spoke to His disciples of old. I know some don't believe God talks to believers today. The biblical fact remains that God is sovereign and can speak and use whomever He chooses without man's approval or opinion on the matter.

13

SIGNS, WONDERS, AND MIRACLES

And God confirmed the message by giving signs and wonders and various miracles and gifts of the Holy Spirit whenever he chose.
—HEBREWS 2:4 NLT

God speaks and confirms His own words through miracles, signs, and wonders. He confirms His words by His actions. In other words, God backs up what He says. Jesus was accustomed to this in His life and ministry here on earth. It was not limited to Jesus but was extended to Jesus' disciples, and that includes you as well. The Scripture speaks many times over of God working with those who are His with miraculous signs and kingdom power demonstrated.

The Scriptures are prophetic, God-breathed, and when we speak, hear, and receive God's Word by faith He begins to move suddenly and miraculously on our behalf. He only confirms His words, not our words. Everything was created miraculously by His words. God's spoken word is equally powerful when we hear it and respond in obedience.

Signs, wonders, and miracles reveal God's mercy and character (Ps. 136:4-25). God performed miracles in Egypt to bring deliverance and freedom to His people, both to reveal Himself to the nations but also to show Israel that He truly is God (Exod. 10:2). The glory of God was a constant reminder of God's presence, but it also provided direction as a navigational system for Israel. The prophetic voice of God gave Israel direction, guidance, and provision.

Miraculous tongues confirmed to the apostles of the New Testament that the Gentiles had indeed received the baptism of the Holy Spirit (Acts 11:15-18). Miracles were a confirmation that the preaching was of God and was anointed (Mark 16:20; Heb. 2:2-4). When a believer hears and obeys the instructions, principles, and laws of God spoken by the voice of God, blessings, provision, and favor are released to them (Deut. 28).

Nowhere in Scripture are we told that miracles, signs, and wonders would cease. We must understand that God doesn't change His mind or His will concerning your destiny and purpose. God's purposes do not change, so His purpose for the miraculous would logically remain the same. God still speaks just as He is still in the business of performing miracles.

Then and now, miracles reveal His character, power, mercy, and love. They display His greatness and glory to His people, confirming the preaching with signs and miracles. This confirms the presence of the Holy Spirit in the life of those anointed by God. So why are there still many churches and sincere Christians who do not see miracles today or fail to hear the prophetic voice of the Lord speaking? Second Timothy 3:1-5 tells us that in the last days there will be many who have a form of godliness but deny the power of God.

The Bible is not a fairytale or fiction, but 66 books divided into two testaments, written and inspired by God through men. It was relevant then and is today and for generations to come. God speaks through miracles and speaks miracles into being. Time and time again this Holy Canon is laced with the power of God's voice, acts, and those who believed and did mighty exploits in Jesus's name.

There are modern-day teachers who claim that God doesn't do miracles anymore, and we may have accepted what they taught us in the past. Why not? Why not trust your Bible teachers? If there are no miracles happening in your midst, why not accept the explanation of those who teach you? As I matured in God, I saw God work miracles. It contradicted what I was once taught. God was speaking to me directly through stories, testimonies, and through His miraculous acts. What would I deem as truth? My teachers, who didn't believe miracles were for today, or what God demonstrated personally?

He said to them, "Go into all the world and preach the gospel to all creation. Whoever believes and is baptized will be saved, but whoever does not believe will be condemned. And these signs will accompany those who believe: In my name they will drive out demons; they will speak in new tongues" (Mark 16:15-17).

The Word of God is the truth because God spoke it. I realized that miracles are released simply through faith in the Word. If we limit what we believe the Word reveals, then we will block the supernatural occurrence of God in our own lives. God still can supersede our belief system to create a space for us to believe that He is God. He does that from time to time. But my point is that signs will follow those who believe in them and, of course, the One who performs them.

Faith and our belief system must agree with what the Word says we can have, do, and receive. In the name of Jesus, healing, deliverance, miracles, and supernatural gifts are unleashed in us and through us by the Holy Spirit. Truth is that light dispels darkness (error). Faith to hear God speak is not only to me a miracle but it's an honor to hear the voice of the Father. Jesus was the earthly model and template for His disciples to duplicate in their own lives and ministry.

The truth is, regardless what teachings are out there opposing the prophetic, miracles, tongues, and deliverance, God still does miracles today! He still confirms His Word with miracles as He did in Bible days. Moreover, He still proves without a shadow of a doubt His greatness and awesomeness by amazing deeds, signs, and wonders.

Nowhere in Scripture are we told that God Himself will cease from performing the miracles. There is only one verse some Bible teachers use to give a biblical explanation for miracles ceasing; that is First Corinthians 13:10, which says, *"But when that which is perfect has come, then that which is in part will be done away"* (NKJV).

Their interpretation is to say that when we have the canonized Bible there is no more need for miracles or such supernatural activities of God; therefore, they believe that God will stop doing miracles or speaking prophetically and directly to His people, because we now have God's perfect written Word (the Bible) and we don't need anything else.

And in the last days it shall be, God declares, that I will pour out my Spirit on all flesh, and your sons and your daughters shall prophesy, and your young men shall see visions, and your old men shall dream dreams; even on my male servants and female servants in those days I will pour out my Spirit, and they shall prophesy. And I will show wonders in the heavens above and signs on the earth below, blood, and fire, and vapor of smoke; the sun shall be turned to darkness and the moon to blood, before the day of the Lord comes, the great and magnificent day (Acts 2:17-20 ESV).

We can see clearly that after the prophetic spirit and outpouring occurred, dreams and visions were released. But most importantly, God showed signs in the heavens and wonders in the earth. God performs supernatural things when His prophetic Spirit is released upon His people. The prophetic spirit releases the supernatural. I always say that the prophetic spirit is the doorway to the supernatural.

This passage of Scripture proves my point is not a theory. God speaks by showing His wonders and signs in the heavens and earth. The God of all creation speaks to His people throughout all biblical history. He performs miracles; gives people such as kings, prophets, and ordinary men and women dreams and visions; sends angelic help; and so much more. But now, all of a sudden, God has sent us the Bible and decided to vacate the premises and stop performing mighty acts?

Sadly, at one point in my life at an early age I used to believe such teachings, but God proved those teaching and theories wrong by personal encounters. He did it by giving me dreams and visions, speaking to me audibly, performing miracles in my life, and so much more. He made supernatural revelation a reality in my life.

I have personally experienced the supernatural protection of God when I was stuck in traffic for two hours and later found out there was a fatal accident. God was speaking to me by protecting me from unseen danger. The voice of the Lord can be comprehended through a miracle. When my great-aunt was in a coma and the family wanted to pull the plug, I interceded that His will be done and overrode their decision. Later, she came out of the coma eating apple sauce and coherent. We must see the voice of God working in our lives through the supernatural.

14

LOVE AND COMPASSION

Remember, Lord, your great mercy and love, for they are from of old.
—PSALM 25:6

One of the greatest things that drew me to the Lord was His love. We know that the Bible says that God is love. It is His very nature. He loved the world so much that He gave us His only begotten Son. That is the greatest display and supernatural love that anyone can give.

Can you imagine God asking you to give up one of your children? I am sure all of you who are parents would have a very hard time obeying that instruction. But Abraham understood that if he killed his only son on the altar, the same God who gave that instruction could resurrect Isaac.

God's love is expressive and that is why we are commanded to love each other. The Cross of Calvary is a supernatural sign of the love and nature of God. Jesus was the Lamb of God slain before the foundation of the earth. Love was hanging from the Cross; He carried our diseases, sickness, iniquity, and sin (Isa. 53:3-4). God will speak to us through His abiding love. We must understand that we didn't choose Him—God chose us first.

The Bible says we can't come to the Father unless the Father draws us. His love drew you into a laid-down-lover, covenant relationship with the Father. When you fall short of the glory of God, His abiding love through the Holy Spirit speaks to us to arise and shine for our light has come and the glory of the Lord shall be risen upon us, according to Isaiah 60. God's love covers a multitude of sins. God will speak to us through His unconditional love. When you are going astray, His still small voice and love will remind you that God will never leave you or forsake you.

As children of God, His love toward us at times will chasten us. He corrects or chastens those He loves, the Bible declares. God's love doesn't condone sin but convicts us of wrong acts, and His love doesn't condemn us but covers us. The Bible says He draws us with loving kindness and mercy. God is love and shows loving kindness as well. It other words, God is merciful toward us even when we sin or fall short.

One of the powerful and primary ways God speaks to me especially in prophetic ministry is by moving my heart with compassion. He also does that to me in my day-to-day involvement with people when I ask Him to teach me how to love like Jesus. I can't tell you how many times I have been in a public place—a restaurant, on break at work, behind the pulpit, in Times Square in Manhattan, or running some sort of errand and not even thinking about ministering to anyone—when God speaks.

Suddenly, someone catches my eye or stands out to me and my heart is moved with compassion to prophesy. I can't get their face out of my head and God zooms in on them like eagle eyes. That's when I know the Holy Spirit is up to something and I start inquiring of the Lord for prophetic insight as I approach the individual, ready to jump into the next God adventure. I feel my heart being moved with compassion and I hear the voice of the Lord as God begins to speak to me concerning this individual. God uses love through the lens of compassion to share His heart with a complete stranger through me.

After talking to many evangelists and those called to curbside ministry throughout the years, I've come to the conclusion that the compassion and love of Christ usually is the number-one way God grabs our attention to respond. I didn't realize praying for more of the love of Christ would amplify my ability to feel and hear the heartbeat of the Father toward someone. God will speak if we ask Him for more love. Jesus understood and exemplified what love looks like when He died on the Cross. Even in Jesus's ministry here on earth He was moved by compassion.

Throughout the Gospels we can read fourteen times that Jesus was moved by compassion for other people. Matthew 20:34 shares an example: *"Jesus had compassion on them and touched their eyes.*" The fascinating part about this is whenever Jesus embodied compassion through what He felt, He would stop everything He was doing and would focus His entire attention on the individual His heart was being stirred up and moved for.

I think it's safe to say that compassion was a big part of how the Spirit led Jesus in His ministry. How much does it influence you in your daily decisions? I love this quote from Heidi Baker, a loving and compassionate woman of God whose ministry serves in the most desolate places on earth: *"Never be too busy to stop for the one."*

One of my spiritual papas, Leif Hetland, who is called an apostle of love, shared with my brother and me one day that *"love is what God looks like."* Compassion is seeing with God's eyes. I believe it takes faith to love and love to have faith in others. Fear to love can kill compassion. We need compassion that stirs up faith to love like Jesus. Fear is the opposite of faith and hate is the opposite of love. Compassion and love are linked to faith. Faith without works is dead. We have to use the compassion of Christ to get results as Christians.

God wants to speak to you through the lens of compassion. I learn compassion by loving the most unlovable people. I learn mercy by needing mercy I don't deserve. The love of God that some people will experience is through you—the believer.

15

STILLNESS AND QUIETNESS

Be still and know (recognize, understand) that I am God. I will
be exalted among the nations! I will be exalted in the earth.
—Psalm 46:10 AMP

God wants to speak to us when we are still. I couldn't hear God when I was going through personal turmoil and spiritual attacks. It was like looking for my car keys. I would mess up the whole bedroom trying to find them, and once I calmed down and settled myself, my keys were right in front of me the whole time. God wants to settle the noise and distractions in our lives and speak to us when we are still. Noise and stillness live within the heart. There are even thought distractions that come to make us weary in the mind.

We must relax, exhale, and close our eyes and think about the goodness of the Lord. As we meditate on God, He will calm the boisterous waves in our life. Sometimes our emotions can get the best of us when abrupt things happen. Our minds can wander at times, and struggles of life can put a good beating on our faith. But getting still before the Lord will cause Him to rebuke and speak to any life-altering storm or situation that arises.

I am reminded of the disciples who were afraid for their lives when the storms beat up against the boat. Jesus was asleep while the disciples were awake frantically unaware of the position of Jesus. They were up worrying and Jesus was snoozing. They woke Him up and He challenged their faith and addressed their fear. Fear is the opposite of faith. Jesus had to adjust their fear to instill faith to believe for the impossible. Jesus spoke to the storm and sea and it obeyed Him.

Some things in our lives may come as a surprise and may be out of our control. Worrying will not change anything, but having peace and stillness will give you the advantage. Have faith in Jesus that He can calm your uneasy mind and rebuke every situation that is contrary to God's will for your life.

Jesus wants us to rest in the boats of our lives. I'm not saying that life will be comfortable but that you will not be shipwrecked but will be in a partnership with Him in prayer to cease all storms and raging seas in your life. We must rest and be still before Him. God loves to speak when we are quiet and still before Him. Most of my answers come to me when I have calmed down to think and gather my thoughts. Just like the car keys I was looking for, I would have saved myself a lot of time if I did that first. Instead, I made the situation worse by messing up the bedroom when the whole time the keys were right in front of me.

You must know by faith that your answer in life is in front of you. The Lord Jesus holds the keys to success and your destiny. Why? Because He has been where you are going and He knows the outcome. Jesus holds the answers to your problems and wants to release them prophetically to you as you are still before Him. Quiet your spirit and allow the voice of the Lord to be amplified in your life.

For me, it took a great deal of discipline and obedience to hear God's voice accurately. I needed to be mature enough in the spirit with spiritual disciplines to able to calm down and hear God's voice clearly. God is requiring us as His sons and daughters to seek a deeper relationship that will unlock supernatural encounters with God and allow us to hear His voice whispering or speaking to us even in our most challenging times. I love this quote about a deeper walk with God in hearing His voice:

> The depth of your walk with God is directly proportional to the zeal with which you seek him. If you seek after God in a halfhearted, inconsistent manner, you cannot expect to hear Him speaking at the deepest levels. But if you will discipline yourself to concentrate

on the Lord and if you diligently obey everything He says, then you will be prepared to experience God at an increasingly profound and personal level. God has invited you to go deeper in your relationship with Him. The depth of that relationship ultimately rests with you.[1]

God made this promise to His people: *"And ye shall seek me, and find me, when ye shall search for me with all your heart"* (Jer. 29:13 KJV). God keeps His promises. Seek Him with all of your heart, and you will hear His voice. By abiding in His presence, we can actually be doing or thinking something else and still hear His quickening prophetic words in all forms.

The storm's purpose was destruction, and Jesus reversed it with the power of the spoken word. Jesus reassured the disciples' faith in the one whom the winds, storms, and seas obeyed. We must follow Jesus's example on the boat, resting and asleep during the storm, and just rest when things happen. Notice that the storm didn't wake Jesus up. Jesus didn't allow the storm to control His peace and rest. Don't lose sleep over something that is not life threatening. There have been times I have slept through unpredicted hurricanes, blizzards, and strange weather patterns. I would awaken and say to myself, "Wow, I didn't know that happened," because I was sound asleep.

Rest in faith in your God and hear His words of reassurance. I believe that stillness of the heart is essential to hearing the prophetic voice of the Lord. Shift your thoughts and silence the noise of life that comes as a distraction or decoy to slow your destiny momentum. Tune out the voices and thoughts that plague or flutter your mind. Rest in God's Word that will drown out the noise.

NOTE

1. Henry and Richard Blackaby, *Hearing God's Voice* (Nashville, TN: Broadman & Holman, 2002), 246.

16

DEFINING MOMENTS

*They triumphed over him by the blood of the Lamb
and by the word of their testimony; they did not love
their lives so much as to shrink from death.*
—REVELATION 12:11

In our lives God uses defining moments to shape and reshape us. Life can throw us curve balls while at the same time experience can often be our best teacher. God permits things to occur to speak to us through those situations or events. Why? He wants to see how we take His instructions, warning, guidance, and leading. Current situations can also be the result of a bad experience. We can change things by deciding to heed the voice of the Lord in the midst of it. I love this quote: "When a defining moment comes along, you define the moment or the moment defines you."

I have heard the voice of God in the most unusual times and places. He is a Father and coach who wants nothing but the best for His children. There is a prophetic advantage when we can look at past or present moments, events, life experiences, and supernatural encounters and come away with a powerful testimony of God's delivering, saving, and unconditional love toward us. God speaks through life experiences, tests, events, and moments to navigate our steps toward purpose and destiny.

What is a defining moment? It's an event that determines all subsequent related occurrences. I believe there are defining moments throughout life. A defining moment is any turn of events in your life in which a choice that you make or an incident that happens causes something in your life to shift, change, or alter. It's a turning point in your life that defines, shapes, and cultivates your life from that moment forward. Throughout a lifetime you will have many defining moments.

A defining moment can be viewed as simply a person moving from one state to another. Someone getting married, having their first child, the death of a loved one, graduation, or a major promotion on a job. A defining moment can be simply one who moves from being a child to a teenager and teenager to adulthood. God speak to us in those moments that shape our thought processes and allow us to overcome life.

As a believer, you too will experience many defining moments spiritually and literally in your walk with Christ—giving your life to the Lord, getting baptized, receiving the gift of tongues, preaching your first sermon, and moving in the gifts of the Holy Spirit. Defining moments and events will ultimately happen throughout your spiritual life and walk with Jesus. The first day you became a believer in Christ was a defining moment. When I first gave my life to the Lord, several months later I was faced with opposition as a newbie in Christ; that was a defining moment.

Furthermore, a defining moment could be when you weathered a tough storm in your life or when you discovered a biblical truth for the first time by revelation given by the Holy Spirit. You can see that in all of these situations you heard the voice of God working through the defining moment. There are two truths concerning defining moments in a person's life. One, people are not limited to having only one defining moment in their lives. Two, defining moments will have a huge, revolutionary impact upon your life when they do occur. Most likely, once you have a defining moment you are not the same again.

Throughout biblical history and modern history we have many defining moments in the lives of human beings that changed the course of history and created destiny. Men and women who have shaped history as we know it had many defining moments. In the Word of God, there are men and women who were noted for their faith in hearing God and obedience to His voice in defining moments. The Word of God is a great place to start and receive great examples of defining moments in the lives of those God anointed and called.

Moses had various defining moments in his life. He was adopted by Pharaoh's daughter, killed an Egyptian, received the Ten Commandments, and parted the Red Sea—all defining moments used by God to speak to Moses. A famous defining moment was when he found the burning bush and God spoke to him.

We also have Daniel and the three Hebrew boys Shadrach, Meshach, and Abednego who experienced supernatural defining moments when they were taken into captivity. Moreover, Daniel had a defining moment when he was thrown into a den full of hungry, ferocious lions. Shadrach, Meshach, and Abednego had a defining moment when they were thrown into a fiery furnace and a fourth man was in there with them and they were not touched by fire nor smelled like smoke. We can see God speaking and intervening in times that define us and change our course forever.

Moreover, we can look at King David who had some interesting defining moments in his life that affected him in negative and positive ways. Our decision in a defining moment can be the wrong decision if we don't seek the counsel and wisdom of the Lord. Every decision we make must be infused by the wisdom of God and direction of the Holy Spirit. We can see that David made the decision to sin with Bathsheba; it was a defining moment that over time made things worse, not better. Later confronted by Nathan about the sin, David entered into another defining moment that challenged his heart condition. God spoke to David by the prophet, as He still speaks in times when we make decisions that are life altering.

The apostle Paul had at least three defining moments—when Stephen was stoned, when he was on the road to Damascus and saw Jesus, and when he accepted Jesus as his Savior.

There are a plethora of examples we can take away from the Word of God of people who experienced personally defining moments that caused them to encounter something that was beyond their human experience. An encounter with the Holy Spirit can create a defining moment that transcends a person and shifts them radically out of their paradigm of life. I would say that a life-altering encounter is a defining moment that God uses to move a person outside the box.

Deliverance or receiving a healing touch can be a defining moment initiated by the Holy Spirit. When we have a personal, revolutionary experience with God we are never the same again. Take Joshua, for instance. He had many defining moments that eventually caused the whole nation of Israel to have a defining moment thanks to his obedience. In Exodus 33, we see a glimpse of a defining moment for Joshua in verse 11, where it reveals to us that when Moses left the Tent of Meeting Joshua would not leave the tent. Joshua stayed put to spend some quality time with God on his face, and it was life changing. Because of the one-on-one dialogue, I classify it as a defining moment.

Furthermore, in Deuteronomy 31 Moses anoints and chooses Joshua as the military general to succeed him as the leader of the Israelites and to take them into the Promised Land. That was a defining moment in history. Supernaturally, Joshua came to the Jordan River at flood stage once again— another defining moment for Joshua and for the nation. We can see that hearing God and obeying His voice in your life creates defining moments and has the potential to create defining moments for those who follow you. Joshua's defining moments lead the nation of Israel to their defining moment.

Defining moments, experiences, and encounters are shaped by our decisions. When the Israelites stood at the banks of the Jordan River, they had to make a decision to follow God and cross the flooded river or to stay put and die off like the previous generation. This event defined them as a nation who obeyed their God and trusted solely in Him to provide a way of escape when there seemed to be no way. Moreover, as the water began to split ways and the people proceeded to cross over into the Promised Land on dry ground, they entered into a seasonal shift called a defining moment.

After the children of Israel crossed over, they were suddenly met with another choice to make. Now they were faced with an impossible task while standing outside of the city of Jericho, the first city to conquer, and the people who occupied it were strong and well protected. It was far beyond their ability to penetrate the walls of this fortified city, and yet they obeyed the voice of the Lord and had a defining moment when they let God win the battle for them. They followed through on every detail of what He said to do through the leadership of Joshua.

17

MEDITATION

This book of the law shall not depart out of thy mouth; but thou shalt meditate therein day and night, that thou mayest observe to do according to all that is written therein: for then thou shalt make thy way prosperous, and then thou shalt have good success.
—JOSHUA 1:8 KJV

We must understand that God will speak to us through our meditation on His Word. In Joshua 1, we can see that they he was instructed to study by meditating on the book of the law. He was to meditate day and night and to observe by doing what was written in it. Joshua prospered and had great success as he meditated on the Word of God.

The Hebrew word for "meditate" is the word *hagah*, which means "to murmur (in pleasure or anger); by implication, to ponder, imagine, meditate, mourn, mutter, roar, sore, speak, study, talk, and utter" (Strong's #H1897). Meditating will give you the ability to prophetically retain, recall, remember, and recite what God's will is and what you are to do.

God wants to hold a conversation with us as we meditate upon His Word daily. We are not just to meditate on the Word of God, but there are times I go back and listen to a prophetic word that I have received. I meditate on what God is saying, and wisdom is released for me to fulfill that personal prophecy. Faith comes by hearing the Word of God.

I recall a time when I was studying the Word and there was one particular Scripture in Isaiah 60 about the glory of God. As I continued to rehearse and play the verse over and over in my head, out of nowhere God brought instant revelation of what that Scripture verse meant. I was only trying to memorize the verse, but God imprinted it on my spirit and it spoke volumes to me and I heard His audible inner voice.

Sometimes I meditate on something in the Word of God, and later when I am ministering to someone God brings that Scripture back to my remembrance and tells me that it's a prophetic word for that person. God has me speak the Scripture verse with authority, power, and in my own unique way. He takes that word I meditated upon and makes it a *rhema* prophetic word. In other words, God speaks to me through His *logos* (written Word) and makes it a prophetic *rhema* (proceeding right now) word for that person.

Meditation is a powerful tool for believers, and we must practice often in order to adapt to the voice of God and have a trained ear to hear what the Spirit of the Lord is saying at any given time. I used to practice martial arts with my uncle Craig Collins and my late father Eric Guy, both high-degree black belts. They taught me the art of meditation and stretching. Meditation stretches our mental capacity and settles, quiets, and brings peace to us even when the world around us is in chaos. Meditation makes us become one with the Word of God, reflect on the Word, and make the Word of God alive and effective in our lives. Moreover, meditation can sharpen you and cause you to be in tune with God—mind, body, and soul.

Whenever I meditate on a prophetic word or dream, I journal it and then God speaks to me with the interpretation or meaning. We are to remind God of His Word, not because He doesn't know what He said but to show Him that we know it and recall it.

Eve misquoted God with regard to the tree of the knowledge of good and evil. God told her not to eat of that particular tree in the midst of the garden. But she told the serpent God said not to eat or touch of the fruit of the tree of the knowledge of good and evil. They could have touched it, but they weren't permitted to eat of it. Touching and eating are two different actions. But her curiosity caused her to touch it, and touching it may have caused her to eat of it and disobey God.

My point is that we are to know the Word of God. Meditating on it and reciting it, at times out loud, will help us to retain it and memorize it. Meditation is memorization, repetition, and prayerful rumination on Scripture texts.

> *How blessed is the man who does not walk in the counsel of the wicked, nor stand in the path of sinners, nor sit in the seat of scoffers! But his delight is in the law of the Lord, and in His law he meditates day and night. He will be like a tree firmly planted by streams of water, which yields its fruit in its season and its leaf does not wither; and in whatever he does, he prospers* (Psalm 1:1-3 NASB).

> *Let the words of my mouth and the meditation of my heart be acceptable in Your sight, O Lord, my rock and my Redeemer* (Psalm 19:14 NASB).

Meditating on the Word of God is a discipline. As a prophet I had to learn the principle of waiting on God, listening, and being still before God. God speaks through us meditating and waiting on Him and His word. Meditate with your eyes closed, rehearsing over and over the Scriptures that you have heard or studied. You will feel the presence of God and you will hear His voice through your thoughts. In meditation, supernatural things begin to occur, such as visions, trances, being transported in the spirit, and angelic visitations.

When we meditate on Jesus we engage Him through concentrating on God's presence and Word. We are to ponder, reflect, contemplate, and center our focus on things of God and getting lost in Christ where our purpose is found and discovered. We are called to think on those things above and not beneath. Colossians 3:2 declares, *"Set your minds on things that are above, not on things that are on earth"* (ESV).

18

WISDOM OF GOD

Instruct the wise, and they will be even wiser. Teach the righteous,
and they will learn even more. Fear of the Lord is the foundation
of wisdom. Knowledge of the Holy One results in good judgment.
Wisdom will multiply your days and add years to your life.
—**PROVERBS 9:9-11 NLT**

God speaks prophetically to us through the Holy Spirit and gives us wisdom and understanding. There is a wisdom and understanding that comes only from God that will give us access to divine blessings and success. King Solomon, the son of King David, inquired of the Lord, and He asked Solomon what he wanted. Solomon, being very young as David's heir, asked for wisdom to lead God's people (2 Chron. 1:7-12).

Solomon didn't ask for wealth, possessions, honor, or glory—not even for death to his enemies—but for wisdom and knowledge instead. God gave him his heart's desire and then gave him what he didn't ask for as well, more than any king before him. Wisdom and knowledge caused him to inherit not just the kingdom but also the benefits of the kingdom. Wisdom is the Hebrew word *biynah*, which means "knowledge which is perfect, understanding, wisdom" (Strong's #H998). Read the below passages of Scripture regarding wisdom:

> *But where shall wisdom be found? and where is the place of understanding?* (Job 28:12 KJV)

> *And unto man he said, Behold, the fear of the Lord, that is wisdom; and to depart from evil is understanding* (Job 28:28 KJV).

> *If now thou hast understanding, hear this: hearken to the voice of my words* (Job 34:16 KJV).

God speaks to us from the place of wisdom to give us understanding, which is perfect knowledge through His Spirit. We can ask for godly wisdom. The fear of the Lord is the beginning of wisdom, and to separate from evil is understanding. God gives us wisdom and understanding in life situations. In other words, He gives us the why and how of things that we need and ask Him for. First Kings 3:10-15 says that God was pleased that Solomon asked for wisdom and a discerning heart. Wisdom gives us a discerning heart to understand. Solomon was wise enough to ask for godly wisdom. He needed the counsel and direction of the Lord to govern and rule. Many people can lead but are unable to rule because of lack of wisdom and understanding.

God's people often perish because of lack of knowledge. Ignorance is a deadly weapon against the believer in Christ. God is please when we ask for spiritual things and not material possessions. God was pleased that Solomon asked for wisdom and understanding to fulfill his calling. What are we asking God concerning our callings, gifts, and ministry? Are we asking for God to equip and educate us with know-how and purpose to fulfill them? Because Solomon asked God for wisdom, God granted him that and wealth, possessions, honor, favor, and long life if he obeyed. God spoke to Solomon by appearing to him in a dream, and in the dream Solomon asked and it happened.

Before I move on to the other prophetic ways God speaks, we cannot mix up or confuse godly wisdom verses worldly wisdom. In other words, there is earthly wisdom and there is heavenly wisdom. There is a difference between the two. As we grow in godly wisdom we will hear the voice of the Lord and His direction in everything we decide to do. Sometimes we think God is speaking to us in our decisions, but it is the wisdom of man. Let me create several examples briefly of what earthly wisdom looks like compared to godly wisdom. Then as believers we can discern the difference as we process the voice of God. Earthly wisdom is a result of being self-focused instead of God-focused!

I love how James described spiritual wisdom in James 3:13: *"Who is wise and understanding among you? Let them show it by their good life, by deeds done in the humility that comes from wisdom."* The Greek word that describes our English word humility means "gentleness of spirit or mildness of disposition." It is said a horse that had been broken is an illustration of humility.

You can't reason with a horse that has never been ridden or talk it into letting you ride on its back. You just have to jump on its back and ride until the horse realizes that you are the boss and you are in control. The horse comes under subjection to your will and recognizes your authority. But here is the kicker (pun intended)—a broken horse still has all the ability, power, and strength that it once had. The difference is, now its will, ability, and power are under the control of someone else. The horse yields himself to the rider and the rider takes full control.

Godly wisdom doesn't surrender its ability, power, and will totally over; it just places it under new management. In other words, the horse decided to submit and yield itself to new management. But at any time, if it wants to rebel it can kick the rider off with the same power, ability, and force it uses to submit.

Imagine what revelation the apostle James gained about spiritual wisdom from the wisdom of King Solomon. We must understand that humility brings about wisdom and pride brings about disgrace (1 Kings 3:1-14; 4:29-34). *"When pride comes, then comes disgrace, but with humility comes wisdom"* (Prov. 11:2).

19

SELF-DENIAL AND HUMILITY

Then Jesus said to his disciples, "Whoever wants to be my disciple
must deny themselves and take up their cross and follow me."
—MATTHEW 16:24

Something powerful happens when we deny ourselves and receive God's embrace. We can hear the voice of the Lord more when we humble ourselves. Many people don't understand how vital self-denial is. One of the most sobering things that God will require out of us is a daily sacrifice that will cause us to come to a place of self-denial. This is a place like the Garden of Gethsemane, where Jesus understood that it was not His own will but the will of the Father for Him to go to the Cross. Gethsemane was a place of great agony and pressure, but Jesus understood it was His purpose to go the Cross.

As modern-day disciples of Christ we are to humble ourselves and follow after Christ. God will speak to us as a reminder to remain humble and stay focused on the course that He has outline for us. I hear God speaking to me the most when I get a little ahead of myself. God often has to speak to me in a loving tone for me to tone it down and hide myself in Him.

The most powerful people are those who have learned the art of self-denial. I believe its spiritual maturity and discipline when a believer knows how to put their flesh and their own will, agenda, and emotions under control. Yielding to the Holy Spirit and walking in humility is self-denial. Leaders and believers have to learn this great biblical principle. Jesus is that self-denial model for us as children of God.

Whenever I sense pride or haughtiness grip by heart, I immediately repent, renounce, and discard it. God exalts the humble and makes base the ones who exalt themselves. Self-denial is a great reminder to live like Christ did and follow His example:

> Then Jesus told his disciples, "If anyone would come after me, let him deny himself and take up his cross and follow me. For whoever would save his life will lose it, but whoever loses his life for my sake will find it. For what will it profit a man if he gains the whole world and forfeits his soul? Or what shall a man give in return for his soul?" (Matthew 16:24-26 ESV)

Personally, this can be a painful place to be, but it has glorious incentives and benefits of a multiplied life. Jesus, our example and model, chose to yield His own will and lay His life down as a righteous seed for the sake of multiplying that seed to all who will believe on His name. We must understand that He denied Himself so that we may not be denied and may be given full access to eternal life. His death on the Cross produced a seed of righteousness for the entire human race (1 Cor. 3:6-9).

Moreover, like Jesus, when we go through death to self, Daddy-God selects what fruit our yieldedness will ultimately produce. I believe every Spirit-filled believer will produce a different harvest that will be based off of their obedience, submission, and yieldedness to die to self and their own will to fulfill the will of the Father in their lives. The Father chose that Jesus' physical death would be multiplied beyond the tomb and grave by producing the harvest fruit of eternal salvation for anyone who partakes of that fruit. Jesus is the righteous seed that produces a righteous harvest. As we draw near to God, he will draw near to us (James 4:8).

The closer we draw to God and give up our own desires, the more we will see the blessing of God manifest. God speaks clearly to us as we die to our own purposes to fulfill His purpose no matter what. Death to self will not be a first priority for everyone. But those who want the Lord more than the world and mammon (material things) and are willing to follow Jesus Christ even to the cross or even unto death will hear God on earth and inherit the earth in the greatest available harvest ever. We have to be like Jesus and say, "Not my will, Father, but Your will be done in my life."

There is nothing wrong with denying your own appetites. I am reminded of a car that has to yield to oncoming traffic. Sometimes God speaks to us by the Holy Spirit so that we don't launch out into oncoming traffic. In our yielding we allow others to go before us, which makes a clear path to our own purpose and destiny without any collisions, accidents, or even premature deaths.

Jesus was all human and all God at the same time. But at Gethsemane, you could say Jesus's human side kicked in with the reality of death on the Cross approaching, and He asked God that the cup would pass from Him. After that natural moment of human emotions, suddenly the quickening power of God and the reality of His purpose for humanity transcended it. Jesus came to Himself as God in the flesh and yielded to the will of the Father through self-denial. His self-denial gave us a corporate purpose of destiny and eternal life in Christ. Jesus's natural human emotions didn't want to die for that moment, but the God-given quickening the soul and flesh. God's will for our lives far transcends our own will and plans.

20

LIMITED FLEECING

Then Gideon said to God, "If you will save Israel by my hand, as you have said, behold, I am laying a fleece of wool on the threshing floor. If there is dew on the fleece alone, and it is dry on all the ground, then I shall know that you will save Israel by my hand, as you have said." And it was so. When he rose early next morning and squeezed the fleece, he wrung enough dew from the fleece to fill a bowl with water. Then Gideon said to God, "Let not your anger burn against me; let me speak just once more. Please let me test just once more with the fleece. Please let it be dry on the fleece only, and on all the ground let there be dew." And God did so that night; and it was dry on the fleece only, and on all the ground there was dew.
—JUDGES 6:36-40 ESV

I remember early in my Christian walk there were times that I wasn't sure God heard my prayers. I would ask Him for a sign or to confirm it. There was nothing wrong with that, but there came a time when God stopped showing me confirmation. Why? I was at the stage of spiritual maturation that I didn't need to ask for confirmation or a sign. I got frustrated that God stopped showing me signs, so I would try to negotiate with the Lord by saying, "If He does this, then I will do that." This was not good at all, nor is this the way we approach a holy and sovereign God. I was fleecing the Lord. I was making it based on *my terms that He should answer my prayers or fulfill something by confirmation.*

It should never be on our terms that we go before the Lord but always on the terms and conditions that He has set out for us. God will at times speak to us through a fleece, but that is not the best practice. Mature believers must seek the Lord for His will, wisdom, and direction through the Holy Spirit. We don't bargain with the Lord. What He says goes and is final. I was still immature in my faith and needed reassurance by the Lord. As we grow in our relationship with Daddy-God, we don't have to fleece Him for anything. God is sovereign and doesn't move on our terms or conditions but on His only.

There are some biblical examples of "fleecing" that was acceptable for God's intervention and confirmation. But we should not have to fleece God when we walk by faith.

Fleecing to me is like someone saying to God, "If You do this than I will do that, and if You show me a sign that it's You than I will finally obey." It is like you have to bargain and ask God to prove Himself on your terms. Fleecing is not faith; obedience is faith in what God is speaking. You have to trust without a shadow of a doubt what God is saying. Prophecy is conditional and must be followed through with obedience and faith. Prophecy doesn't need fleecing.

Knowing this first of all, that no prophecy of Scripture comes from someone's own interpretation (2 Peter 1:20 ESV).

21

PRAYER

Hear my prayer, O God; give ear to the words of my mouth.
—PSALM 54:2 NKJV

Prayer is one of the greatest communication vehicles that God uses to speak to His people and His people use to speak to Him. I believe that prayer becomes the spiritual altar where God visits, speaks, and lives within the believer. I often say that a prayerless believer is a powerless believer. Prayer is the doorway or portal (entryway) from Heaven to earth and earth to Heaven. The Bible says that men should always pray. They are admonished and encouraged to never cease from praying. To stop praying is to stop communicating with the Father and Son through the Holy Spirit.

God also speaks to us when we pray. Unfortunately, many of us have the mistaken idea that the purpose of prayer is to change God's mind. We think, "If I can just plead with God long enough and hard enough, He'll give me what I'm asking for." Prayer is not a way to twist God's arm. Prayer is God's means of getting through to us so that we can do things for Him!

As we pray, God takes our focus off of our needs and puts our focus on His love and His power. Through prayer, God changes our perspective to conform to His purposes; He establishes His priorities for our lives; He leads us into all truth. Through prayer God will filter your requests to make sure they align to His Word first and second to His divine will, purpose, and destiny for your life. Prayer is the open channel through faith that accesses things from the invisible realm into the visible realm. Noah, Moses, Abraham, Isaac, Jacob,

Solomon, and others built altars for God. They built altars at times because God appeared and spoke to them. When we pray and build spiritual altars, God comes down and speaks to us.

God spoke to the young prophet and priest Samuel and called him into the prophetic office. God speaks to us in a still small voice in prayer. Prayer is the main communication system that God speaks through. The Holy Spirit gives us the spirit language of Heaven to communicate to God. Prayer is not a one-way communication method but it goes both ways.

What is prayer? I believe that prayer, very simply, is talking to God. Prayer should not be viewed as a mere religious act but a daily conversation with a loved one who is our heavenly Father. We pray and communicate with Him through the Holy Spirit. Prayer is our direct line to Heaven from earth. I liken prayer to a phone call from one dimension to another. Prayer is how we hear the voice of God.

Prayer is like when we call upon the Lord and in the realm of Heaven He answers us and releases what we are requesting according to His will. We must understand that prayer is a communication process that allows us to talk to our Father. In turn, God loves to talk with His children and wants us to communicate with Him daily, like a person-to-person phone call. We hear the voice of God talking in prayer.

Prayer should be the lifestyle of every Christian. We are told to pray without ceasing! God's communication will not become a dropped call. As children of God we should pray boldly, knowing that no matter how far we travel, our connection to the Father can never be lost or disconnected. It is in the place of prayer that God softens our heart and gives us a spiritual heart transplant. The Father's heartbeat and love overshadow me daily as He speaks to me.

I believe if we are praying often we can hear the voice of God speaking often. When we don't pray at all there are things we can miss out on that the Father wants to disclose privately and personally. The Bible says, *"One day Jesus told his disciples a story to show that they should always pray and never give up"* (Luke 18:1 NLT).

Prayer to me is not only talking to God but God talking to those who make themselves available. Prayer is a powerful means to connect to the God of Heaven. Praying to the Lord consists of making daily requests or petitions, offering up thanksgiving, as well as the giving of praise and being still before Him to wait on His response. Hearing the voice of God through prayer benefits the believer who is praying and should not be thought of as a favor we are doing for God.

I believe that we pray because we need the Lord; it's not that God needs us. One of the greatest keys in hearing the voice of God in prayer is learning the principle of listening. We will never be able to discern, recognize, and hear the voice of the God if we don't learn how to listen first. It is easy to do all the talking in prayer, but God loves to speak too and He is also an amazing listener.

We have to learn how to listen by being quiet and still before Him in our prayer time. In addition, there are other powerful fundamental principles we must follow for our prayers to be what they ought to be. First, when we pray it should always be done in Jesus's name (Col. 3:17), which simply means Jesus is our Mediator and we can offer things up to God through His Son (1 Tim. 2:5).

Second, as children of God when we pray it should be done with absolute faith without doubting or questioning (James 1:6-7) and our prayers it must done in accordance with His Word and His will and not ours (1 John 5:14; James 4:13-15). We must be earnest in our prayers, and we must be seeking to live righteously ourselves (James 5:16).

We must not be in a position of fleecing God to do something for us that is not in His will or Word. Our prayers should be clearly that the Father's will be done in all things in our lives, even if it means He's answering our requests with a "no," "wait," or "not yet" (Matt. 26:39; 2 Cor. 12:7-10). When God gives us a no answer, are we still going to seek Him and maintain that love relationship? It should be a covenant relationship with the Father and not conditional based on convenience.

If we expect God to forgive us when we pray, then we must be willing to forgive others (Matt. 6:14). Two great primary biblical examples of prayer are Jesus's model prayer (Matt. 6:9-13) and the apostles' prayer after Peter and John's release (Acts 4:24-30). Praying is connected to our hearing and hearing is connected to our prayer life. We should always pray to be able to hear the voice of the Father daily. God wants to talk to us through the vehicle of prayer if we just lend Him our ear to hear.

> *And after he had dismissed the crowds, he went up on the moun-*
> *tain by himself to pray. When evening came, he was there alone*
> (Matthew 14:23 ESV).

I believe that prayer is the delivery room for our prophetic purpose and destiny to be birthed. God uses prayer and intercession as a way to communicate and release what He desires to do. We are admonished to pray the Lord's will and Kingdom into the realm of reality. God's glory realm is the reality of Heaven. God speaks through us by what we decree and say. We don't name and claim but decree and declare, command and confess the Word of God in our lives. Angels respond to what we pray when it's in accordance with God's Word and will. God speaks to His people through the vehicle of prayer that establishes a personal altar between you and Daddy-God.

We must understand that meditation or passive reflection is not praying. When we pray and hear His voice it is directly addressed to the Father. God, who is the creator of the human soul, communicates with His people through prayer. Hearing God through prayer can be audible or silent, private or public, formal or informal, direct or indirect. As we pray, all prayers should be done and offered in faith (James 1:6), in the name of the Lord Jesus (John 16:23) and in the power of the Holy Spirit (Rom. 8:26).

22

WORSHIP AND PRAISE

Praise the Lord! Praise the Lord, O my soul! I will praise the Lord as
long as I live; I will sing praises to my God while I have my being.
—Psalm 146:1-2 ESV

Oh come, let us worship and bow down; let us
kneel before the Lord, our Maker!
—Psalm 95:6 ESV

Hearing the voice of God through worship and praise is an amazing feel-ing. God speaks to those who will become laid-down lovers of Him and open their hearts for Him to flood them. One of our most important times in the presence of the Lord is when singers are ushering us into worship and praise.

God is gentle at times and doesn't force His will on us. He is looking to speak to those who are vulnerable before God. When I open myself up in worship and total surrender, God speaks to my heart and I begin to feel His presence surrounding me. I weep in worship and I leap in praise before God. There is nothing like worshiping your Creator and giving Him praise.

> *Know that the Lord is God. It is he who made us, and we are*
> *his; we are his people, the sheep of his pasture. Enter his gates*
> *with thanksgiving and his courts with praise; give thanks to him*
> *and praise his name. For the Lord is good and his love endures*

forever; his faithfulness continues through all generations (Psalm 100:3-5).

When we come before the Lord and when we enter into the courts, gates, and presence of the King, worship and praise unlock our ability to hear the voice of God clearly. Whether it's your own personal worship and praise that you do daily or if you are in a church, meeting, or worship concert—He speaks through worship and praise. God becomes the lamb in our worship and the lion in our praise. There is nothing like hearing the Lord say He loves you back and He rejoices and smiles over you. We can see what this passage of Scripture says about the Lord singing over you:

> *The Lord your God is with you, the Mighty Warrior who saves. He will take great delight in you; in his love he will no longer rebuke you, but will rejoice over you with singing* (Zephaniah 3:17).

> *God smile on you and gift you* (Numbers 6:25 MSG).

There are spiritual protocols when we go before the King. The Bible says that those who worship God must worship Him in Spirit and truth (John 4:24). Another powerful way that God speaks to His people prophetically is through worship. Worship, like prayer, is an amazing way to get God's attention. God searches the earth looking for someone who will worship Him. The 24 elders are assigned around the throne, casting down their crowns and worshiping the Lord, crying, "Holy, holy, holy is the Lamb of God." There is something about worship that pleases God.

God loves when we praise Him as well. I call worship and praise fraternal twins. They are connected and both are needed but they look and sound different. Praise can be used to scatter and confuse the enemy. The Bible says that we can enter into His presence with thanksgiving and enter His courts with praise. There is a protocol in worship and praise that will get the King of Glory's attention and blessings. Worship and praise are vital in hearing the voice of God.

In Second Chronicles 20, King Jehoshaphat faced a huge army of enemies who could have easily destroyed his people, but he did a strange thing. With a declaration that his eyes were on God, he sent in a choir of praise singers:

"Jehoshaphat appointed men to sing to the Lord and to praise him for the splendor of his holiness as they went out at the head of the army, saying: 'Give thanks to the Lord, for his love endures forever'" (2 Chron. 20:21). God released His power, and Jehoshaphat's army defeated their enemies!

Praise confuses the enemy and worship causes God to respond on our behalf. When I am going through a rough time or season I go into a praise break. God would speak to me and give me a strategy of victory. He will tell me to praise Him and make Him big—to magnify the Lord in my praise and intensify my worship. Not long after, I start having perpetual breakthroughs. I often say praise gets God's attention but worship draws Him closer to you.

We have to understand that worship and praise are connected to our covenant with God. He lives in our praise and worship. The Bible says that He inhabits the praises of His people. God lives in our praise and causes us to fill our mouths with words that only bring glory to His name. Here are a few Scriptures that will makes sense of what worship and praise mean to God and those who know their God intimately:

> *He is the one you praise; he is your God, who performed for you those great and awesome wonders you saw with your own eyes* (Deuteronomy 10:21).
>
> *Let them praise your great and awesome name—he is holy* (Psalm 99:3).
>
> *Exalt the Lord our God and worship at his holy mountain, for the Lord our God is holy* (Psalm 99:9).
>
> *And he has raised up for his people a horn, the praise of all his faithful servants, of Israel, the people close to his heart. Praise the Lord* (Psalm 148:14).
>
> *Yet you are holy, enthroned on the praises of Israel* (Psalm 22:3 NLT).

We crown God with our worship. Worshiping God in the spirit is just like praying in the spirit because it's a supernatural activity that God can relate to. Hearing the voice of God in worship and even in prayer is something that every believer can tap into. It's not hard to hear the voice of the Lord in worship and in praise, but it must be done through the Holy Spirit.

23

LIFE PAUSES AND
SELAH MOMENTS

Many are saying of my soul, "There is no deliverance for him in
God." Selah. But You, O Lord, are a shield about me, my glory,
and the One who lifts my head. I was crying to the Lord with my
voice, and He answered me from His holy mountain. Selah.
—PSALM 3:2-4 NASB

L ife at times can throw us a curve ball in our plans. We are living in a
fast and evolving world. I am part of the millennial generation that wants
things fast and wants them now. However, that type of mentality and character dynamic can work against me. God can be speaking but I will miss the
details of what He wants to warn me about or give me wisdom concerning
something I am not aware of. Doing things in a rush will cause us to miss very
simple details.

I used to work in banking, and I was very good at what I did. I worked
with large amounts of money, but one of the major requirements was that we
were to pay attention to detail. If we transferred money to the wrong account
then we were legally responsible for the loss and would be terminated from
employment. We had dual control to protect against any human errors, but
that monitoring still couldn't prevent millions of dollars hitting the wrong person's bank account. We were responsible to verify that our entries in the system
were accurate and legit.

For example, if I entered a dollar amount in the system, another employee had to verify my entry before sending the funds out the door to the account holder. If what I entered was incorrect or there was an error in the spelling, then the other employee would correct it and the system would send it back to me to re-verify and then send it out. My point is that I had to pause and take my time. I had to learn not to rush through the process in order to avoid errors and bank losses.

We have to pause at times and wait on the Lord's directives and voice. God speaks to us when we wait on Him and take a deep breath and listen. There is a relief in the sighing and pauses. Pauses allow us to hear the voice of God and regain control over the situation that tries to control us through our emotions and mind. God slows us down a bit so that we will not exhaust ourselves and crash and burn. The Lord uses pauses to allow us to regain renewed strength and initiate wisdom in the midst of a storm.

God gets our attention when we pause and regroup. He uses it to allow us to release life's pressures and unnecessary demands. When we pause we open ourselves up to make us available for the Lord to speak suddenly. There's nothing like rest and peace in the midst of a life-challenging situation. There are times I take a drive in my car to just get away and place things on pause to hear God. Those moments when I decide to pause are some of the greatest personal revivals I encounter with the Lord. In the Song of Solomon 2:9-11, is a love poem that says, *"My beloved is like a gazelle or a young stag. Look! There he stands behind our wall, gazing through the windows, peering through the lattice. My beloved spoke and said to me, 'Arise, my darling, my beautiful one, come with me. See! The winter is past; the rains are over and gone.'"*

This text above is an invitation for us as believers to arise and come away with the Lord. There are seasons to break away and come to a place of stillness, to be loved, poured into, and refreshed by the Holy Spirit. Pausing, to me, is like a mini vacation to just rest and be at peace in the stillness of God. I am reminded of watching a good movie—I don't want to miss anything if the phone rings. I pick up the remote control and hit the pause button. Many of us are missing what God wants to do in our lives. We are constantly busy, distracted, and engulfed in what we are doing.

We have to allow the Holy Spirit to speak to us in those critical moments to indicate we need to pause for a second. Oftentimes, without noticing, we have accommodated others over ourselves and put our life on pause to assist others. We then miss vital times and opportunities. I believe God wants to redeem the time that we lost by regaining and taking control over what we can manage presently.

Life may be moving a bit fast for you, but I have found that those who pause and reflect on what's going on have the upper hand and advantage. Even though I knew my job responsibilities like the back of my hand, attention to detail was a must. God wants us to wait upon Him and pause for a moment to regroup, gather our thoughts, and proceed with caution.

> *"All the earth worships you and sings praises to you; they sing praises to your name." Selah* (Psalm 66:4 ESV).

God speaks prophetically in *selah* moments of our lives. You often see the word selah at the end of a Scripture verse in the Book of Psalms and may ask, "What does *selah* mean in the Bible?" The word *selah* is found in the Old Testament; it appears 71 times in Psalms, as well as three times in the third chapter of the minor prophet Habakkuk.

In some charismatic circles we have praise breaks. I would consider it a *selah* to take a moment to lift God up. In worship times, we pause to lift our hands while lifting God up with our voices. In Psalm 66:4, I believe they were pausing to praise the One about whom the song was speaking, perhaps even lifting their hands in worship. Selah is an action—all the earth bows down to the Lord. The author using the word *selah* after the verse is expecting a response. The meaning of the word *selah* would encompass all this—"praise," "lift up," and "pause." When we consider the three verses in Habakkuk, we also see how *selah* could mean to "pause and praise."

The Amplified Bible inserts the command "pause and calmly think about that" after each verse where *selah* appears. When we see the word *selah* in a psalm or in Habakkuk 3, we should pause to carefully weigh the meaning of what we have just read or heard, lifting up our hearts in praise to God for His great truths. God uses *selah* moments and times to speak to us. The voice of God is amplified in *selah* times in our lives.

24

WISE COUNSEL FROM OTHERS

Then you will discern the fear of the Lord and discover the knowledge of God. For the Lord gives wisdom; from His mouth come knowledge and understanding. He stores up sound wisdom for the upright; He is a shield to those who walk in integrity.
—PROVERBS 2:5-7 NASB

God speaks prophetically through godly wisdom and advice. When I was in one of the most critical seasons in my life, I needed the wisdom and advice from those I could trust. I needed their wisdom and guidance on a certain matter that was life altering. Often we need the wisdom and counsel of others who are qualified to make good, sound judgments and release the wisdom of God to bring confirmation or direction. A wise man will seek wise counsel. There is biblical encouragement to seek godly counsel of others. In Acts 6:1-7, the apostles came together for counsel to address a problem.

There may be times you do not know what to do in a potentially detrimental matter. Seek godly counsel to be the mediator in the situation. God uses this method of communication to bring peace among believers in Christ. It is always wise to get others' input so that you are accountable as well. I believe this is a safeguard and brings healthy dialogue.

Personally, when I seek my pastors, business partners, peers, colleagues in ministry, or spiritual leaders to whom I am accountable, they usually confirm what I was setting out to do. Sometimes they give me a better plan of action and allow me to rethink things strategically, spiritually, and maturely. The Bible says iron sharpens iron and you must remain sharp, surrounding yourself with men and women of integrity.

Seeking godly wisdom and counsel is not just in conversation but includes those who teach and communicate spiritual truth to us. One of the fascinating ways that God speaks and we at times don't even recognize it is through mentors, tutors, wise advisors, and people who have done what we are trying to accomplish. We don't know everything, and in today's society we have access to a wealth of books, resources, and information God can use to speak prophetically to us.

Many of the mistakes I have made throughout life were due to not seeking wise counsel on a decision. At times, my personal pride got in the way and prevented me from asking for help or wisdom in a specific area. The Bible says in all our getting we must get understanding. Life can teach us valuable lessons. Personal experiences can teach wisdom as well. If we have faced mishaps, setbacks, failures, persecutions, jealousy, envy, demonic opposition, and rejection in our Christian walk, it can be tempting to isolate ourselves and do things on our own.

Some people keep doing the same thing expecting a different result or outcome. The spirit of wisdom, counsel, and might breaks the spirit and power of insanity. God want to change the rhythm of our lives and break demonic cycles, strongholds, and limitations that come to set us back and not forward. The Lord has a prophetic blueprint for our lives that can help accelerate us.

The Holy Spirit will quicken your spirit and lead you to the right voices who have the godly wisdom to thrust you into your purpose and destiny. I truly believe that divine connections will help us fan into flame the gift of God on the inside through the prophetic words released. But it is our responsibility to keep the flame continually kindled and apply the wisdom that we obtain. Applied knowledge is wisdom and lack of knowledge is ignorance.

I love Second Timothy 3:16, which says that all Scripture is "God-breathed." God speaks through His Word and gives us warnings, words of encouragement, or lessons for life. The Bible is a historical book, but it's also an inspired book as well. It's "His-story" written and laced with His love as

God's guide for life so that the man of God may be thoroughly equipped for every good work. His wisdom and lovingkindness is expressed through His Word. When God speaks through others and gives us wisdom that is according to His Word it simply means God is whispering, and sometimes shouting, giving us instructions and principles for our life and destiny.

As we interpret Scripture with Scripture, we avoid the false logic and misinterpretation that comes invading into our world. If a person said something like, "God told me steal back what someone owes me!" would you believe him? Of course not! You automatically know that wasn't God speaking and that's not wisdom at all to take what you were owed. God would never violate or contradict His own Word. That "voice" does not belong to God. Seeking wisdom from others who are seasoned in God's Word and mature in age can save our life, time, and money.

I love what Proverbs 11:13-14 says: *"A gossip betrays a confidence, but a trustworthy person keeps a secret. For lack of guidance a nation falls, but victory is won through many advisers."* There is a profound wisdom in those who know how to keep things confidential. Gossipers know how to reveal secrets, but a man or woman of God will conceal matters. Nations will fall if there is no wise counsel in important matters. When there is an advisory board that has the wisdom of God then there is healing, deliverance, and success. We need the wisdom that comes from others.

One of the wise safeguards to prophecy, dreams, visions, prophetic encounters, and hearing the voice of God is to first make sure its biblical and Holy Spirit-directed. Bringing those types of prophetic encounters to those who are seasoned to make sure you are accountable. There is safety, victory, success, and deliverance in a multitude of advisors. We can hear God through the wisdom of others.

25

FASTING

David pleaded with God for the child. He fasted and
spent the nights lying in sackcloth on the ground.
—2 SAMUEL 12:16

When we fast, God will speak. Notice that I didn't say "if" you fast but "when" you fast God will speak to you. Fasting is a biblical fact that breaks poverty and the bands of wickedness; releases revelation and answered prayers; heals diseases and sickness; and overcomes the lust of the flesh, lust of the eyes, and the pride of life. Fasting should be a regular routine and lifestyle of the Christian. Other religions fast and incorporate it in their religious programs.

As you know, God loves to speak to those who will do what it takes to position themselves to hear His voice daily. There are powerful spiritual principles and biblical truths that give us access to hearing the voice of the Lord more precisely and regularly. Fasting is one of them that I have benefited from. Whenever I get to a place of fasting I tend to have a spiritual awakening but also a spiritual cleansing. Fasting causes me to go through detoxification. God begins to empty out anything that is toxic to my soul and revive me through eating the Word of God.

My question to you is, are you hungry for more of the move of God in your life? Are you ready to hear His voice and draw closer to your Father in Heaven? Do you want to grow spiritually? Are you longing for a spiritual refreshing and breakthrough? If you have answered yes to one or more of these questions, you are on your way to hearing God in ways you never imagined. I would say to lend God your undivided attention through biblical fasting and watch God move supernaturally. I have personally come away knowing the voice of God for myself as a result of making fasting a part of my Christian walk.

> *Is not this the fast that I choose: to loose the bonds of wickedness, to undo the straps of the yoke, to let the oppressed go free, and to break every yoke?* (Isaiah 58:6 ESV)

People often ask me, "When is the best time to fast or when should we fast?" My answer to their question is that fasting is not a question of *if but when.* Jesus clearly said "when you fast" not "if you fast," as we can see in Matthew 6:16-18:

> *And when you fast, do not look gloomy like the hypocrites, for they disfigure their faces that their fasting may be seen by others. Truly, I say to you, they have received their reward. But when you fast, anoint your head and wash your face, that your fasting may not be seen by others but by your Father who is in secret. And your Father who sees in secret will reward you* (ESV).

There are believers who fast religiously, without God's direction, and there are those who fast to appear super-spiritual or deep. If that's the case, then check your motives for fasting because fasting creates a space for self-denial and humility. When God calls you to fast, then obey His voice and direction.

Fasting should not become a ritualistic practice or be used to fleece God. We should make that sacrifice out of worship and humility. When I fast, God has already laid it on my heart for a definite reason and speaks to me profoundly. Below I have provided seven benefits of fasting:

1. Divine protection (Esther 4:16; Ezra 8:21-23; 2 Chron. 20:1-25)

2. Victory over temptation (Matt. 4:1-11)

3. Ordination, preparation, and commissioning into ministry (Acts 13:2-3; Acts 14:23)

4. Access to the heart of God (Jonah 3:4-10)

5. Personal deliverance (Mark 9:28-29; Isa. 58:6)

6. Preparation for new seasons of ministry (Matt. 4:1-17)

7. Divine healing and spiritual health (Isa. 58:8)

Fasting not only gives spiritual benefits but physical ones as well:

> Fasting cleanses the body from built-up chemicals, metals, and other toxins. When you fast, your cells, tissues, and organs dump out the accumulated waste products of cellular metabolism as well as chemicals, heavy metals, pesticides, and solvents. Fasting revitalizes you in every way: mentally, physically, and spiritually. It also allows the overburdened liver to "catch up" on its detoxification work.[1]

Remember, when you fast, the time you would usually spend eating is spent with the Lord instead. Write down your questions, any struggles you may be facing during the fast, and what God is showing you in your journal. Go back later in the fast and read what you wrote. Often you will gain more revelation or see the answers to your questions as God completes the work He is doing. Whatever the purpose of your fast, it will strengthen your walk with God. Fasting will cause you to thrive spiritually.

Fasting and prayer is a power combo that Jesus emphatically taught His disciples they should do often. In deliverance, fasting and prayer has the power to deliver from demonic strongholds and stubborn spirits. There are times that revolutionize my life when the Lord calls upon me to fast. Fasting is necessary to produce and maintain a healthy Christian walk and lifestyle. Fasting will crucify all fleshly appetite so that you can feast on the goodness of Jesus and desire spiritual things.

Each way that God speaks to us today meshes into the other. God often speaks to us through His Spirit, through prayer. We may not know how to pray, but God's Word tells us His Spirit makes intercession for us (Rom. 8:26-27). There is no such thing as a fast without prayer. A fast without prayer is just going hungry, and you're accomplishing nothing at all. While fasting is not necessary for salvation, it is essential to your Christian walk of faith and highly recommended.

In fact, Jesus expects believers to embrace fasting as regular routine in their spiritual walk. Fasting will assist anyone who is seeking a more intimate relationship with Christ. I know when I was young I fasted for three days and I not only heard God's voice audibly but had several spiritual encounters with angels. This may not be the case for everyone, but I guarantee that you will recognize a big difference when you do and when you don't fast.

Fasting will ultimately assist a believer to overcome sin and temptation, break bad habits, and help open your spiritual eyes to things that are displeasing to the Father in your life. Fasting breaks your appetite and changes your palate for the things of the Lord. Fasting benefits your spirit man and aligns your soul to discipline and overcome fleshly agendas and appetites. As well as fasting and praying, incorporate a time to separate from your regular life activities, patterns, and from things of the world that will prevent you from having a closer access to the Lord.

We are not to make spiritual disciplines complicated. Fasting should not be one of those spiritual things we often dread because there are so many benefits and reasons for fasting and so many ways to do it to make it at least tolerable. As you research and grow in your faith with God you know personally what works best for you. Find out the best method for you and stick to it throughout the whole process.

In addition, I would suggest that you find out the purpose for your fast and how long you are planning to do it by seeking the Lord. God will speak to you in a still small voice or there will be an inner witness that will confirm that you should. Always trust your prophetic instinct that is leading you to do something that is uncomfortable. Keep in mind the Holy Spirit doesn't force you not to eat. It's solely up to you, and God honors that and will speak to you in many different ways described throughout this book.

Often through a combination of fasting and prayer our minds become clearer, keener, and our hearts are more sensitive to the voice and moves of God. Again, we may not hear God's literal voice at first, but His Spirit will eventually confirm a certain direction or answer for you that you were waiting for. As the distractions fade, you will overtime throughout the fast and prayer will sense the strong presence and leading of the Holy Spirit in a new way.

Does this type of encounter happen suddenly? Not always; it depends on each case or situation. There have been occasions when I still had no clue what to do, but in faith I was thankful that God showed me something small that got my attention because I obeyed Him and did a fast. In addition, I am thankful whenever and however God answers me in prayer through a fast. God will speak to you in so many ways because of the fast you did voluntarily.

NOTE

1. Don Colbert, *The Seven Pillars of Health (Carol Stream, IL: Oasis, 2008)*, *177.*

26

DREAMS

Your sons and your daughters shall prophesy, your old men
shall dream dreams, your young men shall see visions.
—JOEL 2:28 NKJV

Godly dreams are very common and biblical. Often God speaks to us while we are asleep—when we can actually maintain the kind of peace, silence, and quietness that is required for us to receive spiritual and prophetic instructions, directives, and guidance from the Lord. God uses the vehicle of dreams to speak to us. There are Spirit-filled dreams that the Lord gives us. There are times when the Lord will appear to us in a dream. We have to be able to recognize it's Him.

Dreams and visions are of God, and there are also soulish dreams that we may have as well. We have to be able to distinguish soul-type dreams from divine dreams sent by God. In Matthew 12, an angel of the Lord appeared to Joseph in a dream and gave him clear instructions. Can you imagine the outcome if Joseph didn't pay attention to the instructions of the Lord in his dream concerning Jesus's life? The enemy was after Jesus and the Lord used several dreams to lead him. God will at times appear to you in a dream as He did in Gibeon to Solomon.

> *In Gibeon the Lord appeared to Solomon in a dream at night;*
> *and God said, "Ask what you wish Me to give you"* (1 Kings 3:5
> NASB).

In this dream, we know that Solomon asked for wisdom and later it was granted unto him. Never ignore your dreams because God uses them to speak to you and prepare you for what is next. I recall a dream where I was climbing the fence of a park, and I saw my cousin in the dream. As I was trying to get over the fence to the basketball court, I heard loud gunshots, and a bullet passed my head toward my cousin on the other side. I actually fell over the fence and I woke up.

Later that day, my twin brother Naim called me to inform me that our cousin was killed. I asked him where and he stated that Greg was killed outside of his home. Where my cousin lived was in front of the same basketball court fence I was trying to climb over in my dream. My cousin was shot and he succumbed to his injuries. Dreams can speak hidden messages that are prophetic in nature, and we must pay attention to them so that we can pray, fast, and intercede for ourselves and others.

Some of the Spirit-filled dreams I receive are complex and may take days, weeks, months, or even years to get the full interpretation. Dreams are normally meant for us to chew upon and are not immediately understood in every detail. Most dreams are symbolic or allegorical.

With prophetic dreams we have to wait on the Lord for the interpretation and ponder our findings while permitting the Lord to unfold, unravel, and disclose His revelation to us. The more complex the allegory in the dream, the stronger the content of the dream becomes and needs revelation, interpretation, and clarification by the Holy Spirit. We must understand that the tougher meat takes time to digest and should not be impulsively assimilated.

Dreamers of dreams, seers of visions, or prophetic visionaries will hear the voice of the Lord and respond in faith to release the supernatural power of God. As we ask God to speak to us more in dreams, He is just and merciful to answer our request. If it is your heart's desire to really hear from the Lord, God through the Holy Spirit will assist you. I have come to the realization that a true, prophetic, Spirit-filled dream initiated by the Lord will come to pass in every detail in my life. Dreams, like prophecy, should also bring confirmation and revelation to the hearer. The Bible says out of the mouth of two or three witnesses let His Word be established. Dreams and visions must be confirmed as well.

Why do you complain against Him that He does not give an account of all His doings? Indeed God speaks once, or twice, yet no one notices it. In a dream, a vision of the night, when sound sleep falls on men, while they slumber in their beds (Job 33:13-15 NASB).

We can see from the above passage that God speaks once or twice yet no one notices that it's Him. God will speak several times in dreams, called visions of the night, and we must be sensitive and aware of His confirming voice. I normally will know that it's the Lord revealing something to me when I have the same type of dream repeatedly. Some dreams are more vivid than others and I won't need Him to give me that dream again. It will take some work and effort to get familiar with how dreams speak to you personally and prophetically.

We must know that a true Holy Spirit-filled dream will never violate Scripture or God's divine attributes. Holy Spirit-filled dreams are sent to us from the Lord and given to us to fulfill a specific purpose in life. If a dream is lacking the above characteristics, it does not mean it is not a pure, Holy Spirit-filled dream, but it may be something lodged in your soul. A pure dream can be a simple allegory that is a teaching or form of direction, guidance, or even alignment that you need. A Holy Spirit-filled dream will reflect God's goodness, love, mercy, and grace.

Moreover, a Holy Spirit-filled dream will also have the absence of the characteristics of a soul dream. A soul dream will contain what is in our mind, will, and emotions that will come up eventually while we are asleep. Soul dreams can contain good ideas, but a good idea is not a God idea. We need God-idea dreams that are His perfect will for our lives. There are Spirit-filled dreams, visions, mental pictures, and Holy Spirit expressions that God uses to speak to His people.

The people of the Bible were familiar with dreams and visions, angelic and supernatural occurrences. We must be the same in our walk with God and by faith trust what He is revealing, speaking, and expressing to us through dreams and visions. Holy Spirit-filled dreams will always be a method of communication that God uses regardless if one is saved or not. God spoke to ungodly kings, leaders, and normal people to get His word across. We not only need to open ourselves to allow God to speak to us through dreams, we must ask Him to speak the interpretation as well—or send someone who has the gift to interpret dreams of God.

We must be able to decode the dream language of God. There are several types of dreams in which the Lord speaks, including *literal* and *symbolic* dreams. Sometimes dreams can only be interpreted or revealed by the Holy Spirit. Discernment is also a major component of uncovering the meaning of dreams.

Holy Spirit-filled dreams given by the Lord are a common form of communication from God. While we are dreaming, the Father is able to bypass the reasoning of our natural thought patterns, mindsets, and paradigms to convey His message. While we are asleep, we are not asking the question in our mind, "Is this God or is this just me thinking this?"

Some dreams from the Lord will have a major impact on our heart, mind, soul, and spirit. Holy Spirit-filled dreams can even keep us from hell, warn us of danger, correct us, align us, and give us a prophetic forecast of what's next. Pray that God will give you the ability to recognize and discern Holy Spirit-filled dreams, filter them through the Word of God, and receive confirmation from spiritually seasoned men and women.

> *In a dream, a vision of the night, when sound sleep falls on men, while they slumber in their beds, then He opens the ears of men, and seals their instruction, that He may turn man aside from his conduct, and keep man from pride; He keeps back his soul from the pit, and his life from passing over into Sheol* (Job 33:15-18 NASB).

God opens the ears of men, and that can be any person—saved or not. He seals their instruction so that they will turn aside from their conduct. God will not waste time giving you a dream if He's not serious about your life and conduct. He requires us to obey His instructions. God wants to keep His people from going to hell and to fulfill their destiny and purpose in Him. The most powerful prophetic words I have received came through warnings in dreams. God knows the plans of the enemy and always will give us a way of escape.

He will also tell us through our dreams what we are to do and what season we are in.

Moreover, God can give you a dream directly from the Holy Spirit. Another term that you may hear for dreams is "visions of the night." Throughout the Bible there are a plethora of examples of people receiving dreams from God. One example was when the Lord used an angel in a dream to tell Joseph to immediately flee to Egypt right after Jesus had been born, as Herod was getting ready to assassinate all of the male babies. In the days of Daniel, King Nebuchadnezzar was given dreams of end-time events, but he needed Daniel the prophet to interpret those dreams for him. Daniel himself was also given dreams and visions concerning the state of the kingdom and pending judgments.

The time of a dream is very important, and I've gotten into the habit of journaling and watching the clock upon awakening. I always get these God-dreams close to when I am getting ready to wake up. For instance, if I go to bed at 1 A.M. and I am going to be getting up at about 5 A.M., the dream will be coming in between 3 and 4 A.M. The reason He does this with me is so the dream is basically right in my face as I am starting to come out of that deep sleep.

Throughout the day I also take naps and have prophetic dreams, and I still look at the time when I wake up. For example, if I wake up from a dream at 9:01 A.M., I time stamp my journal with 9:01 A.M. and then the Lord will speak to me by giving me a Scripture such as Psalm 91. How powerful is that! God will do these amazing things so that I will know with certainty that the dream is coming in directly from Him.

Most dreams you have during the night you will either have no memory of or you'll only remember vague details within the first one to three hours. After three hours have passed, you will have forgotten about the dream altogether. That is why it's important to get in the habit of journaling immediately while your mind is still fresh. I have found that most direct dreams from the Lord I am able to recall in detail. These Holy Spirit-filled dreams do not fade away. They are as clear in your mind's eye six hours later as when you first woke up. They will stay with you for days, if not forever.

I suggest that you pay attention to all of your dreams even though they may not all be directly from the Lord. My point is, the Lord wants you to know how He speaks to you, and He does use your dreams. You can become an expert in interpreting your own dreams if you put in the work.

27

VISIONS

*In the last days, God says, I will pour out my Spirit on all
people. Your sons and daughters will prophesy, your young
men will see visions, your old men will dream dreams.*
—ACTS 2:17

One of the powerful ways God speaks prophetically is through visions.
Dreams only happen when you are asleep, while visions occur when you
are awake. Visions are a special and unique way of hearing the voice of the
Lord. Some speak of vision as a general term, as in visualizing a future perspective or objective. There are godly visions that God uses to speak to His
people. These supernatural visions given by the Lord can be open visions or
inner visions within your spirit.

When God poured out His prophetic Spirit on all flesh there was a divine
awakening that caused supernatural things to occur. Furthermore, God ignited
dreams, visions, prophetic utterances, and spiritual activities directly. Keep in
mind that prophetic visions, dreams, and utterances are Holy Spirit workings.
God will use these types of encounters for believers today as He did in the
Word of God. The supernatural outpouring of God's Spirit is coming upon
all flesh according to Joel 2:28 and Act 2:17. God is using these supernatural
encounters to reveal His power and glory. The prophetic nature and outpouring of God's Spirit has already started and will continue. Furthermore, God's
prophetic Spirit will usher in a global awakening and harvest of souls. All

kinds of people from all over the world are encountering God through prophetic dreams, visions, and prophetic utterances.

There are three types of visions:

1.   Visions of the mind, internal visions, or closed visions

2.   Open visions or external visions

3.   Pictorial visions

The prophet Daniel received fresh revelation from God through internal visions or what is called a closed vision. These types of divine communication through the Holy Spirit are actually images, portraits, visuals, projections, and pictorial screenshots or pictures projected on the Spirit-filled believer's mind. The Holy Spirit uses a believer's mind as a blackboard on which He paints portraits, draw images, or projects mental photos.

The second type of vision is an *open-eyed vision* or *open vision* when one is awake but can see image(s) with their natural eyes. God is a prophetic, speaking Spirit who releases these visions and images to young men and women. Joel spoke of a future time when God would pour out His Spirit on all mankind and they would come into spiritual supernatural encounters: *"That I will pour out My Spirit on all mankind; and your sons and daughters will prophesy, your old men will dream dreams, your young men will see visions"* (Joel 2:28 NASB). Open eye visions or external visions happen when your natural eyes are open and the Holy Spirit projects visions upon the screen of your mind or imagination.

I remember sitting with a friend talking about the goodness of the Lord and while talking I had an open-eyed vision or external vision. My natural eyes were open and I could see what was going on all around me. I was clearly aware of the surroundings of the room and could hear and see my friend, but this movie screen was before me. It was like someone put a movie projector in front of my eyes and I was able to see a vivid scene of myself running through a cornfield and next I saw ocean water and then a forest of trees. I was very surprised by this supernatural occurrence.

The strange thing about this vision was that I was able to hear and see my friend in my peripheral vision. God was showing me a season of harvest, fruitfulness, and abundance that was coming to me. Through this open-eyed vision God spoke to me of the harvest field of ministry that He was sending me out to gather. That same year of the open-eyed vision I was sent out and ordained as a prophet in my church.

The third type of vision is a called a *pictorial vision, glimpses,* or *flash visions.* This type of vision is low-level revelation that can be activated by our imagination. Simply, this can be called a "sanctified imagination" or an imagination influenced by the Holy Spirit. Most often, this is how the Holy Spirit speaks to us and allows us see the prophetic message of God through the lens of our mind's eye and imagination. When I am ministering to people prophetically I have glimpses and pictorial flashes in my mind as I share what God is saying through these types of visions.

A biblical vision is a literal, spiritual, and oftentimes a physical happening. We must understand that it's not something you can ignite or initiate on your own with your reasoning, logic, or mind. Receiving a vision is a gift from the Father—a supernatural encounter of sight. God uses them to get our undivided attention. We don't seek after visions but must realize that they are a gift of God and always will be a gift.

28

VISUALIZATION

*Then the Lord answered me and said, "Record the vision
and inscribe it on tablets, that the one who reads it may
run. For the vision is yet for the appointed time; it hastens
toward the goal and it will not fail. Though it tarries, wait
for it; for it will certainly come, it will not delay."*
—HABAKKUK 2:2-3 NASB

We must understand that visualizations or images are another type of vision given by the Lord. That is why it is important that we keep our minds pure and in a right place. My late spiritual prophetic papa Bob Jones told Naim and me, as prophets and seers, to have a sanctified imagination. He stated that "the mind is the headquarters of the Holy Spirit to speak to us." I believe that our imagination is a powerful tool for connecting with the spirit world. That's why the apostle Paul gives us wisdom that we can command our imagination and thoughts to align with the knowledge of God (2 Cor. 10:5).

> *And now, dear brothers and sisters, one final thing. Fix your
> thoughts on what is true, and honorable, and right, and pure, and
> lovely, and admirable. Think about things that are excellent and
> worthy of praise* (Philippians 4:8 NLT).

God speaks through visualizations and inner pictures of the Spirit. There are times in the prophetic when I receive pictures in my mind concerning an individual I am praying for. I see snapshots of their past and I share with the hearer the details of what I am seeing. I may see them as a child and share with them around what age they were and what happened to them based off of the picture I receive by the Holy Spirit. I may see other individuals in the pictures who are friends or family members. The hearer may weep or look amazed at the detail of the word of knowledge. This type of communication is parabolic and needs divine interpretation of the vision or picture.

Visualization is the process of forming mental images. We must be careful that we don't use visualization as mean of tapping into the demonic realm. Oftentimes I say that if we can see it than we can seize it—that should always be based on God's Word. I believe we can develop our spiritual senses to grow in the gifts of God. Oftentimes, visualization involves envisioning events or situations that don't exist or that have not happened yet.

Prophetically, God will give us a word that will activate visualization that will bring about realization. The enemy will try to pervert anything that God does. So we are to be careful and check our motives for visualizing. Visualization can be spiritually healthy or spiritually unhealthy, depending on the situation and the reasons for the visualization.

An NFL quarterback may visualize himself making a difficult throw to a wide receiver in the end zone before he actually throws the football, or an Olympic swimmer may picture herself making a record-breaking dive before she mounts the platform. Musicians, actors, writers, and other artists may use visualization to create a picture in their minds before writing it down or acting it out. Visualization to me is gazing at an end result or outcome that will motivate a person to act on what they want to accomplish.

Visualization is not always something that will come to pass or come true. If I am bald, I can visualize hair, but that doesn't mean I will eventually grow hair. This is not the purpose of visualization. It should be used to see from God's view and lens for you, according to God's Word and will for your life.

Everyone uses visualization to some extent. We picture what we want to eat before we make or buy the food. We picture and envision what we want to wear before we put it on. I often will see something I like when shopping and visualize myself in it without even trying it on. When I purchase the clothes, it is usually what I have envisioned and the results are better in real time.

I always ask God to speak to me through visualization and He shows me a mental picture or image when I am driving. You will be surprised when you ask the Lord to speak to you in this manner the amazing things that will happen. I envision something and obey as I feel the Lord is leading me, and I cross paths with a divine connection all of a sudden.

God may give me a mental picture of someone I haven't seen in many years and their face will come before me in my mind's eye out of nowhere. Then, in my travels, I suddenly run into them. God wants us to have Holy Spirit-filled visualization. Moreover, as I move in healing and miracle ministry, God gives me flashes of pictures of health conditions or words of knowledge of a person's sickness in my mind.

Visualization is a way we prepare ourselves before taking action. We imagine conversations happening before they happen. There is nothing unbiblical about the tendency for humans to visualize in this way. In fact, it is wise to consider outcomes before taking action (Luke 14:28).

I want to share four great points to teach you how to train your imagination to recognize the voice of the Lord through visualization.

1. Pray and yield your imagination to the Holy Spirit by asking Him to wash and cleanse you. Ask the Holy Spirit to give you a sanctified imagination and cut off anything that would come into your eye, ear, and mouth gates that will contaminate what you imagination. Repent and close any door that was open to pornography, dirty conversation, filthy gossip, slander, and anything that violates the Word of God.

2. Understand that your imagination can become a canvas that the Holy Spirit can paint upon. Ask the Holy Spirit to paint the picture and create the portrait that He wants to show you and give you the interpretation of that vision, trance, or picture.

3. Read, study, and listen to Scripture and picture the stories in your mind's eye. Activate your imagination by visualization and picture yourself as one of the Bible characters to get the meaning. In other words, picture yourself like Daniel in the

lions' den as God supernaturally turn the hungry lions into sleeping, harmless cubs.

4.   Proverbs 4:23 AMP says, *"Watch over your heart with all diligence, for from it flow the springs of life."* We must guard what we are feeding our imaginations and heart. We have to become a watchman over what we see, hear, and listen to that will impact our heart and subconscious. When you pray for or with others, pause in God's presence to see if He has anything to reveal to you as a word of knowledge.

God will begin to show you things by way of impressions, visions, mental flashes, physical impressions for healing, etc. Always note sudden pictures or images you receive that pass through your imagination. Train your mind to be keen and attentive to the small things that God wants to communicate. As you become more alert and aware of these images, visions, and prophetic impressions, God will give you more.

29

TRANCES

The next day, as they went on their journey and drew near the
city, Peter went up on the housetop to pray, about the sixth hour.
Then he became very hungry and wanted to eat; but while they
made ready, he fell into a trance and saw heaven opened and an
object like a great sheet bound at the four corners, descending to
him and let down to the earth. In it were all kinds of four-footed
animals of the earth, wild beasts, creeping things, and birds of the
air. And a voice came to him, "Rise, Peter; kill and eat." But Peter
said, "Not so, Lord! For I have never eaten anything common or
unclean." And a voice spoke to him again the second time, "What
God has cleansed you must not call common." This was done
three times. And the object was taken up into heaven again.
—ACTS 10:9-16 NKJV

What is a trance? According to *Merriam-Webster Dictionary* a trance is
a "sleeplike state (as of deep hypnosis) usually characterized by partly
suspended animation with diminished or absent sensory and motor activity."[1]
God caused prophets of the Bible to encounter a stupor or supernatural daze
where He spoke to them in these deep sleep states to bring revelation.

God speaks through trances. There are times when I will be praying and I
will fall into a deep sleep-like state. I wouldn't be sleepy at first, but while praying and meditating I find myself in a trance. Peter fell into a trance and saw
the same vision three times about the Gentiles (Acts 10:10-16). God wanted to

get Peter's attention and was very serious about changing Peter's preconceived religious bias about the Gentiles. Through obedience, Peter heeded to the prophetic instructions of the Lord given in the trance and received a revelation that was to open the way for the Gentiles as well as the Jews (Acts 10:34). When he acted on this message, the door of faith was opened to the Gentiles. Paul also would fall into a trance while praying in Acts 22:17-21.

A trance is the Greek word *ekstasis*, from which we get the word *ecstasy*, which denotes the state of one who is "out of himself" (Strong's #G1611). It means "a displacement of the mind, to remove out of its place or state, i.e. bewilderment, or ecstasy." Such were the trances of Peter and Paul—ecstasies, "a preternatural, absorbed state of mind preparing for the reception of the vision" (2 Cor. 12:1-4). In Mark 5:42 and Luke 5:26, the Greek word is rendered "astonishment" and "amazement" (Mark 16:8; Acts 3:10).

God can communicate to us through Holy Spirit-filled trances. Trances are high-level encounters and many may not have these types of experiences, but don't count them out because God uses them and they are biblical. We are not to throw the baby out with the bathwater if we are not familiar with a supernatural way God speaks and does things. The only premise we can go by is in the Word of God. You may not know if you fall into a trance until after the encounter. I had trances often when I was younger in the faith, and they happen when I come out of prayer and in meditation.

When God use trances as a method of communicating to us, rejoice in it that He decided to do something *wow* in your Christian experience. Trances are not something you can initiate on your own or try to activate. They are a sovereign working of God. New Age teaches and practices traveling and astral projection that is self-induced or controlled by a hypnotist. I am not referring to anything self-initiated like that. You know it was God when it just happens. A trance given by the Holy Spirit is an experience where you suddenly find yourself losing control of your own actions and see visions or receive some divine instruction.

This type of trance happened to John in Revelation 1:10-13:

> *On the Lord's Day I was in the Spirit, and I heard behind me a loud voice like a trumpet, which said: "Write on a scroll what you see and send it to the seven churches: to Ephesus, Smyrna,*

Pergamum, Thyatira, Sardis, Philadelphia and Laodicea." I turned around to see the voice that was speaking to me. And when I turned I saw seven golden lampstands, and among the lamp-stands was someone like a son of man, dressed in a robe reaching down to his feet and with a golden sash around his chest.

John received a revelation—the voice of the Lord speaking to him through a trance. The apostle Paul fell into a trance in Acts 22:17-21:

After that, I returned to Jerusalem. While I was praying in the temple courtyard, I fell into a trance and saw the Lord. He told me, "Hurry! Get out of Jerusalem immediately. The people here won't accept your testimony about me." I said, "Lord, people here know that I went from synagogue to synagogue to imprison and whip those who believe in you. When Stephen, who witnessed about you, was being killed, I was standing there. I approved of his death and guarded the coats of those who were murdering him." But the Lord told me, "Go! I'll send you on a mission. You'll go far away to people who aren't Jewish" (GW).

When I was growing in the prophetic and establishing a strong prayer life as a young prophet, God would allow me to fall into trances and show me heavenly things that were so clear, and when I came out of the trance the time had gone by so fast. I pray for an hour without realizing time had passed. I want you to understand that God can and will speak through a trance. He did it in the Bible and He will surely do it today.

You may fall asleep or lose consciousness of your immediate surroundings and see things you weren't thinking of or pondering on. Let me be clear that these short moments of sleep visions or trance visions are not to be categorized as a dream because trances come and go in a flash. Often, we may not able to comprehend what's going on when trance visions and encounters happen. We miss the move of God and the unusual prophetic ways He speaks because we want to encounter a spectacular supernatural manifestation of God. We must be faithful in the low-level ways He speaks in order for us to appreciate and value the higher levels as well.

Personally, I journal and get the habit of writing out any trances, dreams, and open visions and prophecies I receive. I become a good steward not only of the true Word of God but of the many ways He decides to sovereignly speak to me. I suggest that the first step to understanding God's message and hearing His voice through a trance is to take great notes of whatever sudden visions you have.

The problem is, we want to interpret the meaning of the trance first without detailing and journaling the trance encounters. There are times the interpretation is self-explanatory and other times the meaning will become clear later. Peter didn't understand the meaning of the vision and God's prophetic message until some events took place surrounding the trance.

I want to give a better explanation of what a trance looks like. Some people don't realize that God does speak through prophetic supernatural encounters. Trances are one of those means, and I want to encourage you if this happens to you not to be afraid. We can clearly see that trances are found in the New Testament. God can speak to you the same way today.

During a trance, most if not all awareness of a person's natural and external surroundings is obscured, and they are transfixed on the events in the trance. This is unlike an open-eyed vision where the individual is able to observe something transpiring. In a trance, a person is participating in the scene through their own actions. There have been instances when the Lord would take me in a trance-like state and I was the main character acting in the vision.

A trance can last any length of time, from a few seconds to several hours depending on the message God is conveying. The history of the church is filled with accounts of God speaking through trances. Keep in mind that trances are a higher level of revelation given by the Lord than simply a dream or glimpse/pictorial vision because they are less subjective in nature. You cannot make yourself have a trance; they come from the Lord and do not stop until He decides to end them.

NOTE

1. *Merriam-Webster Dictionary*, s.v. "trance," accessed April 18, 2019, https://www.merriam-webster.com/dictionary/trance.

30

TRANSLATION AND TRANSPORTED IN THE SPIRIT

He reached out what seemed to be a hand and took me by the hair. Then the Spirit lifted me up into the sky and transported me to Jerusalem in a vision from God. I was taken to the north gate of the inner courtyard of the Temple, where there is a large idol that has made the Lord very jealous.
—EZEKIEL 8:3 NLT

God will speak to His people through translation and being transported in the Spirit of God. We have to embrace and understand biblically these high-level prophetic ways God speaks to His people. There are demonic and counterfeit encounters such as astral projection. I am not going to address or cover that, but I will focus briefly on divine translations, transporting, and being caught up, which are biblical terms and experiences by the Spirit of God. Below I will share three different ways God communicates to us prophetically through the supernatural:

1. Translation is God moving your spirit.

2. Transportation is God moving your physical body

3. Being caught up is God moving of your spirit or natural body
    to the heavenly realm.

This is another type of experience that a believer cannot activate or initiate at will. These are God's special invitations to a person He chooses. God does the inviting, but we must be open and positioned by being ready when God does this sovereignly. Jesus was transported several times in Scripture after His resurrection (Matt. 28:8-10; Luke 24:13-43).

God will bring you into divine translations and transportation. Being transported physically or translated in the spirit is when you are taken away to another place to deliver a message or prophetic word of God. Probably the most quoted transportation is Phillip's, found in the Book of Acts. It appears that Phillip was transported to another location in the flesh in an instant. His whole body, soul, and spirit were transported:

> *So he commanded the chariot to stand still. And both Philip and the eunuch went down into the water, and he baptized him. Now when they came up out of the water, the Spirit of the Lord caught Philip away, so that the eunuch saw him no more; and he went on his way rejoicing. But Philip was found at Azotus. And passing through, he preached in all the cities till he came to Caesarea* (Acts 8:38-40 NKJV).

When he was done witnessing to the Ethiopian eunuch, Philip was taken to preach in another city. I love what the text says—that the Spirit of the Lord "snatched" Philip away (NLT) and the eunuch no longer saw him. Later, Philip found himself at Azotus—that basically means that he was in one place physically and ended up in another place miraculously. He was seen no more, which leads me to believe that he was there physically in sight and later wasn't. Philip was in one place and translated to another place by the same source—the Spirit of God. Since I was a young Christian I have heard people talking about Phillip's transportation in the Spirit, and I wanted to have that same kind of encounter. I wondered how it would be. I have been translated and transported places in the spirit but not physically like Philip.

After Philip baptized the Ethiopian treasurer we can read that Philip appeared at Azotus and traveled about. Luke, the author of Acts, would have heard about this event directly from Philip as he stayed with him in Caesarea (Acts 21:8-9).

As we look deep into this type of supernatural way God speaks to His people, we can see that what happened to Philip is described by the Greek word *harpazo* (Strong's #G726), which is translated as "suddenly took" in the NIV. The other occasion Luke uses this Greek word is when the apostle Paul was in Jerusalem and the Jews falsely accused him of speaking against their religion:

> *The dispute became so violent that the commander was afraid Paul would be torn to pieces by them. He ordered the troops to go down and **take him away from them by force** and bring him into the barracks* (Acts 23:10).

Here the word *harpazo* is translated "take by force." Both usages of the word harpazo are powerful and are similar in expression. We can see in both cases the person in the text was suddenly moved away or taken away by force from where they were presently in eyesight and then seen in another location. It is as though someone seized them as police would when they come to make an arrest. In the second case it was by means of the troops and in the first case it was by means of the Holy Spirit.

Likewise, the apostle Paul wasn't sure if he had been carried away in body or just in Spirit:

> *I know a man in Christ who fourteen years ago was caught up to the third heaven. Whether it was in the body or out of the body I do not know—God knows. And I know that this man—whether in the body or apart from the body I do not know, but God knows— was caught up to paradise and heard inexpressible things, things that no one is permitted to tell* (2 Corinthians 12:2-4).

The word used for "caught up" is, again, *harpazo*. Paul uses this word again in First Thessalonians 4:17 to speak of the Christian believers who are alive and remain at the coming of Christ and who will be "caught up" to meet Him in the air.

Ordinary men encountered the power of God through being caught up, transported, or translated in the Spirit. Ezekiel was lifted up in one text of the

Scripture and another stated that a hand took him by the hair. Ezekiel was translated into the future:

> *Then the Spirit lifted me up, and I heard behind me the voice of a great earthquake: "Blessed be the glory of the Lord from its place!" It was the sound of the wings of the living creatures as they touched one another, and the sound of the wheels beside them, and the sound of a great earthquake* (Ezekiel 3:12-13 ESV).

In the Old Testament, we can presume that being transported was a fairly common occurrence for the prophet Elijah from the instant reaction the sons of the prophets had to Elisha when he stated that his master (Elijah) had been taken (2 Kings 2:16-18). The sons of the prophets sent out 50 men to look for Elijah to verify the disappearance, saying, *"Perhaps the Spirit of the Lord has picked him up and set him down on some mountain or in some valley."* Also, when the servant of Ahab came to Elijah he was afraid that Elijah would be transported somewhere, and in the following Scripture he openly expressed his concerns and fear:

> *And now you say, "Go, tell your master, 'Elijah is here'"! And it shall come to pass, as soon as I am gone from you, that the Spirit of the Lord will carry you to a place I do not know; so when I go and tell Ahab, and he cannot find you, he will kill me. But I your servant have feared the Lord from my youth* (1 Kings 18:11-12 NKJV).

As we know, translation is when the Lord moves you in the spirit, such as when Elisha's spirit was divinely translated in Second Kings 5:26. With regard to transportation the Lord moved Enoch in the physical body to another place (Gen. 5:24; Heb. 11:5). Elijah was taken up or caught physically in his body by God through the means of a whirlwind. He was caught up into Heaven physically, while the apostle Paul spoke of being carried away into the third heaven in Second Corinthians 12:2:

> *I know a man in Christ who fourteen years ago was caught up to the third heaven. Whether it was in the body or out of the body I do not know—God knows.*

What is the "third heaven" referred to by Paul? The very first verse of the Bible tells us, *"In the beginning God created the heavens and the earth."* So what is the third heaven? The only reference to the "third heaven" in Scripture is found in Second Corinthians 12, speaking of the apostle Paul. Paul was basically saying of his dramatic experience that he never knew how this prophetic encounter happened, so we can be quite sure that we can't know. Nevertheless, the Bible sheds light on individuals caught up in the body, translated, or transported with out-of-the-body experiences.

Both Enoch and Elijah didn't see death but were caught up the same way. This wasn't something made up; it's biblical fact found in the Old Testament. We can see that happening in a different way with Philip being translated or transported in the Spirit.

In *Awakening the Prophet in You,* author Abraham Peters states that "Out-of-body encounters are biblical! God still uses these types of supernatural encounters to speak to us today. While we cannot make these types of experiences happen, we can position ourselves and make ourselves available by removing doubt and unbelief. If we would only believe, then all things are possible." The prophet was carried away, transported, or caught up by the Spirit. This is a prophetic encounter that God uses to reveal specific life-altering things to you. There are times in the Bible that prophets were carried away or translated by the Spirit of God into visions and supernatural encounters.

It is very important to understand that we can hear the voice of God when we have these high-level encounters. God doesn't allow us to have these experiences in vain. God does them on purpose to shift and change the way you think about God and yourself. I don't have a lot of these types of encounters, but when I do I am changed forever! One may ask, "Is it safe to ask the Lord for them?" I never asked to have them; they happened sovereignly. For me, when they first happened to me the first thing I did was go to the Word of God to make sure this wasn't something demonic.

I found that it was in fact biblical and something that people of God such as Paul, Ezekiel, Philip, and Elijah experienced. We can make ourselves available for these experiences by simply telling God that we submit to His will and are ready to be used by Him however He would wish.

31

SPIRITUAL SIGHT

Then Elisha prayed, "Lord, please open his eyes so that he may see." The Lord opened the servant's eyes and let him see. The mountain around Elisha was full of fiery horses and chariots.
—2 KINGS 6:17 GW

Using the model of our five physical senses—*sight, hearing, smell, taste, and touch*—we discover that God can prophetically speak to us through all five. God uses our natural senses to speak to us through physical impressions. He will give us spiritual revelation through seeing, hearing, smelling, tasting, and touching spiritually. Although this may initially sound strange, there are scriptural precedents for God speaking to us through our "spiritual senses."

We cannot control our natural senses because they operate automatically, but we can train our spiritual senses to smell, see, hear, taste, and feel what God wants us to by the Holy Spirit. As our natural eyes give sight and vision, we are given spiritual sight, insight, hindsight, and foresight. God can speak through our spiritual sense of sight to see into His plans, purposes, and will and also discern the works of darkness against us.

What is the spiritual sense of sight? Prophets were often called "seers" in the Old Testament. They were given spiritual sight to discern through their eyes what God was saying and doing. In Second Kings 2, we find a biblical example of the gift of discerning of spirits operating through spiritual sight. When Elijah was translated to Heaven, Elisha received a double portion of the spirit that was upon him, and he also received Elijah's mantle for ministry. Consider what the sons of the prophets said when they saw him:

> *Now when the sons of the prophets who were at Jericho saw him opposite them, they said, "The spirit of Elijah rests on Elisha." And they came to meet him and bowed to the ground before him* (2 Kings 2:15 ESV).

As Spirit-filled believers, we have the ability to see spiritually. The prophets in the prophetic university saw the mantle representing the authority, power, and spirit on Elisha. They were able to detect spiritual things. They were keen in discerning spiritual movements and operations. These young men "saw" something, and what was that? They saw that the spirit of Elijah was now resting on Elisha. What did they see specifically? Was there some physical change in Elisha's appearance that they saw? Or was it a spiritual shift that they could discern with their spiritual eyes?

There was a spiritual presence that was once upon Elijah that they now "saw" resting upon Elisha, which gave them the indication that Elisha was now in charge. This was the prophetic mantle or authority in which Elijah had walked and now Elisha was the successor to occupy Elijah's prophetic responsibilities.

Oftentimes, God will reveal to me a person's calling, and I can identify it by what I see on them. I spiritually see a person's mantle (anointing by the Spirit). For example, I may be ministering to someone and see a healing mantle, and I identify the scope of that person's ministry based off of Paul's healing mantle in the Bible.

I like this particular way that God speaks because He uses our literal eyes to show us things spiritually. I would say that it's like having spiritual blinders on and suddenly they're removed. This is a wonderful way that God gets our attention. God opens our eye gates to the spiritual realm. He has given us eyes to see naturally and He desires for us to see in the spirit.

> *So he answered, "Do not fear, for those who are with us are more than those who are with them." Then Elisha prayed and said, "O Lord, I pray, open his eyes that he may see." And the Lord opened the servant's eyes and he saw; and behold, the mountain was full of horses and chariots of fire all around Elisha. When they came*

down to him, Elisha prayed to the Lord and said, "Strike this people with blindness, I pray." So He struck them with blindness according to the word of Elisha (2 Kings 6:16-18 NASB).

We can see that Elisha the prophet prayed for the eyes of the servant to open that he may see. He needed to see in the realm of the spirit what Elisha already knew and saw. We can ask God to open our spiritual eyes and for the eyes of our understanding be enlightened.

I pray that the eyes of your heart may be enlightened, so that you will know what is the hope of His calling, what are the riches of the glory of His inheritance in the saints (Ephesians 1:18 NASB).

There are times in the prophetic ministry when God will open my eyes to the spiritual realm. I see angels, demons, sickness, disease, and different types of spirits on people. In addition, I recall a time when I was praying for a couple. While I was praying for them, God gave me a supernatural ultrasound vision where I was able to see a baby in the spirit and the woman pregnant. Furthermore, I saw that the baby was a boy. I began to prophesy to them what I saw, and they were weeping because they desired to have a baby boy but couldn't because of prior health issues. God fulfilled their hearts' desire, and nine months later the prophetic word came to pass. They had a healthy, beautiful baby boy, and two years later they were able to have another baby boy.

"Hear, now, and I will speak; I will ask You, and You instruct me." I have heard of You by the hearing of the ear; but now my eye sees You (Job 42:4-5 NASB).

We must know that God communicates through our literal (natural) eyes and uses them as gates to open them up to the world of the spirit. The Lord must open our spiritual senses.

32

SPIRITUAL HEARING

He who has ears to hear, let him hear.
—MATTHEW 11:15 ESV

Anyone with ears to hear must listen to the Spirit and understand what he is saying to the churches.
—REVELATION 2:29 NLT

Hearing in the natural is powerful in itself because we are able to hear sound waves even though we can't see them. Hearing in the spirit or having *spiritual hearing* is also profound because we are able to hear the sound waves of Heaven. The voice of the Lord can be heard spiritually with our natural ears. Spiritual hearing, I believe, is another remarkable prophetic way God gives revelation. Like spiritual sight, God will give us revelation through what we hear, as clear as someone calling your name audibly.

In the same way that God can open our sight, He is able to speak to us through our ear gates. God has given us one mouth and two ears on purpose. We must be able to hear what the Spirit of the Lord is saying to us—the church. We have the ability by the Holy Spirit to hear the audible voice of God, angelic voices, heavenly instruments and music, and even the voice of the Holy Spirit quickening us.

I remember a time when God opened my eyes in the realm of the spirit to hear His small still voice. I was in prayer and worship and weeping before the Lord concerning the decision to resign from my job. I didn't hear the Lord in prayer, but when I got to work ready to do my daily assignment, I heard the Lord say to me aloud in my right ear, "Hakeem, today is your last day." I was first taken by surprise because I was saying to myself, "Why, Father, did You wait for me to get all the way to work to say that to me?" But the Lord was testing my faith and knew that if He told me in prayer or in the car on the way to work, I wouldn't obey Him. He waited for me to clock in to work to ultimately clock out once and for all.

When I heard the Lord tell me it was my last day, I immediately went to human resources and resigned without a two weeks' notice. Ever since that day on September 16, 2016, I never looked back and the Lord catapulted me into full-time ministry. God has given us ears to hear and with that we must listen to understand what He is saying to us daily. God wants to cause our ears to incline to His prophetic voice daily. I love what Isaiah 50:4 declares: *"The Sovereign Lord has given me a well-instructed tongue, to know the word that sustains the weary. He wakens me morning by morning, wakens my ear to listen like one being instructed."*

God doesn't just want us to hear His voice daily but heed His instructions. We can train our ears to hear the voice of the Lord. Look at a few Scriptures below:

> *Now then go, and I, even I, will be with your mouth, and teach you what you are to say* (Exodus 4:12 NASB).

> *In the morning, O Lord, You will hear my voice; in the morning I will order my prayer to You and eagerly watch* (Psalm 5:3 NASB).

> *But I, O Lord, have cried out to You for help, and in the morning my prayer comes before You* (Psalm 88:13 NASB).

> *I rise before dawn and cry for help; I wait for Your words* (Psalm 119:147 NASB).

God will give us prophetic instructions daily as we listen attentively with an open heart and mind. To know the voice of God is to know His ways, will, word, and heart. Spending time with the Lord daily will increase our ability to know the voice of God and how He communicates to each of us in a unique way.

When someone calls me and I don't recognize the voice on the other end of the phone, I will respond, "Who is this?" or, "May I ask who's calling?" But if I regularly speak to someone, I instantly know the person's voice and wouldn't have to ask, "Who's speaking?" Many of us have to speak to the Lord and allow Him to speak back to us daily in order to know Him more and more. Communing with God sharpens the communication between our Father and His children—speaking of you.

33

SPIRITUAL SMELL
AND SCENTS

*So he went to him and kissed him. When Isaac caught the
smell of his clothes, he blessed him and said, "Ah, the smell of
my son is like the smell of a field that the Lord has blessed."*
—GENESIS 27:27

I personally love dogs and have heard that a dog's sense of smell is ten times stronger than humans. I would love to smell what they smell and at the extent they smell it. For me, the smell of fresh apple or sweet potato pie whets my appetite. So I can only imagine what it smells like to have a dog. God uses the nose of our spirit to smell things in the spirit, which I call *spiritual smell*.

The Lord will speak to us through our spiritual sense of smell. God want to sharpen our nose (discerner) of the spirit to smell what He wants us to inhale. James W. Goll, a pioneering prophet and my spiritual prophetic father, says in his book *The Discerner*, "Our goal should be to share the fragrance of Heaven that we have inhaled."

"At the moment I have all I need—and more! I am generously supplied with the gifts you sent me with Epaphroditus. They are a sweet-smelling sacrifice that is acceptable and pleasing to God" (Phil. 4:18 NLT). Your spiritual sense of smell becomes keener with knowing and studying the Word of God. The Word of God is a discerner that can help us sense good and evil, right from wrong, angelic or demonic, error and truth. Hebrews 4:12 KJV says, *"For the word of*

God is quick, and powerful, and sharper than any two edged sword, piercing even to the dividing asunder of soul and spirit, and of the joints and marrow, and is a discerner of the thoughts and intents of the heart." Through the spiritual sense of scent or smell God can reveal a divine revelations or messages. In addition, the Lord can validate His work as well as the devil's. We must know that God has created all of our five senses for a specific natural purpose.

That being said, we also have five spiritual senses that God uses to identify specific things. We are naturally hardwired and created to smell. The Lord created our sense of smell for our understanding what is bad or good. In other words, if we smell a rotten egg how do we know its rotten? It's because the smell of it causes us to know it's bad. And we identified that it's an egg through our sense of smell. God most definitely utilizes our sense of smell to speak to us. Good or pungent smells can indicate various things.

Over time, God will train our sense of smell to discern things based off of their scent. A police sniffer dog is trained at an early age to discern and distinguish bad things like drugs, bombs, missing persons, and criminals on the run. It can use the scent or odor from a person's clothing to find someone. It's a powerful natural sense that is equally powerful in the spirit. It is no surprise in different cultures and regions that worship is connected to what they smell or through the sense of smell. There is a sweet aroma of Christ, an awesome fragrance. I have smelled many times the fragrance of Christ and presence of God.

> *And walk in love, just as Christ also loved you and gave Himself up for us, an offering and a sacrifice to God as a fragrant aroma* (Ephesians 5:2 NASB).

However, throughout my prophetic ministry I have encountered strange demonic odors of death, sickness, disease, infirmity, and so forth on people and in particular meetings. God speaks to us through these spiritual scents to target what is going on in the atmosphere or even in a person who may need healing, deliverance, and breakthrough. God has opened up my spiritual sense of smell many times to speak to me concerning a sickness, illness, spirit of infirmity, perversion, sin, angelic presence, the glory of God, and more.

There was a time when I was in prayer and worship weeping before the Lord. After an hour or so on the floor, I left my prayer room to use the bathroom. When I returned I was hit with a strong baby powder smell and fresh scent of roses in my room. I couldn't believe what I was sensing because it was so intense that it was on all my clothes, bedsheets, and even carpet. God opened up my spiritual sense of smell to discern His presence. There is a sweet aroma of God's presence when intense prayer and worship is released.

Several times in ministry God used me in healing and deliverance by letting me spiritually smell strong odors from people's bodies. One service the Lord gave me a word of knowledge that someone needed healing from cancer. A woman came forward and I began to pray for her and cast out spirits of infirmity and sickness. There came from her this foul odor like rotten eggs. It was a pungent smell, so profuse I was gaging because I didn't expect to smell such a thing. A month later, the woman received a report that the cancer that was in her blood was no longer there.

Another time, I was with a relative of mine who came to pick me up. He wanted to talk with me, and as we were driving along chatting I suddenly smelled a strong skunk odor. I asked my cousin if he smelled it and he looked around surprised, saying, "No, I don't smell anything."

I said, "Really? You don't smell that skunk smell?"

He said, "No, not at all."

I thought I was smelling things. The more he talked, the more the smell got stronger. I hear the Lord speak to me and say, "It's him!" As I looked at my cousin, I was able to discern that there was a foul, perverted spirit operating on the inside of him.

Later that evening after he dropped me off, I asked my cousin what was going on with him, and he said that before he picked me up to talk, he was looking for male prostitutes. My cousin struggled with immortality and perversion and what I smelled were the spirits of toxicity that were keeping him bound. God will speak to us through our sense of smell if we allow Him to.

34

SPIRITUAL TOUCH

Therefore, since we have a great high priest who has ascended into heaven, Jesus the Son of God, let us hold firmly to the faith we profess. For we do not have a high priest who is unable to empathize with our weaknesses, but we have one who has been tempted in every way, just as we are—yet he did not sin. Let us then approach God's throne of grace with confidence, so that we may receive mercy and find grace to help us in our time of need.
—HEBREWS 4:14-16

I have come to notice that God frequently speaks to me through the sense of touch. Jesus also received information and knowledge through the sense of touch when He felt virtue leave Him when the woman with the issue of blood touched the hem of His garment. The power of feeling and touch is great to experience. In the realm of worshiping God we have the ability to feel or sense the presence of the Lord. When I move in the prophetic or healing I am oftentimes able to feel people's pain, injuries, or bodily afflictions. God speaks through the sense of spiritual touch or feeling. Some people also receive prophetic revelation by physically touching an individual.

And a woman was there who had been subject to bleeding for twelve years. She had suffered a great deal under the care of many doctors and had spent all she had, yet instead of getting better she grew worse. When she heard about Jesus, she came up behind him in the crowd and touched his cloak, because she thought, "If I just touch his clothes, I will be healed." Immediately her bleeding stopped and she felt in her body that she was freed from her suffering (Mark 5:25-29).

We can see that she didn't touch Jesus's body per se but touched His clothing and He felt healing virtue leave Him. I believe that if we are anointed by the Holy Spirit, anything that is on us can be anointed as well. Jesus's garment was saturated with power. We can see that Jesus was able to discern that someone touched Him when in fact they didn't touch His physical body but the hem of His garment. In Mark 5:31 it says:

And His disciples said to Him, "You see the crowd pressing in on You, and You say, 'Who touched Me?'" (NASB)

He asked the question, "Who touched Me?" which indicates that He didn't know who touched Him per se but that He was able to feel and sense spiritual virtue was pulled from Him physically speaking. He was able to sense spiritually and naturally what was going on.

God sometimes speaks to me concerning someone who is in need of healing breakthrough. The Lord will use the sense of touch to identify what is going on with someone. In other words, I will feel an impression to indicate what is going on in someone else's body.

For example, I receive a word of knowledge and I feel warmth in my knees, ankles, hands, neck, eyes, back, or whatever area God highlights, and I ask who is having any pain in this particular area. A hundred percent of the time it is someone in the meeting. There are times in prayer, worship, and intercession when I feel in my body the actual pain or wounds of another. God will open our senses so that we can be used as His healing agents.

I recall a time when I was ministering a message on the healing power of God. I received a word of knowledge and a burning sensation in my stomach. I said that there was someone there who had pain in the female organs and was unable to digest her food. A man and woman came forth and I laid my hands on them both and I felt heat in my hands and the man fell out under the power of God and the woman yelled that she felt heat shoot through her stomach. A week later, I received an email from the woman that she was able to keep her food down and digest it and had no more pain in her stomach.

Jesus was moved with compassion through natural feelings. I recall a time when I was in a service ministering in deliverance and I sensed a strong demonic presence next to a man who was manifesting and instantly my hands began to tingle like electricity or static. I began to pray for him and call out spirits that were oppressing him. When I laid my tingling hands on his stomach, he began to cry and later vomit. There was a strong odor that came from his body. I knew that he was touched with the delivering power of God through my hands. As I used that same hand to touch people, many were yelling out, falling under the power of God, and even healed.

God wants to use our bodies for His glory. As God uses me in the prophetic, there are times I don't get a strong impression or word from God until I lay my hands on people or touch them. As a seer prophet I understand that the Lord uses my five senses to speak to me. We must know that our spiritual sense of touch and feeling can be activated. We can simply ask the Father to open them and He will do just that by our faith. We are to present and yield ourselves for His use. Here are a few Scriptures about the touch and power of God:

> *Jesus stretched out His hand and touched him, saying, "I am willing; be cleansed." And immediately his leprosy was cleansed* (Matthew 8:3 NASB).
>
> *Moved with compassion, Jesus stretched out His hand and touched him, and said to him, "I am willing; be cleansed"* (Mark 1:41 NASB).

> God uses the sense of touch to let us experience His power in our physical bodies. That is why we must as believers and leaders take care of our physical bodies or physical temples. Why? Our bodies are to host the Holy Spirit and how we treat our bodies will impact the anointing and power of the Holy Spirit flowing in and through you.

35

SPIRITUAL TASTE

I took the little scroll from the angel's hand and ate
it. It tasted as sweet as honey in my mouth, but
when I had eaten it, my stomach turned sour.
—REVELATION 10:10

I recall when our spiritual father, the late Bob Jones, who was a seer prophet, activated Naim and me in the five spiritual senses. He told us if God says hot, fresh bread and we don't see it, what happens? And we said we taste bread that is hot in our mouth. He said that was the correct answer, because God told us it was hot, fresh bread and we were able to taste it by hearing what God was speaking. That's what tapping into your spiritual taste buds is like. God speaks to us prophetically through what I call *spiritual taste.*

The Holy Spirit can cause a Spirit-filled believer to receive revelation through their spiritual taste buds. God uses what you are familiar with to get your attention. God will use your spiritual taste to speak something familiar to us. If I blindfold most of you and did a taste test survey, many of you would be able to identify apple, pumpkin, or lemon pie. Likewise, with our spiritual sense of taste we are able to identify things as well and call to our memory certain tastes that were bitter, sweet, salty, hot, cold, or warm. Ezekiel understood this when he was given the scroll to eat.

> *So I opened my mouth, and He fed me this scroll. He said to me,*
> *"Son of man, feed your stomach and fill your body with this scroll*

*which I am giving you." Then I ate it, and it was sweet as honey
in my mouth. Then He said to me, "Son of man, go to the house of
Israel and speak with My words to them* (Ezekiel 3:2-4 NASB).

God can speak to us through our sense of taste. When we ask the Lord to
use us for His glory, God does just that. He has created our bodies to function through messages between the brain and the body. God speaks to our
imagination and sends messages through our bodies to respond. The brain is
the control center of the body. God uses the brain through our imagination to
communicate what is on His heart and mind. Through the Holy Spirit we can
ascend to the throne room of God in one thought and be seated in heavenly
places with Christ Jesus here and now.

I can recall a time I was in Huntington, West Virginia attending Marshall
University. I was in my dorm room recreational center talking to a room-
mate. As we were talking about track and field and our interest in the sport,
I suddenly was interrupted by a sour taste in my mouth. It was like someone
squeezed a lemon in my mouth. I didn't understand why I was tasting this out
of nowhere. This taste came suddenly as I was talking to my friend who ran
track. I tried to discount what I was tasting and continued on with the conversation, and the more I looked at my friend the more bitter the taste got. I
didn't understand what was going on or why I was having these strange tastes
when suddenly the Lord spoke to me about him.

God begin to give me a word of knowledge (specific details or information
about a person past, present, or even future). He told me that there was bitterness, unforgiveness, and resentment in my friend's heart. I started to inquire
more about the specifics of what He was revealing to me through my taste
buds. God initiated a dialogue like a friend would have with another friend.
The Lord gave me more prophetic intelligence in my mind concerning a bitter
root issue that needed to be resolved.

The interesting thing about it was that God used my taste buds to identify the taste of a lemon to speak to me what was going on in his heart toward
someone dear to him. I didn't know at first that he was upset. God knew and
began to show me through my personal familiarity with the taste of lemons.
The lemon taste was the unforgiveness that God used to help me see what was
deep-rooted in his soul and impacting his life negatively.

It all started to make sense as I was talking to the Lord. I inquired of the Lord what the bitterness was a result of and the Lord said clearly, "His father!" I shared with my friend that the Lord spoke to me concerning his bitterness in his heart concerning his father. His father abandoned him at a young age and God wanted him to forgive his father and be healed.

Suddenly, he began to break down crying like a baby and I went over to him and hugged him like a father. I started to pray for him and have him renounce some things and forgive his father for what he had done to him and his mother. I was so surprised that God would speak to me with just a simple lemon taste in my mouth. We should never limit how God speaks to us. When we make ourselves available God will call on us for His work.

The Bible says Psalm 34:8, *"Taste and see that the Lord is good; blessed is the one who takes refuge in him."* We can taste the goodness of God's Word and find safety in His presence. Do you ever study and read God's Word and it's so good that you come away full or satisfied? Yes, that is what happens when God speaks to us daily and we feast on His fresh manna. God will allow us to taste and digest what He reveals to us.

36

UNDER AN OPEN HEAVEN

After these things I looked, and behold, a door standing open in heaven, and the first voice which I had heard, like the sound of a trumpet speaking with me, said, "Come up here, and I will show you what must take place after these things."
—**REVELATION 4:1 NASB**

An open Heaven is a divine supernatural encounter where the voice of the Lord is released. Jesus Christ was announced by the Father at the Jordan River through an open heaven experience at His baptism. Matthew 3:16-17 declares:

> *As soon as Jesus was baptized, he went up out of the water. At that moment heaven was opened, and he saw the Spirit of God descending like a dove and alighting on him. And a voice from heaven said, "This is my Son, whom I love; with him I am well pleased."*

We can see from the above text that a voice from heaven spoke and declared who Jesus was—the beloved Son of the Father. God will speak to you through an open heaven and declare not only your relationship with Him but others will hear the announcement or divine broadcast of heaven over your life. I can remember being ordained to the ministry office of the prophet by my local apostolic leaders—heaven literally opened while Apostle Dale Mast was prophesying over Naim and me.

Oddly, I didn't hear Apostle Dale but the voice of the Lord thundering through him. Others who were at the ordination service witnessed the glory and light of the anointing shine upon those who were being ordained, and the power of God was present. One person said that they saw angles around us when we were getting released into prophetic ministry. God speaks through times of open heaven activities.

In open heaven encounters the voice of God speaks, prophetic visions are released, the anointing and spiritual mantles are identified, ministry credentials are announced, and angels are seen. There are many Old and New Testament accounts of the Lord speaking to His people from Heaven. Look at several Scriptures that prove my point. God wants to speak to us in many ways through an open heaven encounter:

> *Now it came about in the thirtieth year, on the fifth day of the fourth month, while I was by the river Chebar among the exiles, the heavens were opened and I saw visions of God* (Ezekiel 1:1 NASB).

> *As soon as Jesus was baptized, he went up out of the water. At that moment heaven was opened, and he saw the Spirit of God descending like a dove and alighting on him* (Matthew 3:16)

> *He then added, "Very truly I tell you, you will see 'heaven open, and the angels of God ascending and descending on' the Son of Man"* (John 1:51)

There are many Scriptures that prove that God speaks from Heaven to His prophets and apostles.

> *Then the Lord said to Moses, "Thus you shall say to the sons of Israel, 'You yourselves have seen that I have spoken to you from heaven'"* (Exodus 20:22 NASB).

> *Out of the heavens He let you hear His voice to discipline you; and on earth He let you see His great fire, and you heard His words from the midst of the fire* (Deuteronomy 4:36 NASB).

> *Then You came down on Mount Sinai, and spoke with them from*
> *heaven; You gave them just ordinances and true laws, good stat-*
> *utes and commandments* (Nehemiah 9:13 NASB).

It's very clear that the voice of God is connected to the heavens being opened. God speaks when there is a rending of the heavens. God speaks His Word from His throne in Heaven and we can hear Him through the Holy Spirit.

37

HOLY SPIRIT ENCOUNTERS

Do not get drunk on wine, which leads to debauchery.
Instead, be filled with the Spirit.
—EPHESIANS 5:18

God will often speak through unusual activities of the Holy Spirit. Most charismatic movements or Pentecostal expressions will have Holy Spirit encounters where God will speak dramatically in those moments. I have fallen under the power of the Holy Spirit and seen an angel. The words *drunk, slain,* and *soaking* don't make sense to those who are not spiritually minded. They will ask, "How can you be drunk or intoxicated by the Holy Spirit? Or how can the Spirit of God slay you if you are still alive? Or how can you be soaking when you are still dry?"

We have to understand that these terms should be taken spiritually—being drunk or intoxicated not with natural wine but full of the Spirit of God. In addition, being slain in the Spirit is speaking of death to self, fleshly appetites, and daily sacrifices to kill any ungodly desires. Soaking in the Spirit is being immersed in God's Spirit when we are waiting on Him to fill us up with His glory. These words or terms are used as an expression of things we understand.

Encounter is a phenomenal experience with God without words, but leaving an overwhelming message or strong impression.

The Lord reigns; let the peoples tremble! He sits enthroned upon the cherubim; let the earth quake! (Psalm 99:1 ESV)

O mountains, that you skip like rams? O hills, like lambs? Tremble, O earth, before the Lord, before the God of Jacob, who turned the rock into a pool of water, the flint into a fountain of water (Psalm 114:6-8 NASB).

Hear the word of the Lord, ye that tremble at his word; Your brethren that hated you, that cast you out for my name's sake, said, Let the Lord be glorified: but he shall appear to your joy, and they shall be ashamed (Isaiah 66:5 KJV).

There are times when the Spirit of God will minister to you when you are under the influence of the Holy Spirit. I have been in intense worship, deliverance, and prophetic services where the Holy Spirit came upon me and I was trembling uncontrollably. My hands began to shake and I knew that the Lord was actively present on me. In addition, there are times I am soaking or marinating in His presence. I am lying prostrate before the Lord waiting on Him to impart, revive, refresh, and awaken me.

In Charismatic or Pentecostal circles this is normal. To soak or marinate in His presence is to wait on the Lord and bask in His abiding love. In those types of positions we receive the greatest impartation and life-changing results. I have received personal deliverance, healing, and direction by God through the Holy Spirit while soaking, marinating, and trembling under the power of God. Just like food that is marinated with a particular sauce, soaking in God's presence is the same way. We get seasoned and juicy with more of God and less of us. Intimacy with God begins when we radically pursue Him with our whole heart.

38

ANGELS

Are they not all ministering spirits, sent out to render
service for the sake of those who will inherit salvation?
—Hebrews 1:14 NASB

Angels are supernatural beings created for the eternal purposes of God. The powerful thing about them is their holy reverence to the Lord and His will, their important role, and their total understanding of the prophetic Word of God. Angels are messengers of God. Throughout Scripture, angels were assigned to carry messages from the heavenly realm to men and women in the earthly realm. They themselves are very much acquainted with releasing what God has said.

Angels not only have the ability to hear the voice of the Lord and respond to it but they carry it out, fulfilling His word accurately in our lives. Angels have a great mandate to also minister, protect, strengthen, and go before us to bring prophetic words for us to speak, deliver spiritual gifts, and release the kingdom, power, and glory of the Lord. Angels are another voice from the heavenly realm. Throughout the New Testament, angels visited and spoke to people concerning what they should do.

We have the ability to see angels with our natural eyes or in our mind with the eyes of our understanding. We never know who we will encounter in life with a prophetic word from the Lord. God uses angels to send prophetic words and we have the ability to hear God through them. However, everyone claiming that they are sent to you is not sent by the Lord. The Bible admonishes us: *"Do not neglect to show hospitality to strangers, for by this some have entertained angels without knowing it"* (Heb. 13:2 NASB). Demons are fallen angels as well, so we have to be careful who we entertain because both angels and demons are real and don't look like what we were taught.

We can see in the Book of Acts that an angel appeared to Phillip to tell him to get up to speak to the Ethiopian eunuch: *"But an angel of the Lord spoke to Philip saying, 'Get up and go south to the road that descends from Jerusalem to Gaza.' ...So he got up and went; and there was an Ethiopian eunuch"* (Acts 8:26-27 NASB). Angelic visitation also came to the apostle Paul. He heard the voice of the Lord through angelic experiences in the New Testament (Acts 27:23; Heb. 1:7).

God sends angels on purpose to fulfill His agenda. Angels come to declare and carry out God's will. Hearing the voice of the Lord through angels is another high level of revelation by God that a believer can experience. I believe that every Spirit-filled believer has been given an angel or angel(s) at birth. Angels are prophetic because they are like mail carriers—they deliver a message. They only respond to the voice of the Lord.

We as believers and children of God should take a lesson in our own lives from angels who, in total faith and reliance, are obedient to the voice of the Lord. God's angels are great servant messengers who obey the instructions of the Lord. In other words, angels come to deliver what God has spoken. They make sure what God has commanded is fulfilled. Angels help fulfill the personal prophecies over your life. The apostle Paul was no stranger to angels. We can see that an angel appeared to Paul concerning going to Rome:

> For this very night an angel of the God to whom I belong and whom I serve stood before me, saying, "Do not be afraid, Paul; you must stand before Caesar" (Acts 27:23-24 NASB).

God can and wants to speak to us and show us His mighty acts, but we must be open to receive them by faith. Angel sightings, appearances, and involvement in the early church were so common that when Peter was released from prison and knocked on the door of the room where the apostles were, they were more able to believe it was his angel than Peter!

> *When he knocked at the door of the gate, a servant-girl named*
> *Rhoda came to answer. When she recognized Peter's voice, because*
> *of her joy she did not open the gate, but ran in and announced that*
> *Peter was standing in front of the gate. They said to her, "You are*
> *out of your mind!" But she kept insisting that it was so. They kept*
> *saying, "It is his angel"* (Acts 12:13-15 NASB).

Angelic communication and visitation is prophetic in essence. God uses angels to communicate His eternal purposes, while we have the ability to hear the voice of God through angels. Prophets are also called messengers of God and they operate in the realm of the angelic through they are given direct, indirect, and divine messages from the Lord. One of the most fascinating things to happen in a believer's life is to encounter one of God's angelic messengers. It is imperative to biblically understand God's angelic messengers that He sends to minister to us.

We must be spiritually sensitive to the voice of God through these angelic messengers. These heavenly messengers come to declare and speak the oracles of God to man. We cannot summon or command angels, but we can ask God for them to help us fulfill our prophetic purpose.

Angelic communication and activity in the affairs of humans is found throughout Scripture, Old and New Testament. Angels are instrumental in our lives for they serve us as a gift from the Lord. God send them to help us, encourage us, war on our behalf, and bring blessings, provision, and breakthrough. Angels are dispatched with divine assignments at the moment we pray, just as Daniel 10:12 declares:

> *Then he continued, "Do not be afraid, Daniel. Since the first day*
> *that you set your mind to gain understanding and to humble your-*
> *self before your God, your words were heard, and I have come in*
> *response to them."*

39

HIS GLORY

Arise, shine; for thy light is come, and the glory of the Lord is
risen upon thee. For, behold, the darkness shall cover the earth,
and gross darkness the people: but the Lord shall arise upon thee,
and his glory shall be seen upon thee. And the Gentiles shall
come to thy light, and kings to the brightness of thy rising.
—Isaiah 60:1-3 KJV

There is a powerful force of God that comes when His heavy weight of glory comes on you. I have had many personal prophetic moments in God's presence when He did things that only God can do. I am not trying to be like Moses the prophet, asking to see His glory, but I want to carry it. God is raising up glory carriers who are able to release it to see societal, spiritual, economical, and holistic transformation. God's glory brings change, blessings, favor, power, and correction or judgment to anything that is not like God.

There is nothing like the glory of God operating in your life. Why? Because miracles, signs, wonders, and the prophetic voice of God are manifested. God doesn't just want to anoint us with His Holy Spirit but to anoint us with His glory as His children. God speaks through His glory, which is manifested in the supernatural results that you witness.

When the glory of God is present upon a person, it causes them to bow down and bow out and become subject to the King of Glory. The priests in the Old Testament couldn't stand to minister because of the glory. The glory of

God is not something we are to take lightly. The glory of God speaks of God's creativity and nature. The glory of God is found in this particular Scripture:

> *The heavens declare the glory of God; and the firmament sheweth his handywork. Day unto day uttereth speech, and night unto night sheweth knowledge. There is no speech nor language, where their voice is not heard. Their line is gone out through all the earth, and their words to the end of the world. In them hath he set a tabernacle for the sun* (Psalm 19:1-4 KJV).

The glory of God reveals the beauty of His spirit. We must understand that the glory of the Lord is not an aesthetic beauty or a material beauty, but it is the beauty that emanates from the Lord's character and from all that He is, was, and is to become. James 1:10 illustrates the word *glory* when it calls on a rich man to *"glory in his humiliation,"* indicating a glory that does not mean natural, worldly riches or power, fame, or material beauty. The glory of the Lord can fill the earth or crown humanity.

Furthermore, the glory of the Lord can be visibly seen within man and witnessed in the earth realm, but it is not of them; this glory is of and from God. The glory of man is the beauty of man's spirit, which is fallible and will over time pass away, and is therefore humiliating. But the glory of God is eternal and does not pass away because His glory is manifested in all His attributes together.

In the glory we can hear the voice of the Lord as well as feel the weight of His presence. There are times when I hear the voice of God in His presence in prayer or worship. I love what Isaiah 43:7 shares—that God created us for His glory. In context with the other verses, it can be said that man "glorifies" God because through man God's glory can be seen in things such as worship, prayer, love, music, heroism, mercy, grace, praise, and so on—such things belonging to the Lord Himself that we are carrying *"in jars of clay"* (see 2 Cor. 4:7).

We were created for His glory and we become vessels that are able to host His presence. We become "glory vessels" who contain and release His glory. Our source is found in God, and we are able to do all things. God interacts with nature, as nature created by God also exhibits His glory. His glory is revealed to man's mind through the material world in many ways, and often in different ways to different people.

When I look at the vastness of the sea, I think about the awesomeness of God's glory and what He created with His Word. Some people are awe-struck by the sight of the sun, moon, stars, or snow-capped mountains, while another person loves the beauty of forest or ocean. But that which is behind it all (God's glory) speaks to both people and connects them to God.

My second book, called *Heaven Declares: Prophetic Decrees to Start Your Day,* which is a 90-day devotional, helps readers to hear the voice of God while understanding His glory in what He has created. God desires to speak simply through what He has created. God is more than able to reveal Himself to all men, no matter their background, race, age, heritage, or geographical location.

The heavens are speaking of the glory of God and declaring the works of God's hands. Each day pours forth speech, and night after night brings revelation knowledge. We can hear the voice of God anywhere, any place, to the four corners of the earth. It doesn't matter where you are in life, God will break through to speak to you personally while revealing His glory to you daily and nightly. We must understand that God will always speak when we spend time with Him in His presence.

God's presence will also speak of His glory. When we soak and marinate in the presence of God, He will come to speak! The glory of God is so weighty that a person can't even stand or speak. When I am worship, prayer, fasting, or studying the Word of God, the presence of God is so thick and strong that I hear or feel His presence moving upon me. I often cry, fall on my face, or be still before Him. I just love being in the presence of God. In His glory is where I get a lot of personal healing, deliverance, correction, and refreshing. The Bible says in Acts 3:20, *"that times of refreshing may come from the Lord, and that he may send the Messiah, who has been appointed for you."* If you want to continue to hear the voice of God and stay refreshed, make sure you stay in the presence of God and keep your heart pure.

40

APOSTLES

And He Himself gave some to be apostles, some prophets, some evangelists, and some pastors and teachers, for the equipping of the saints for the work of ministry, for the edifying of the body of Christ.
—EPHESIANS 4:11-12 NKJV

God speaks through the modern-day apostles who are sent by God with a special message. Those who may be called to this ministry and office must know what an apostle is. This ministry is a New Testament ministry office that God has set in the church. God is raising up anointed men and women called to apostolic work. The apostolic ministry didn't cease with the first century apostles, but there is a continuation of the ministry of Christ through sent ones who are commissioned through the local church as the Holy Spirit directs. Apostles can and should be prophetic in nature because of the Holy Spirit.

Apostles today should hear and know the voice of the Lord and teach those they are leading, fathering, and equipping to as well. Those who come into contact with modern-day apostles will be able to benefit greatly through their ministry. Teaching, preaching, prophesying, training, and most of all love and truth will be the earmark of who they are. The word *apostle* means "one who is sent out." In the New Testament, there are two primary usages of the word *apostle*. The first is in specifically referring to the 12 apostles of Jesus Christ, and the second is generically referring to other individuals who are sent out by the Holy Spirit to be messengers or ambassadors of Jesus Christ through the church.

An apostle is sent forth by the Lord to minister with delegated authority given by him through the Holy Spirit to the churches. They are called of God and sent by God, not man. An apostle has a pioneering grace to establish churches, ministries, and movements; they equip believers and lay foundational truth in the lives of God's people (Eph. 2:20). Apostles could be called "spiritual builders" (1 Cor. 3:10). They have oversight of the body (1 Cor. 4:15).

The 12 apostles held a unique position. In referring to the New Jerusalem, Revelation 21:14 states, *"The wall of the city had twelve foundations, and on them were the names of the twelve apostles of the Lamb."* The 12 apostles are also referred to in Matthew 10:2; Mark 3:14; 4:10; 6:7; 9:35; 14:10,17,20; Luke 6:13; 9:1; 22:14; John 6:71; Acts 6:2; and First Corinthians 15:5. These 12 apostles were the first messengers of the Gospel after the death and resurrection of Jesus Christ.

These 12 apostles were the foundation of the church, with Jesus being the cornerstone (Eph. 2:20). God uses modern-day apostles to speak God's Word and establish God's people in truth. We can hear the voice of God through men and women who are anointed by God to equip, train, and educate us to fulfill our divine calling in Christ. Apostles are needed today so that we are able to hear the voice of God for ourselves and be established.

41

PROPHETS

And He Himself gave some to be apostles, some prophets, some evangelists, and some pastors and teachers, for the equipping of the saints for the work of ministry, for the edifying of the body of Christ.
—EPHESIANS 4:11-12 NKJV

God speaks through prophets today as He did in the past. A prophet is one who speaks for God to man. He does not necessarily have to foretell the future, although that is a valid prophetic ministry. He does foretell a word from God that reveals God's plans for the church, city, region, people, or territory. Prophets can and do know the voice of God. Oftentimes, if you are not a prophet yourself but have the Holy Spirit, you are able to hear the voice of God speaking through a prophet.

Prophets also have to hear the voice of God for themselves through the Holy Spirit just as Spirit-filled believers should. God uses prophets to give direction and correction to the Body of Christ. According to First Corinthians 14:3, the prophetic gifts are given for edification, exhortation, and comfort to the believer. In other words, prophecy should build up, stir up, and cheer up. Prophecy is one of the ways God speaks to His people and a way we can hear the voice of God. Prophetic words that tear down the body and depress the people are not from God. Prophecy given by a prophet or a prophetic believer should construct not destruct.

The prophet does more than prophesy, but they are relatively associated with prophecy that serves to encourage and strengthen. However, a hard prophetic message, or word of correction, may come forth, such as a call to repentance, but it will always result in establishing, not in destroying. God used a prophetic apostle in the New Testament by the name of Barnabas, who is called "son of encouragement" (other translations say "consolation" or "exhortation") (Acts 4:36).

He was able to hear God's voice and speak it forth to exhort or bring consolation. Barnabas had an innate prophetic gift that exhorted the body to purposefully and steadfastly hold on to the Lord (Acts 11:23-24). Moreover, there were New Testament prophets like John the Baptist (Luke 1:76) and Agabus (Acts 11:27-28; 21:10-13) who heard the voice of God and spoke for Him. John was sent forth to speak as a prophet through the tender mercy of God (Luke 1:78). True prophecy will always be tempered with love, mercy, and wisdom.

There are Christians who believe that they have to be a prophet to hear God's voice, but that's not biblical. Every child of God can and should hear the voice of God. In addition, every believer can prophesy, even though every believer is not called to be a prophet. My point is that God still speaks today and He will continue to use modern-day prophets to speak for Him. We are not to replace the Holy Spirit with prophets. We call can hear the voice of God for ourselves, but we are not to ignore one of the foundational ministry gifts and offices that God has set in the Body of Christ.

However, there are many false prophets and teachers out there against whom we must safeguard ourselves. But we are also are not to be so turned off by the false that we neglect the true or authentic prophets God is raising up and using. Prophecy is God's idea and prophets are God's mouthpieces in His divine plan. In a general sense, a prophet is a person who speaks God's truth to others. The English word *prophet* comes from the Greek word *prophetes*, which can mean "one who speaks forth" or "advocate." Prophets are also called "seers" because of their spiritual insight or their ability to "see" the future.

In the Word of God, prophets often had a dual teaching and revelatory responsibility, proclaiming God's truth on contemporary, social, and church issues while also revealing details about the destiny of the Church. Isaiah's ministry, for example, touched on both the present and the future. He preached boldly against the corruption of his day (Isa. 1:4) and delivered grand visions of the future of Israel (Isa. 25:8).

Prophets had tremendous responsibility to not only hear the voice of God but speak God's Word to His people. We can hear God's truth and prosper through the prophesying by the prophets. In Ezra 6:14 it says, *"So the elders of the Jews continued to build and prosper under the preaching of Haggai the prophet and Zechariah, a descendant of Iddo. They finished building the temple according to the command of the God of Israel and the decrees of Cyrus, Darius and Artaxerxes, kings of Persia."* We can see how powerful it is to hear and respond to the voice of God through prophets.

The Jewish leadership finished rebuilding the temple through the prophetic Word of the Lord. When we obey the voice of the Lord through the Holy Spirit speaking through prophets, we will prosper and be established to complete what God has called us to finish. In addition, prophets were very instrumental in guiding the nation of Israel and establishing the church. God's household is *"built on the foundation of the apostles and prophets, with Christ Jesus himself as the chief cornerstone"* (Eph. 2:20).

The early church also had prophets like Ananias, who was given a prophecy about the apostle Paul's future (Acts 9:10-18). In addition, there were four daughters of Philip who had the ability to speak for God through the gift of prophesying. We must know that prophecy or the prophetic gift is listed as a spiritual gift in First Corinthians 12 and 14. In the last days, referring to eschatology, the two "witnesses will prophesy from Jerusalem (Rev. 11).

Usually, the prophets God sends are greatly despised, rejected, and prophecies are oftentimes unheeded. I am reminded of the prophet Isaiah who described the nation he was sent to as a *"rebellious people, deceitful children, children unwilling to listen to the Lord's instruction. They say to the seers, 'See no more visions!' and to the prophets, 'Give us no more visions of what is right! Tell us pleasant things, prophesy illusions'"* (Isa. 30:9-10). Jesus lamented that Jerusalem had killed the prophets God had sent to them (see Luke 13:34).

A true prophet of God is only committed to speaking God's truth. He or she will never contradict God's revealed Word. Like the prophet Micaiah just before his fateful confrontation with Ahab, a modern-day prophet of God will declare, *"As surely as the Lord lives, I can tell him only what my God says"* (2 Chron. 18:13).

42

EVANGELISTS

And He Himself gave some to be apostles, some prophets, some evangelists, and some pastors and teachers, for the equipping of the saints for the work of ministry, for the edifying of the body of Christ.
—EPHESIANS 4:11-12 NKJV

God still speaks and uses anointed, soul-winning evangelists today. Like apostles and prophets, we can hear the voice of God through these ministry gifts. I can remember when I was in college and I would hear Billy Graham preaching a message of salvation. The evangelist is a messenger who proclaims the good news. He or she brings the lost to salvation and exhorts Christians to witness for Christ. Phillip was a New Testament evangelist who preached the Word with signs following. His preaching and miracles led to revival and great joy in Samaria (Acts 8:5-8).

In the apostle Paul's second letter to Timothy, he sets forth the work of an evangelist. He is to preach the Word, be ready at all times, reprove, rebuke, exhort with patience, be watchful, and endure afflictions (2 Tim. 4:2-5). An evangelist is a proclaimer of the good news. In other words, he or she preaches the Gospel to win souls for Jesus Christ while they are doing missionary work in the field. A person with a heart called to the ministry of evangelism is often an individual who travels from place to place, city to city, country to country to proclaim the Gospel and call many unto repentance.

Philip was an evangelist, and Paul prophetically admonished his spiritual son Timothy to do the work of an evangelist. These are the only three uses of the word *evangelist* in the entire Bible. Other people could be considered "evangelists" in that they preached the Gospel, including Jesus Himself (Luke 20:1) and Paul the apostle (Rom. 1:15), but Philip is the one person specifically called an evangelist in Scripture.

Philip was not only called an evangelist but was one of the seven deacons chosen so that the apostles could do their work of teaching and prayer (Acts 6:3). We must understand that we can hear the voice of God through evangelists sharing the good news. I gave myself to the Lord when I heard the voice of Jesus through my pastor, calling me to give my life totally to Him. My point is we can hear the voice of God through an individual. God uses people to speak, proclaim, preach, prophesy, and teach His Word.

Hearing the voice of God through an individual is easier than God speaking to you directly. We can understand each other's language and culture. God will use evangelists today to cause people to hear God's voice and respond to His love. Philip had a dual function as an evangelist and an ordained deacon in the church as well. Evidently, Philip had settled in Caesarea and had lived there for some 20 years before the apostle Paul came in Acts 21. Philip's previous evangelistic responsibilities were in Samaria (Acts 8:4-8) where he deliberately proclaimed the message of the Messiah, speaking of Jesus to the Samaritans (Acts 8:5). Philip demonstrated the supernatural—that includes healing, miracles, casting out evil spirits, and healing paralytics. It is noteworthy that Philip performed water baptism in the name of Jesus, but the baptism of the Holy Spirit did not occur until the apostles came to Samaria.

Philip's ministry as an evangelist continued in Acts 8 as he was led by an angel to take the desert road to Gaza. On the road he met an Ethiopian eunuch—a court official to the queen of Ethiopia. We can see that Philip was instrumental in opening the man's understanding of the Word of God, and the eunuch was saved. He was able to hear the voice of the Lord through Philip's evangelistic ministry.

God wants us to hear His voice through the message of the Gospel. If you are a person like Philip called to preach and proclaim the good news, many will be given the opportunity to hear the voice of the Lord through you. We can see that Philip later baptized the eunuch, and the Holy Spirit transported Philip away in the spirit (Acts 8:39). Furthermore, we can see that Philip the evangelist later *"appeared at Azotus and traveled about, preaching the gospel in all the towns until he reached Caesarea"* (Acts 8:40). It's important to know that it was Philip's mission, wherever he went, to share the Gospel. That's what evangelists are called to do—become bearers of the good news of Jesus.

Interestingly, the apostle Paul exhorted his spiritual son Timothy to do some pre-salvation preaching—the "work of an evangelist" (2 Tim. 4:5). In other words, there will be some seasons and times when you are not to neglect the preaching of the Gospel even while you are establishing your work or church. This same preaching of the Gospel I believe is a generic apostolic call to the disciples in the Great Commission and to all of us today and to the end of the age (Matt. 28:16-20).

I am reminded of Jude 1:3 where it states that all saints are to contend earnestly for the faith delivered to them, and in verse 23 we are to *"save others by snatching them from the fire."* I truly believe that in today's society the ministry of evangelism has been overlooked. I believe there is coming a great awakening of revival and mass evangelism that will win souls for Jesus. The office of the evangelist will be needed until the church reaches the maturity of Christ Himself (Eph. 4:13).

The good news is to be shared. And we have the best news of all—Jesus died and rose again and saves all who will call on Him (Rom. 10:9-13). We need anointed evangelist through whom we can hear the message of salvation. We can hear God through anointed evangelists who have a heart for souls and a love of Christ that will draw men and women to Christ.

43

PASTORS

And He Himself gave some to be apostles, some prophets, some evangelists, and some pastors and teachers, for the equipping of the saints for the work of ministry, for the edifying of the body of Christ.
—EPHESIANS 4:11-12 NKJV

God speaks through covenant-keeping pastors. We must understand that God is using shepherds today who will have the heart of the Father for His people. Pastors of Christ will demonstrate the love of Christ. We should be able to hear the voice of the Lord through our pastors. Pastors should be able to hear the voice of God. But we shouldn't solely depend on our pastors to hear for us.

As a seven-year-old, I heard the voice of God through the message my blind pastor preached. A good pastor will teach their flock how to mature in the things of God and hear God personally. Pastors should be able to feed their flock to ultimately feed themselves and others. In order to understand the duties of a pastor, we should first ask, "What is a pastor?" However, don't be surprised by the answers you hear to this question—some people are confused about what a pastor is. Some churches have no pastor at all. Instead, they may have individuals in the congregation perform the duties. Many people are confused about who even qualifies to be a pastor according to the Bible. Often churches will have an elder or a bishop who fills the role of a pastor and use these titles in the same way as they would a pastor (1 Tim. 3:1-7; Tit. 1:6-9; 1 Pet. 5:1-4).

We have to understand the difference between a pastor, elder, or bishop; an elder or bishop carries a different meaning than pastor. The Hebrew word for pastor in the Bible literally means to tend a flock, pasture it, or graze it. The English words are often translated to "feed" or "shepherd." It is also translated as herdsman or pastor. Likewise, the Greek word for "pastor" found in the New Testament is most often translated as shepherd. But it is translated only once as pastor in Ephesians 4:11.

A pastor should be able to teach the Word of God that will cause their followers to hear God. The word *pastor* literally means "shepherd." A pastor is the shepherd of a local church flock. A pastor should be responsible to teach, protect, correct, exhort, edify, comfort, and discipline their flock.

He has authority to watch over the flock (Heb. 13:17) and to be an example (1 Pet. 5:2-3). A good shepherd must be able to lead their flock to pasture and water. One of his main roles and responsibilities is to feed the flock (Jer. 3:15; 23:4; Acts 20:28; 1 Pet. 5:2-3). We have false pastors/shepherds who feed themselves rather than their flocks (see Ezek. 34:1-6), but true shepherds are under Jesus, the Chief Shepherd (see 1 Pet. 5:4), and they follow His example (see Ps. 23).

We need pastors who will have the heart of God and hear for you concerning your spiritual welfare. God challenged the people to repent of their sins and turn back to God and that He would bless them with new pastors (see Jer. 3:12-15; 23:3-5). This tells us that the duties of a pastor include being a godly leader.

44

TEACHERS

*And He Himself gave some to be apostles, some prophets, some
evangelists, and some pastors and teachers, for the equipping of the
saints for the work of ministry, for the edifying of the body of Christ.*
—EPHESIANS 4:11-12 NKJV

God speaks through gifted and anointed teachers of the Word of God. We
need teachers who are able to hear the voice of God. Hearing the voice
of God through anointed teachers will cause us to appreciate the teaching of
the Word of God. A teacher is one who expounds and interprets the Word of
God. He or she does not just impart knowledge but living truth, which can be
applied to the lives of God's people. Teachers build on the foundation laid by
the apostles and prophets (1 Cor. 3:10). All those who function in the five-fold
ministry must be "able to teach" (1 Tim. 3:2).

Teaching is and should be a necessary and valuable part of life for a
Christian. Hearing and recognizing the voice of God is imperative when it
comes to knowing the Word of God. There are those who are powerful in
their spiritual gifts or charisma but lack the foundational teaching of God's
Word. I love the teaching ministry and those who are called to teach. They
make the complex simple. A great teacher can expound on the word and make
it comprehensive. God doesn't want us to be ignorant of spiritual things or of
His Word. We don't come into this world automatically geniuses and experts.
Someone has to teach us something in life.

We must be taught language proficiency, motor skills, cultural norms, social customs, manners, moral values—all these and more are the product of the learning process of childhood. Teaching is a key element in acquiring information and developing knowledge, so it is not surprising that the Bible has much to say about teaching.

In the Word of God, teaching is one of the gifts of the Holy Spirit. *"We have different gifts, according to the grace given to each of us. If your gift…is teaching, then teach"* (Rom. 12:6-7). In this context, teaching refers to the God-given ability to explain, expound, and dissect God's Word; the teacher has the supernatural ability to clearly instruct and communicate knowledge, specifically the doctrines of the faith and truths of the Bible (1 Cor. 12:27-29).

Paul understood that we have 10,000 instructors but lack fathers in our lives. Somebody will teach us something regardless of how young or old we may be. We should also be in a position to learn and grow. Hearing God's voice is knowing and recognizing it, as I am doing in this book. I am teaching you the reader how to tap into other streams of prophetic ways that God speaks. Christians should be able to learn and be taught how to hear and discern the voice of the God.

45

CALLING AND SUBMISSION TO LOCAL LEADERSHIP

The voice of God calls each person to a specific area of ministry and to a specific work. He will, in time, reveal it to the church leadership that you are a part of. If not, then wait until it is prophetically confirmed out of the mouth of two or three witnesses. We do not have to make an announcement of what God has called us to or continue to ask to be ordained or sent out or even try to work our way into a specific position. Where the Lord directs us, He will also provide for us! All we must do is obey His voice in that particular season and by faith do what is set before us to do while resting in Him and waiting for God to open doors for leadership. In doing so, our gift will make room for us (Prov. 18:16).

God always prepares before He sends out, and this takes time. Who goes out to battle without proper training and armor? Jesus called 12 men and then prepared them for the work of the ministry. Their only call was to follow Him (Matt. 4:19). A disciple is simply one who follows another's teaching. Many times the disciples just sat and listened to Jesus's teaching, receiving impartation and information. Likewise, we must sit down first before we can be sent out later.

Christians must crawl before they walk, walk before they run, and learn before they teach. Jesus's disciples were called to relationship first, then trained as students, and later they were commissioned as ready apostles. We must follow before we can lead. In other words, Jesus trained, educated, equipped, and prepared His 12 disciples in three basic ways. They were called to be with Him, to obey, and to follow His example as their model. The disciples were called to "*be with him*" (Mark 3:14) so that He might pour Himself into them.

Can you imagine what an education they received by living with Him for three years? They all slept together, walked together, ate together, worked together, lived together, and by simply being with Him they were constantly being prepared for what Jesus was doing. The disciples were also called to obey the commands of Jesus.

If you are called to lead others, you first must put into practice what you will eventually preach. Obedience is a great teacher. Jesus learned obedience in what He suffered. In other words, hearing the voice of God will teach you how to obey the Spirit of God over your flesh. In fact, without obedience it is impossible to learn from Jesus (John 7:17). The Lord continually prepares us as we continually obey Him.

Last, the disciples were called to hear the instructions of Jesus and to follow His example. Jesus set the example for the disciples to follow. He did not just give a few commands to for them to obey, but He lived His life for them to follow and they heard His voice. He is our supreme template, model, and example (John 13:15). They had to know His voice of a Shepherd in order to obey the voice of the Shepherd.

We must obey the voice of the Lord through leadership. If you feel called to some area of ministry then you must find a local place where you can serve and be accountable. God is not raising up freelance leadership and believers who are an island to themselves. God wants a loving, covenant-working relationship with His people.

Moreover, hearing God's voice will be simple if we continue to pray and keep our gaze upon Jesus. To witness to others of the good news we must are able to become witnesses of Jesus working in our own lives first. Not only is Jesus our great model and example, but He also gives believers the power to live life in the earth realm as He did (Acts 1:8). One who is fully prepared for leadership will know God and himself.

God often prepares us by revealing our weaknesses, as He did with Moses. As we grow in our faith and walk with God, I believe we must lean on Him fully, not on our own natural strengths and weaknesses. A great leader will also have a thorough knowledge of God's Word that will give them an ear to hear what the Spirit of the Lord is saying to them personally and to those they are called to lead. In addition, we must keep in mind that one of the prophetic ways God speaks to us is through our local church and through leadership, whether it be those you deem a spiritual father, mother, covering, or network of other leaders. This serves as an accountability protection.

God will not only speak to us for our personal calling but He will send us to places that will confirm and cultivate what God has placed on the inside of us. If I want to be a doctor or surgeon I have to go to school for it. If I need a job I must apply and later get training for a specific position. We don't need any untrained, unequipped, uneducated, and ignorant five-fold emerging leaders or existing ones. We must upgrade in this hour so that we are able to hear God and train others to hear God as well.

God will speak to those who are also submitted and serving a local church. God loves when we are submitted to each other in love and able to work together to advance the King and His Kingdom. There are those who claim to have a call of God on their lives but never submitted and went through the process of discipleship, training, equipping, education, and spiritual maturation. God uses the local church to govern and to establish His rule. We are the *ekkelsia*—the called out ones who are to advance the agenda of heaven on earth in any locale (Strong's #G1577).

God speaks through ordained leadership. We don't solely hear God through men and women, because they are human as well. But God has set in the church His government through gifted men and women to establish His rule in and through our lives. Samuel heard the voice of God only when he was submitted under Eli the high priest. Samuel didn't tap into his prophetic ability and call until later after ministering before the Lord even when he didn't recognize or know God.

God will speak through our leadership, and it's equally important that there is godly leadership that will represent the Kingdom. In addition, we need leadership today that is prophetic—able to hear the voice of God and speak only what He is saying by the Spirit to the churches. God will speak to us about the call to ministry or the marketplace. He will identity His calling and will for our lives through a holy dissatisfaction, discontentment, or frustration.

46

RECURRING AND DIRECTED THOUGHTS

*For "who has known the mind of the Lord that he may
instruct Him?" But we have the mind of Christ.*
—1 CORINTHIANS 2:16 MEV

God wants to speak to us in the plainest way for which we were created.
Our minds were created by God to function and to hear Him. The
Creator knows how our minds work and how we process things. There is a
saying out there that a mind is a terrible thing to waste. We can't waste time
and we can't waste our minds on things that are not purpose-driven or not of
God. The Lord created our minds to align and to be synchronized with His
mind, will, and purpose.

God desires to speak to us through our thoughts. In other words, our
thoughts are not just mere thoughts but they become a gateway into the mind
and heart chamber of the Lord. We have to renew our minds and align our
thoughts daily to God's will and thoughts through His Word.

> *I appeal to you therefore, brothers, by the mercies of God, to present
> your bodies as a living sacrifice, holy and acceptable to God, which
> is your spiritual worship. Do not be conformed to this world, but
> be transformed by the renewal of your mind, that by testing you*

may discern what is the will of God, what is good and acceptable and perfect (Romans 12:1-2 ESV).

We can a have a transformed mind through a daily renewal. The power of discernment is important so that we are able to know the good and acceptable and perfect will of God. God doesn't want us to be double minded, which will bring about instability. God will speak to those who are spiritually stable and have a sure foundation upon the Word of God.

He is a double-minded man, unstable in all his ways (James 1:8 ESV).

Often, people who use to be able to hear God's voice clearly will ask me why they are not hearing God. They fell into sin, and it clogged their ability to hear God. My answer to them is to repent and make it right with the Father and they will be able to hear again. Sin will mute the voice of the Father. It's not that you cannot hear God because you fell—that is not the case. You have ignored and tuned out the voice of the Father.

We destroy arguments and every lofty opinion raised against the knowledge of God, and take every thought captive to obey Christ (2 Corinthians 10:5 ESV).

In Amos 4:13, the Lord makes known His ways to us through our thoughts. Hearing the voice of God is really easier than most people think. God will speak to us in our own language, dialect, and speech, and He understands every culture. God created our thoughts to align and adjust to His will and purpose. Furthermore, in Matthew 1:19-21, while Joseph thought about things, God spoke to him.

We need to be careful here because not every thought that comes to our minds comes from the Lord. Thoughts can also be placed in our minds from the enemy, and we can simply think up things in our own imagination. When it comes to our thoughts, we must always go back to the point of reference and the basis of the Word of God. The Word of God and the Holy Spirit will become the filter system to separate God's voice from our own mind and the enemy. So every time we get a thought, we need to judge if it is from God's Word, will, ways, and purpose. I believe we have to do a self-assessment and evaluation when it comes to our thoughts and screen them through the Word by asking, "Does it align with Scripture? Does it in any way contradict the character of God?"

> *For my thoughts are not your thoughts, neither are your ways my ways, saith the Lord* (Isaiah 55:8 KJV).

God will speak to us giving us what's on His mind. He will superimpose His will and divine plan on our thoughts. We are to have the mind of Christ. I love what First Corinthians 2:10-12 says:

> *These are the things God has revealed to us by his Spirit. The Spirit searches all things, even the deep things of God. For who knows a person's thoughts except their own spirit within them? In the same way no one knows the thoughts of God except the Spirit of God. What we have received is not the spirit of the world, but the Spirit who is from God, so that we may understand what God has freely given us.*

One of the prophetic ways the Lord speaks to us is through directing our thoughts. Directing our thoughts is subjective and we have an active role in it. God lets us be a part of the process when He uses our thoughts but at the same time He gently steers us in the right direction.

> *The king's heart is like a stream of water directed by the Lord; he guides it wherever he pleases* (Proverbs 21:1 NLT).

> *Commit your works to the Lord, and your thoughts will be established* (Proverbs 16:3 NKJV).

The more you feed your mind with filth and toxic spoken words, written words, gossip, and visual sights, the more impure your thoughts will be. We must take a good look at the word *feed*, which should be emphasized. It's not necessarily what a person is exposed to that creates impurity or toxic thoughts; it's what the person feeds on. In other words, what is feeding your thoughts and what do you expose your mind to? If you have a hard time speaking and hearing the Word of God, your thoughts may be tainted, toxic, and unhealthy.

God desires to use those who know how to have the mind of Christ (1 Cor. 2:16). Changing your carnal mind into the mind of Christ is not an overnight process but a step-by-step process of renewal and transformation. The more we feed our thoughts on things of God, the quicker our minds will be transformed. I love what these Scriptures say about the counsel of the Lord:

> *But which of them has stood in the council of the Lord to see or to hear his word? Who has listened and heard his word?* (Jeremiah 23:18)

> *I no longer call you servants, because a servant does not know his master's business. Instead, I have called you friends, for everything that I learned from my Father I have made known to you* (John 15:15).

> *Who has known the mind of the Lord? Or who has been his counselor?* (Romans 11:34)

As children of God, we have access to hear and see the Word of the Lord. We should commit our thoughts unto God and ask Him to direct them. In addition, ask Him to bring an individual, maybe a family member or friend, to mind and direct your thoughts to what that person needs prayer for. Look up a Scripture that is about a specific topic or subject concerning them. Pray for the individual, then pray the Scripture over them, using the Word of God to bring breakthrough to them. This will help you to hear the voice of God as He directs your thoughts and trains your mind. Finally, I would suggest that you contact the person you were praying for and inform them what you have done. You may be surprised to find you have done a prophetic act that brings them confirmation.

God speaks through *recurring thoughts*. We can hear the voice of the Lord through thoughts, images, or memories that come back to our mind. This is another prophetic and common way that God speaks to His people. When this occurs, God is trying to address something specific. God often will bring things back up so that we can address and confront something that He is concerned about.

It is powerful when the Lord speaks over and over through recurring thoughts. He can turn our thoughts in His direction or bring something up repeatedly in our minds. I remember when God wanted to confront me about forgiving someone in my family who hurt and offended me deeply. I wanted God to bless me in a specific area of ministry, but the Lord in prayer would bring up this particular name to my mind every single time. I was ignoring the recurring images of my family member—I thought it was me, continuing to think about it.

Actually, it was the Lord speaking to me to reach out to them and ask for forgiveness. Honestly, I was so hurt that I was not at the place of asking that person to forgive me. In my opinion they should call and ask me to forgive them! But God wouldn't let me off the hook to avoid this family issue. God was not going to bless me while I was holding on to offense or unforgiveness. Everywhere I would go I would hear messages about forgiveness and have this recurring thought of my family member.

Ultimately, I gave in and obeyed the Lord and reached out to my loved one to ask for their forgiveness. To my surprise, before I could even ask they said they were waiting for my call because I'd been on their mind frequently. They asked me to forgive them first, and I began to weep because it only took a phone call to resolve something. I made things hard, but to the Lord it was an easy process. I needed to humble myself and not find fault but operate in the love of Christ.

Recurring thoughts can be the Lord speaking to you and getting your attention. Pay attention to things that come often and suddenly to your mind.

47

GIFT OF WORD OF WISDOM

To one there is given through the Spirit a message of wisdom...
—1 CORINTHIANS 12:8

God speaks through the word of wisdom. This gift is a supernatural revelation or insight into the divine will and purpose, often given by the Spirit to solve perplexing problems and situations. There are times in the prophetic God gives me a word of divine instruction and directive to give to someone, and once they obey the word of God they come back to me saying that if they hadn't made a wise decision it would have cost them their life, business, marriage, family, etc.

We thank God for the gift of the word of wisdom, but what is it? It is an appropriate, instantaneous insight for a particular occasion; to make a right decision; to discern good from evil; or to resolve, help, or heal a particular situation or need.

The first gift Paul mentions is the gift of wisdom. It is listed first perhaps because it is foundational to the church and this is a gift that the believer can earnestly desire (1 Cor. 12:31). Wisdom is clearly taught in the Word of God, and, *"The fear of the Lord is the beginning of wisdom; all who follow his precepts have good understanding"* (Ps. 111:10). This is the precious gift that Solomon asked for and received from God to be able to rightly rule God's nation (1 Kings 3:12). With this wisdom, Solomon could understand what do in difficult decisions.

Wisdom is also associated with fearing the Lord. Fear is simply standing in awe of God in reverence and respect. It entails loving His Word and being obedient to what it says. There is no wisdom in disobedience. This gift is of supreme importance for members in the Body of Christ, for if we can love God and our neighbor, we can greatly contribute to the church and those outside of the church. This love is another way of attracting unbelievers to Christ (John 13:35).

God will use the word of wisdom to speak to you about what decision you should make. God will use this gift to cause you to make the right decision with godly wisdom so that you will not walk through life in error. This is a powerful gift that any believer can ask for. In addition, when this supernatural gift of word of wisdom is in operation, it can help people walk in the will and purpose of God. This gift is one of my strongest gifts and its one of the nine supernatural gifts of the Holy Spirit and is part of the revelatory gifts. God speaks through this gift to those are ready to fulfill their God-given purpose. Possessing the gift of the word of wisdom is knowing what to do by the Spirit of God.

48

GIFT OF WORD OF
KNOWLEDGE

...to another a message of knowledge by means of the same Spirit.
—1 CORINTHIANS 12:8

The word of knowledge is a supernatural revelation of divine knowledge or insight into the divine mind, will, or plan, to know things that could not be known otherwise. God will give supernatural data concerning a person, place, or thing so that we can pray about it and receive instructions. He has prophetically given me facts about a person I didn't have previous knowledge or insight about. God gave me a word of knowledge about a person's illness after I prayed for them, and I rebuked and cursed the spirit of infirmity and the person was totally healed. Let me share how God speaks through the gift of word of knowledge.

Most prophets will flow in this gift, and some are stronger in specific areas of the word of knowledge. We must have the gift of discerning of spirits so that we are not deceived when this gift is in operation. There are psychics who operate in the realm of the soul where they can receive data or information, facts, and intelligence about a person. The gift of word of knowledge reveals divine facts and it should bring glory to God and reveal that God who is omniscient knows more about us than any human agent. Below is a brief list of biblical support and examples of how the word of knowledge is and works:

1. Names of people revealed (Acts 9:11)

2. Lost items found (1 Sam. 9:20)

3. Enemy exposed (2 Kings 6:9)

4. Relationships revealed (John 4:16-18)

5. Address revealed (Acts 9:11)

6. Actions revealed (John 1:50)

7. Nations revealed (Acts 16:9)

8. Secrets revealed (Dan. 2:47)

God will reveal specific things about people through the gift of word of knowledge. I remember a time I was looking for my wallet, which I never lose, but I looked everywhere and couldn't find it. I heard the Lord say, "It's in the car." So I looked in the car and I was getting so frustrated because I was looking like a fool, looking multiple times in the same place over and over. I said, "Lord, it's not here," and the Lord said, "Did you look everywhere?" I said yes and He said, "No you didn't!"

I sat down to calm down and I heard the Lord whisper: "Look in the trunk." So I jumped up and looked in the trunk of the car and there was my wallet halfway out of the pocket of a pair of jeans that I had worn. I said, "Father, thank You for that word of knowledge." He was right that I didn't look everywhere. I looked on the inside of the car but never thought that it would be in the trunk in a pair of blue jeans. God is very specific when we stop, calm down, and listen to His voice. The supernatural gift of word of knowledge can also be a fragment of knowledge or disclosure of truth implanted by God—not learned through the mind—about a particular person or situation for a specific purpose.

When this supernatural gift of the Holy Spirit is in operation, God will reveal past, present, and even future details concerning specific information or data. A believer can greatly benefit from this powerful gift and hear God speaking as He can use this gift to help bring resolution, closure, understanding, and peace. Any Spirit-filled believer can ask the Lord to give them this gift of word of knowledge.

49

GIFT OF DISCERNING OF SPIRITS

...to another distinguishing between spirits...
—1 CORINTHIANS 12:10

God can speak profoundly and powerfully through the gift of discerning of spirits. This is a supernatural revelation or insight into the realm of spirits to detect them and their plans in the minds of men. The discerning of spirits tells the difference between the three voices and influences in our lives:

1. Spirit of God or voice of God through the Holy Spirit

2. Human spirit or voice of self (or of others)

3. Demonic spirits or counterfeit voice of the enemy

God wants to give each of us a K-9 sense of discernment. A dog's sense of smell is amplified and higher than a human sense of smell. In deliverance and healing ministry, this gift is essential and vitally important to possess. This powerful gift detects spiritual movements, activities, patterns, etc. I call it the "knower" and the "nose" of the Holy Spirit. I tease my brother Naim a lot because he can sniff out anything that doesn't smell right. His discernment gives him the nose of the Spirit of God to sense, smell, and detect what is God and not.

The gift of distinguishing between spirits is having the gift of discernment. It is the ability to discern Scriptures and their application to believers in the church. It is also being able to tell whether someone is earnest and sincere or they have an agenda. Peter displayed this in Acts 5 when Ananias, together with his wife Sapphira, sold a piece of property and kept back part of the money and brought the rest and put it at the apostles' feet but lied saying they had given it all to the church (Acts 5:1-10).

Jesus said many would come in His name and would deceive many (Matt. 24:4-5), but the gift of discerning spirits is given to the Church to protect it from such as these. Through any spiritual gift, God will use an individual to bring Him glory and to build the Body of Christ. These nine of gifts of the Holy Spirit shouldn't be used as weapons of warfare against another believer but weapons against the enemy.

Those with this gift of discernment or distinguishing between spirits may be able to know whether the church should or should not do particular things. The gift of discerning of spirits or distinguishing of spirits is one of the nine supernatural gifts of the Holy Spirit that believers can possess. This gift has the unique ability to determine the true message of God from that of the deceiver, satan, whose methods include spreading deceptive and erroneous doctrine. I believe every believer should pray and ask the Father for this gift. God will speak through this powerful gift, and you can ask the Lord to give it to you.

50

GIFT OF PROPHECY

...to another prophecy...
—1 CORINTHIANS 12:10

The gift of prophecy is not an office. The gift of prophecy is a speaking gift to build up, cheer up, and call near. Prophecy is a message or utterance through an individual from God to strengthen, encourage, or comfort a person or group of people at a particular time (1 Cor. 14:3).

God is a prophetic Spirit. He can speak through the prophetic gift in Christians. Prophecy is the supernatural utterance or divine communication of the mind of God conveyed in a native tongue. It is a miracle of divine utterance, not conceived by human thought or reasoning. It includes speaking unto men to edification, exhortation, and comfort. I love the prophetic because it's a building gift. God speaks through this gift of prophesying to believers. I have prophesied to hundreds of thousands people and seen many miracles, healings, and breakthroughs taking place because of the prophecy.

God talks to believers through the power of the prophetic. The prophetic is so needed today and in every generation. The prophetic comes through the gifts and voices of believers. We have to look at what *prophecy* means in the Greek. The Greek word is *prophēteia* and properly means "a speaking forth" (Strong's #G4394). According to *Thayer's Greek Lexicon*, the word refers to "discourse emanating from divine inspiration and declaring the purposes of God, whether by reproving and admonishing the wicked, or comforting the afflicted, or revealing things hidden; especially by foretelling future events."

To prophesy is to declare the divine will, to interpret the purposes of God, or to make known in any way the truth of God that is designed to influence people. God wants to speak to you as you hear His voice as He shares and reveals hidden things, foretelling your purpose and destiny. God will use this powerful gift to help you interpret His plan, will, and vision for your life. In addition, He wants to encourage, comfort, and build you up while you are pursuing your destiny in Him by faith.

We must know clearly what the supernatural gift of prophecy does and why God uses it in His Church. We must first know that the gift of prophecy is not for unbelievers but for a sign to believers. First Corinthians 14:22 says clearly, *"Tongues, then, are a sign, not for believers but for unbelievers; prophecy, however, is not for unbelievers but for believers."* This gift of prophecy is one of the most powerful but also sometimes one of the most misunderstood of the nine supernatural gifts from God. It is the forth-telling of a divine revelation, a prophetic message, intended to build up the Body of Christ. Prophetic messages are usually for the purpose of:

- Edification of the Body of Christ by building them up in faith (1 Cor. 14:3)

- Exhortation of the Body of Christ by calling people nearer to God (1 Cor. 14:3)

- Comforting the Body of Christ to set at ease and to encourage (1 Cor. 14:3)

- Convict and convince people of sin leading to repentance and reconciliation (1 Cor. 14:24-25)

- Instruct, discern, and confirm calling and gifting (1 Tim. 4:14-15)

- Testimony of and from Jesus—people realize that Jesus is near by the operation of the gift of prophecy (Rev. 19:10).

The purpose of the gift of prophecy in the New Testament church is described in First Corinthians 14:3: *"But the one who prophesies speaks to people for their strengthening, encouraging and comfort."* We have to understand that the gift of prophecy is to encourage the Church at large or the body of believers with the love and heart of God. In the New Testament Church, we as prophetic people are not called to bring negative words, correction, or call fire down upon people. We are prophets of grace, not prophets of judgment. We do not prophesy people's problems but we prophesy the answers. We are called to bring forth the best in people. The gift of prophecy is to build, exhort, encourage, and comfort believers by the Spirit of God.

51

GIFT OF VARIOUS KINDS OF TONGUES

...to another speaking in different kinds of tongues...
—1 CORINTHIANS 12:10

God speaks through diverse kinds of tongues. This is a supernatural utterance in other languages that are not known to the speaker. I have seen God release words of prophecy through this gift. I will be speaking in an unknown tongue and someone will come up to me and say, "Thank you for sharing that personal prophecy because you answered my prayer." I will be surprised because I wasn't singling out the person and giving a personal prophecy. But through prayer and worship I was speaking in another language by the Holy Spirit, and the hearer caught hold of the prophetic word in their own native language and was blessed.

When I was a sophomore in college attending Marshall University in West Virginia, I would be up at 3 A.M. every day praying in tongues. I had a resident advisor whose room was next door to mine and he would hear me praying in tongues. He stopped me one morning and said, "Hakeem, I didn't know you spoke three different languages." He said that he was an international relations major and was able to understand everything I was saying in a different language. I am not bilingual or trilingual, but through the gift of different kinds of tongues I was able to speak and my resident advisor tranlated what I was saying.

The gift of tongues is a language given by the Holy Spirit and spoken by a believer. We are not talking about the believer's prayer language but a message to a person or congregation that requires interpretation. The supernatural gift of tongues has been one of the most controversial and most misunderstood gifts.

During the original outpouring of the Holy Spirit on Pentecost, there were many speaking in tongues. The literal translation in Greek is *glossa* and means language. This same word *glossa* is used again in Acts 2:11. This means it is a known language not some unknown tongue. Then it says that there were unbelievers present at Pentecost who were hearing God's message in their own *dialektos*—dialects or language (Strong's #G1258): *"Now there were staying in Jerusalem God-fearing Jews from every nation under heaven. When they heard this sound, a crowd came together in bewilderment, because each one heard their own language being spoken"* (Acts 2:5-6).

Paul the apostle wrote about tongues extensively in First Corinthians 12 through 14, but he was reproving the Corinthians for misusing the spiritual gifts without knowledge, training, and protocol. The Corinthians were fascinated by speaking in tongues but lacked prophesying in their native tongue. They had actually prostituted the gift of tongues into something pagan that wasn't even representative of the work of the Spirit.

All you need to do is to go back to Acts 2 and read verse 4: *"All of them were filled with the Holy Spirit and began to speak in other tongues as the Spirit enabled them."* On the day of Pentecost, those present were able to hear and see God moving miraculously. Tongues and prophecy should work together. We should be able to speak supernaturally in various tongues but also prophesy by the gift as well.

52

GIFT OF INTERPRETATION OF TONGUES

...and to still another the interpretation of tongues.
—1 CORINTHIANS 12:10

The gift of interpretation of tongues is a supernatural ability by the Spirit to interpret in the native tongue what is uttered in other languages not known by the one who interprets. This is not translating a language but a supernatural interpretation of what the Spirit is saying through an unknown tongue. If someone is bilingual and can speak English and Spanish, they don't necessarily possess this gift. Keep in mind that there are those who possess a natural gift or ability to learn a foreign language. But God speaks through the *supernatural gift of interpretation of tongues.*

Notice the gift is an interpretation, not a translation. Have you ever heard someone give a long message in tongues and when the interpretation came it seemed much shorter? A translation would be word for word what was spoken. To *interpret* means to paraphrase the meaning. In other words, if I am hearing an unknown tongue spoken, God will then give me an interpretation to sum up the prophetic message. That is why a message in tongues can be long while the interpretation can be much shorter.

I don't speak any language other than English. If I overheard someone speaking in a foreign language, I would have no clue what they were saying. However, if I heard someone speaking by the gift of tongues and I was walking by the Spirit, the gift of interpretation would give me pieces of what was said and I would give a summation in known tongues of what God was saying in unknown tongues.

If someone speaks in tongues in the church, there absolutely has to be someone there to interpret or they need to be silent. In the church of Corinth, those who were speaking in tongues were told to have no more than one individual speaking in tongues and one interpreter translating at a time. If there were many people in the church speaking in tongues at the same time, there would be confusion in the atmosphere, and we know that the Lord is not the author of confusion; He is the God of order (1 Cor. 14:33). It is not edifying to the church to have several speaking in tongues at the same time with no one to interpret.

Let me be clear that there is nothing wrong with believers speaking in tongues that build themselves up in their faith, but when someone bursts out with tongues and doesn't bring forth interpretation then they are clearly violating biblical and spiritual protocols. Biblically, tongues are a sign for unbelievers and not for the church. Paul writes, *"In the Law it is written: 'With other tongues and through the lips of foreigners I will speak to this people, but even then they will not listen to me, says the Lord.' Tongues, then, are a sign, not for believers but for unbelievers"* (1 Cor. 14:21-22).

I love how the apostle quotes Isaiah 28:11-12, where the prophet Isaiah declares, *"For with stammering lips and another tongue will he speak to this people. To whom he said, This is the rest wherewith ye may cause the weary to rest; and this is the refreshing: yet they would not hear"* (KJV). Clearly, here in the Old Testament the gift of tongues is that of a known language as a witness to unbelievers, and Paul makes his point with this quote. The apostle Paul goes on to make sure of the purpose of spiritual gifts and how they should operate. He makes clear that believers should not elevate one gift over another but esteem each as necessary for the completeness of the kingdom.

A believer with the gift of interpretation of tongues can understand what a tongues speaker is saying even though he does not know the language being spoken. The tongues interpreter possessing this vocal gift of the Holy Spirit then communicates the message of the tongues speaker. God wants to speak to us through this gift, and we can hear God through the interpretation of God's prophetic word.

53

GIFTS OF HEALING

...to another gifts of healing by that one Spirit.
—1 CORINTHIANS 12:9

God can speak through any believer who has the gifts of healing. Note that I didn't put *gift of healing,* speaking of one particular healing, but gifts in a plural sense. This is speaking of different types of healing. We can hear the voice of God through someone who possesses this supernatural gift.

God speaks to me through the gifts of healing, which I often operate in. God will give me a word of knowledge concerning a specific sickness or injury and He will release the gifts of healing in that certain part of someone's body and they are healed. I tend to get healing results with back, neck, ankle, and knee problems. When I move in the gifts of healing, the person who receives healing from the Lord doesn't need medicine or medical attention. The gifts of healing are by supernatural power, without human aid or medicine.

This gift was prominent in the New Testament church to confirm that Jesus Christ's name had power and that God was working in the church. The gifts of healing may be coupled with the power of prayer, and we know that the effectual prayer of a righteous man or woman can accomplish miracles (James 5:16). In any event, any healing that is done is *"by that one Spirit"* and not by humans.

In my first preaching engagement at the age of 19 years old, God used me in the gifts of healing to bring healing to people who had back, leg, and ankle problems. I would be able to feel heat or some sensation or physical impression in my body. God was speaking to me through the physical impression—that is another prophetic way God can speak to us. Through these gifts of healing I was able to get instant results. People respond to the voice of the Lord through me when this gift is in operation. They will respond by faith and get healed as I lay my hands on them or cause them to do something they couldn't do before.

With any gift, the enemy will unleash counterfeits, scammers, imposters, and fraudsters. We have to be careful of this—that is why we need the gift of discerning of spirits to detect who's who and what is at work. God will speak through someone with this gift and bring healing. Those possessing the supernatural gifts of healing will release the Spirit of God who will bring healing to those in need, not just believers but anybody who has the faith in God.

54

GIFT OF WORKING OF MIRACLES

To another the working of miracles...
—1 CORINTHIANS 12:10 KJV

The Lord speaks through this powerful gift of working of miracles, which is the supernatural power to intervene in the ordinary course of nature and to counteract natural laws if necessary. God can speak to you about sickness and disease in someone's body, and you can be a healing and miracle conduit of God's power. The greatest miracle that occurs today is the miracle of human salvation. I see this as the greatest miracle of all because only the Spirit of God can illuminate the Word of God and reveal to us who Jesus Christ is (John 6:44; Matt. 16:17).

The gift of miraculous powers is operative and available for today as any other of the nine gifts. Also known as the working of miracles, this is a power sign gift unique to the New Testament church that involves performing supernatural events that could only be attributed to the power of God (Acts 2:22). This supernatural gift was exhibited and demonstrated often in the apostolic ministry of Paul, Peter, Stephen, and Phillip, among others noted in the Bible (Acts 19:11-12; 3:6; 6:8; 8:6-7). Those possessing the gift of miraculous powers or working of miracles operate by the Spirit of God to bring instant recovery, healing, and resurrection.

We can hear the voice of God through the power gift of working of miracles—especially those who are in need of a miracle touch from the Lord. The gift of miraculous powers is categorized with the gift of faith and gifts of healing as the power gifts. God often uses me in this gift of miracles coupled with the gift of faith, which I will talk about next. Any gifts or results are always credited to the Spirit of God and not to humans or to ourselves.

I have seen the Lord speak prophetically to me through this powerful gift to work a miracle. There was a time I was ministering to a woman who was unable to walk, so I prayed over her. This supernatural faith arose on the inside of me and I took her by the hand and lifted her up on her feet. I told her to walk and she looked perplexed as something happened to her and she started crying and began to dance and later run. God performed a miracle instantaneously.

God works miracles through believers by the Holy Spirit to glorify Himself. Arlene, the first administrator for my ministry with my brother Naim, needed a miracle touch because she was battling stage four breast cancer. We knew that she wanted to be totally healed, so we agreed to go over to her house to pray the prayer of faith and release the miracle power of God to Arlene's body. There was a supernatural discontentment against sickness and disease that rose up on the inside of us. We cursed cancer in her body and commanded her body to be made well in Jesus's name, and we cast out the spirit of death and infirmity. It took the gift of faith coupled with the gift of working of miracles and the power of agreement to break the power of darkness, sickness, and disease off her life.

We labored in prayer and faith with her for an hour, and all of a sudden her countenance was different. She was glowing and didn't appear sick at all. Before, she couldn't move or walk, and after praying for her and commanding cancer to go she was running around in the joy of the Lord. Several weeks later during her follow-up, there was no trace of any cancer in Arlene's blood. We gave God glory for what He did because we made ourselves available to activate the gifts of working of miracles.

God doesn't just work in mysterious ways but miraculous ways. God can use you to release the gift of working of miracles. You can ask for this supernatural gift and become a miracle worker. God wants to use you by faith to release His glory and power to those in need.

55

Gift of Faith

...to another faith by the same Spirit...
—1 Corinthians 12:9

We must understand that it's through the gift of faith that other gifts are activated. It takes the gift of faith to prophesy. Just like it takes the gift of faith to believe God for the impossible even when you are low or lack faith. It's a supernatural gift to believe God without human doubt, unbelief, and reasoning.

I recall a time when I needed $20,000 for a co-publishing deal and I was facing a deadline. Not knowing where I would get the money from, I just knew in my heart that I would have the money before or on the deadline. I had no money at the time, and I didn't have many preaching engagements. As the deadline was approaching, my faith was tested. I signed the book deal contract anyway; I just knew without a shadow of a doubt that I would have the money because the Lord told me to submit my manuscript and He would take care of the rest.

I obeyed God, and it wasn't even five months before I had received an influx of money coming from everywhere. People were sowing hundreds and even thousands of dollars. Ministry doors were opening up for me to come and speak, and a week or two before my deadline I had $25,000. God gave me $5,000 more than what I needed.

God will speak through the gift of faith. Faith pleases God, and without it we can't please Him. So we walk by faith and not by sight, but the gift of faith is to believe for the impossible to become possible. We need faith to hear God just as much as we need it to speak for Him and obey Him.

Those with this gift of faith operating in their own life, ministry, business, and church are truly amazing in how they see the Lord unfold things. In my own prophetic ministry, I have to possess the gift of faith to speak for God but also believe for things for others when they don't have the faith to believe for themselves. Through the prophetic gift, the gift of faith will exude confidence in all situations. The Bible says that we can speak those things that are not as though they already exist (see Rom. 4:17). So the gift of faith couples with prophecy, healing, and miracles.

For example, when I am prophesying a Word of the Lord to someone I speak about things by the gift of faith as if they already exist or have come to pass, revealing to the hearer that God is going to do something for them. I recall prophesying to couple wanting to have a baby, but they had health issues and complications that prevented them from getting pregnant. I spoke by the gift of faith as if the baby was already coming in nine months. God spoke about the baby boy they both wanted while the doctor's report said they couldn't have a baby. Supernaturally, the married couple conceived a beautiful, healthy baby boy as I had spoken by faith what I heard and saw in the spirit. God performed a miracle by the power of prophecy through the gift of faith. God is always proven to be right and supersedes the natural mind, but He needs someone with the gift of faith to speak it forth into being.

A Spirit-filled believer with this type of gift is a person more God-like in their thoughts. He or she sees things that aren't as if they already are! The believer who possesses the gift of faith is someone who is given a measure to see things or speak things into being as God's Spirit leads them. Every Spirit-filled believer does possess faith in some measure because it is one of the gifts of the Spirit bestowed on all who come to Christ in faith (Gal. 5:22-23). The spiritual gift of faith is exhibited by one with a strong and unshakeable confidence in God, His Word, His promises, and the power of prayer to impact and effect miracles and the supernatural.

56

LIFE MISTAKES AND BLOOPERS

For though the righteous fall seven times, they rise again,
but the wicked stumble when calamity strikes.
—**PROVERBS 24:16**

In life we will go through some trials. Life can throw curve balls that we are not aware of or ready to catch. We are not called to live perfect lives. But we are called to live life on purpose. In addition, misguided and wrong things will happen to us. We make mistakes and wrong decisions. When we make a mistake we should not beat ourselves up over it but just learn from it and make better judgments going forward. God is forgiving and loving and knows that mistakes and accidents comes with life's territory. God desires to perfect those things that concern us.

There are things that I have experienced in life that I wish I could take back and do all over again. I realize as I mature and gain more wisdom that comes with age that things in life don't just happen to us. I believe that we are in control of the major of things that happen in our lives. They are determined and orchestrated by our decisions. There are things that may or may not be in our control. But when these things happen we are to make a life assessment and learn from them.

God can use life mistakes, misfortunes, mishaps, and accidents as a way to get our attention. It may sound odd that God speaks through life mistakes and bloopers. But I believe wholeheartedly that God has a great sense of humor and like a loving Father wants us to laugh in the midst of life's journey.

I recall a time when I got nice dress shoes and I was so happy to wear them that I never put the grips on the bottoms of the heels. I could hear my mother's voice saying, "Hakeem, make sure you put the sole grips on the bottom of your dress shoes." Ignoring what I heard, I went outside, excited, with a new suit on and dress shoes. I slipped and fell in dirt. I was totally humiliated. If I'd only obeyed my mother's voice and taken the time to put the sole grips on, I wouldn't have fallen. I was embarrassed, but there was no one around who saw me fall. God spoke to me through the voice of my mother and by keeping me from embarrassment. As I processed what happened I had to laugh at myself and make light of the situation.

In life all Christians will make mistakes, but we should all desire to use our mistakes for good and learn from them. Ask yourself—are you gaining wisdom from your mistakes? Sometimes our mistakes are the reason for our trials and tribulations. I remember in my own life when I took counsel from the wrong voices concerning my car and I did my own will instead of God's will. This caused me to lose a few thousand dollars and go through very hard times when I really needed the money. This one mistake I made taught me a valuable lesson to pray fiercely before making any major decisions and continually weigh my motives. God wants to speak to us if we are open to hearing His voice.

God was always faithful through any life mistake that I put myself through by listening to the wrong voices or people. In addition, doing my own thing without the wisdom of God caused me to waste so much time. We must understand that God is a loving, forgiving, patient, merciful Father who will be faithful through any mistake you make even if it may be your fault. God will be with you and get you through it. Praise God! We are to grow in faith and get stronger in our trust and faith in the Lord so we can make fewer mistakes in life.

As a child grows they get wiser, and we're to do the same in Christ as we grow in faith and relationship with the Lord. Children are not going to always do everything right but will make more than a few mistakes. To learn from mistakes, pray continually, walk by the Spirit, receive wise counsel, meditate on the Word of God, put on the full armor of the Lord, be humble, and trust the Lord with all your heart and don't lean on your own understanding. Don't keep returning to those mistakes.

> *As a dog that returns to its vomit, so fools repeat their folly. Do you see a person wise in their own eyes? There is more hope for a fool than for them* (Proverbs 26:11-12).

> *Of them the proverbs are true: "A dog returns to its vomit," and, "A sow that is washed returns to her wallowing in the mud"* (2 Peter 2:22).

Forget! Don't dwell on them that can be dangerous, but instead press forward:

> *Brothers and sisters, I know that I still have a long way to go. But there is one thing I do: I forget what is in the past and try as hard as I can to reach the goal before me* (Philippians 3:13 ERV).

> *Don't remember the prior things; don't ponder ancient history. Look! I'm doing a new thing; now it sprouts up; don't you recognize it? I'm making a way in the desert, paths in the wilderness. The beasts of the field, the jackals and ostriches, will honor me, because I have put water in the desert and streams in the wilderness to give water to my people, my chosen ones* (Isaiah 43:18-20 CEB).

Get up! Never give up after a mistake, but instead learn from it and keep going:

> *For the righteous falls seven times and rises again, but the wicked stumble in times of calamity* (Proverbs 24:16 ESV).

> *The goal I pursue is the prize of God's upward call in Christ Jesus. So all of us who are spiritually mature should think this way, and if anyone thinks differently, God will reveal it to him or her. Only let's live in a way that is consistent with whatever level we have reached* (Philippians 3:14-16 CEB).

We can gain wisdom from any mistakes we make.

> *Foolishness brings joy to one without sense, but a man with understanding walks a straight path. Plans fail when there is no counsel, but with many advisers they succeed. A man takes joy in giving an answer; and a timely word—how good that is!*
> (Proverbs 15:21-23 HCSB)

God speaks through mistakes that we make in our lives to allow us to recognize them and shake ourselves off and move forward. God doesn't embarrass His children nor is He is laughing at you, but like a loving Father He is concerned and wants you to do your best. I do believe that the Father has a good sense of humor and uses bloopers and humor moments in our lives to teach us.

Once I was preaching and there were two bottles of water on the platform and I opened one to take sip. As I was finishing I accidently grabbed the bottle that wasn't open and put it to my mouth with a closed cap. I started laughing and I heard the Lord say to me prophetically through that blooper, "Many prophets are full of My Spirit but they are capped to flow and pour out to others to refresh them." God used that blooper, which was funny to me personally, to speak a prophetic word.

God will use bloopers and funny moments to relieve unnecessary stress. I remember a friend of mine who was so critical of everybody and everything he did that he found himself always making unnecessary mistakes and making things worse. He couldn't understand why everything he tried to perfect kept falling apart. He didn't realize that God was trying to tell him that he was not perfect but to live life stress free.

There is nothing wrong with attention to detail and getting things right. But things will happen and everyone will make mistakes. My friend needed to be personally okay with that. God began to speak to him that He is perfect and not my friend and that he should seek God for wisdom, understanding, and direction.

Today, my friend is stress free and living life with fewer mistakes and pressure free. God will speak to you through life mistakes and bloopers to allow you to pause and hear His voice of reasoning. God will speak wisdom to us in the midst of those things we may not be proud of. The Lord has your best interests at heart. God will never lead you on a fool's errand. God takes every life mistake and turns it into a life lesson that will catapult you forward and impart wisdom for you to assist someone else.

Scripture is clear that the Lord permits sinful humans to make mistakes and reap the consequences of those life mistakes, but only a sovereign God and covenant-keeping Father could also promise that He will make *"in all things God works for the good of those who love him, who have been called according to his purpose"* (Rom. 8:28). In ways known only to God, He takes even our mistakes and unplanned events and weaves them together to fulfill His purposes.

57

IMPRESSIONS

*I perceive that this voyage will be with hurt and much damage,
not only of the lading and ship, but also of our lives.*
—Acts 27:10 KJV

God uses impressions in our bodies to get our attention. In healing and the prophetic the Lord uses certain impressions such as heat, tingling, numbness, nudging, cold sensations, and unique impressions to speak to me. An impression can also be a faint feeling in your spirit that you are supposed to say or do something. Intercessors sometimes say, "You were on my heart or in my spirit while in prayer." I will go further to say that an impression can be a burden from the Lord. Whenever something is weighing heavy or comes up repeatedly in your spirit it is the Lord getting your attention.

We can hear the voice of the Lord through impressions. Impressions are one of the most common ways in which people hear God and which God uses to urge someone to pray. When it comes to impressions, you don't hear the actual voice of God but you feel a strong urge in your spirit and have a knowing that you need to follow through.

Furthermore, impressions can also feel like a thought that is inspired, like when someone or something drops into your mind or spirit. An impression can also move upon your emotions—you will feel empathy, compassion, and a heavy burden. Most intercessors and prophets feel this in prayer and ministering the prophetic Word of the Lord. There are times when God will speak to me through an impression that dropped into my spirit and I will be moved with tears while I am prophesying to someone.

God brings tremendous breakthrough and healing by borrowing my emotions to relay His heart, burden, love, and compassion toward someone. Interestingly, a God-inspired impression can be when a Scripture all of a sudden comes alive to you by revelation and you have a precise knowing or clear understanding of its importance for your own life, present situation, or to assist others.

We have to keep ourselves open to hearing the voice of God through these impressions that can be easily overlooked. However, a Spirit-filled believer may never see the fruit of obedience to instructions through this mode of communication—or they may even overlook how God desires to work in specific situations. God does speak often this way and we should pray for God to speak to us through impressions so that we can obey His leading.

I get impressions when I am speaking to someone and often it starts in my thoughts or in my spirit or gut. I ask them what I sense, and God gives me more details because I was faithful to sense His signals in my body, spirit, or heart. Impressions from the Lord are a great way the Lord speaks, especially when they are obvious impressions that you cannot avoid.

I remember talking to a woman when I was working in banking, and I kept feeling sharp pains in my stomach area. After the feeling became somewhat intense I asked her was she having pain in her stomach and she said yes. I heard the Lord say, "Cramps!" I went on and said, "You are having very bad cramps," and her eyes got big as saucers and she said, "Yes!" I asked her if I could pray for her and I took her by the hand and had her put her other hand on the pain and as soon as I prayed the pain suddenly went away. How was I able to know this? Well, the pain I felt in my stomach went away instantly. Praise God that women received her healing because of a God-inspired impression physically manifesting in my own body.

It's important to follow the Holy Spirit's promptings. Prophetic impressions are not always a dramatic encounter like trances, visions, or third-heaven expressions; they are often very gentle, light, and subtle. Just about every Christian throughout their walk has heard the voice of the Lord through impressions, whether they noticed it or not. Impressions are one of the easiest ways that God's speaks. Prophetic impressions are common among Spirit-filled believers; however, due to the lack of teaching on the subject, many people will discount impressions as their own thoughts.

Many prophetic people experience discernment through impressions without even realizing it. Oftentimes we can sense an evil spirit on someone just by sitting down next to that person. The evil spirit that is troubling the person will begin to trouble us in the same manner. For instance, if a spirit of fear troubles a person in a close geographic area, we can actually begin to feel fearful as well.

If we do not realize our prophetic ability and discernment in this area, we can begin to feel very confused or think we are crazy. Within this viewpoint, it is possible that those diagnosed as "bipolar" may actually be experiencing a powerful level of discernment but do not, unfortunately, know how to use this gift properly.

Discernment is a knowing that God will highlight something in our spirit through an impression. God will speak through the impression and not so much a voice. God speaks in a unique way through impressions and discernment of the way we sense, feel, or think.

I will also say that impressions can be another word for an inward witness of the Holy Spirit. An impression is not a voice but a "knowing" or a "feeling" about something. Impressions are a common way that the Lord communicates.

Below are five other prophetic unique ways that I believe God speaks to us and through us as these can be prophetic notifications:

1. Imagination: inner images or concepts creatively conceived or formed through guided imagery.

2. Impression: inner conviction, direction, or affirmation of a thought that has more strength than a normal thought or "hunch."

3. Intuition: knowing spontaneously the right thing to do or say.

4. Emotions: a gut-level feeling, desire, impulse, impression, arresting concern, or insistent nudge.

5. Common sense: the ordinary use of rational, good judgment through experience and logical thinking.

God speaks through impressions in order for Him to use us for His glory to bring healing, deliverance, and a prophetic word of breakthrough.

58

MEMORIES

I thank my God in all my remembrance of you, always in every
prayer of mine for you all making my prayer with joy, because of
your partnership in the gospel from the first day until now.
—PHILIPPIANS 1:3-5 ESV

The Lord speaks to us both in ways we can understand and ways that we may not understand at first. I have found that God will speak to me through flashbacks and even through memory recall. Oftentimes, we would rather ignore some of the painful memories or simply laugh, cry, and cherish some of them. There is nothing wrong with reflecting on the past and recalling what we have experienced. Through memory we learn the process of life and where we came from. Memories are connected to what happened in a person's life that we may have also experienced.

In Scripture, Jesus often told parables and used examples that related to the people He was speaking to. When Jesus told a parable about sheep, they could relate to that. The Lord can use past events from our life to speak to us or to give us understanding when delivering a prophetic word. For example, you could be delivering a prophetic word to someone and suddenly a memory of a past event may spring forth in your mind. Stop and ask the Lord for understanding. If that event created a sense of fear in you, the Lord could be showing you what the person is experiencing, to give them faith to overcome fear.

We thank God that He doesn't erase or delete any information archives lodged within our memory banks. Memories bring about powerful testimonies of how the Lord has made a way out of no way. We overcome satan by the blood of the Lamb and the word of our testimony. God wants someone to hear the testimony in our memories. Whether they were life lessons, mistakes, or bloopers, He want to use past experiences to bring present healing breakthroughs.

God uses memories to speak to us. He wants us to remember what He has said and spoken. Someone with a good memory can recall things of the past and share in great detail. Studying God's Word and meditating can sharpen your ability to retain information, impartation, and revelation. God loves to bring things to our memory to bless, align, correct, and teach us. Obviously, there are bad and traumatic things that we'd rather not think on. But God does want us to keep in mind and not lose sight of His promises, will, and Word.

In the prophetic, one of the things that I suggest people to do is record their personal prophecies so that they can go back and listen to them. That helps people to remember what was spoken by the Lord through the prophetic word. When I was young in Christ, we would memorize biblical stories and favorite passages of the Bible. I didn't realize that those types of practices caused me to hear God's voice when He drops certain Scriptures into my memory for someone I am prophesying over.

Memory is a great asset to have and we should value it. Could you imagine not remembering anything or having short-term memory loss? God wants to speak to us through His Word and have us reflect on past stories of biblical characters who overcame things that were challenging.

> *But Mary treasured up all these things, pondering them in her heart* (Luke 2:19 ESV).
>
> *But Abraham said, "Child, remember that you in your lifetime received your good things, and Lazarus in like manner bad things; but now he is comforted here, and you are in anguish"* (Luke 16:25 ESV).
>
> *But the Helper, the Holy Spirit, whom the Father will send in my name, he will teach you all things and bring to your remembrance all that I have said to you* (John 14:26 ESV).

I believe that one remarkable way that God speaks to His people is through our memories. As we partner with God we will find out that our partnership with Him will be demonstrated through the memory recall of what the Lord has done in our life. The Lord will highlight His power and wonderful works in our life through our recollection.

There have been times when I was praying concerning something specific and didn't have much faith to believe God would do it for me. Suddenly, the Lord gave me several powerful memories of what He has done, defeating all fears built up in my heart. God has a beautiful way of recalling things thing to our minds. I always say that one thought and memory of God's faithfulness can bring healing, deliverance, and faith. John 14:26 is a great illustration of God's voice present in our memories, where we see the Holy Spirit become our "Advocate" whom the Father will send in His name, who will teach us all things and will remind us of everything God has spoken to us.

This is very powerful when it comes to prophetic words, because there are many personal prophecies that I have received but have forgotten the details, but the Spirit of God will bring what was spoken back to my memory. It doesn't matter how long ago that prophecy or dream was given—the Spirit of God will recall it to us if we ask Him. He proactively and actively speaks to us through our memories in order to bring remembrance of what the Spirit of God has spoken.

We are engineered and wired by the Lord to hear our Creator's voice. Our minds have been created and designed to remember natural things, but spiritual things are supernaturally activated through the voice of the Lord. God's quickening power of His Spirit will recall spiritual and supernatural things to our minds through His voice.

59

COINCIDENCES

*And by a coincidence a certain priest was going down in that
way, and having seen him, he passed over on the opposite side.*
—LUKE 10:31 YLT

At some point in our lives, all of us have had to sit back and think this was a divine setup. There are times when something may have happened so divinely that you knew God was in it. The chips just fell into place, and you didn't know how it happened but later everything made sense. As you think about some of the coincidences you've had in life, you may be glad they happened and that you were at the right place at the right time. God speaks through these coincidence that are often so prophetic in nature.

What is a coincidence? The *Merriam-Webster Dictionary* defines the word *coincidence* as "the occurrence of events that happen at the same time by accident but seem to have some connection."[1] There are events in our lives that seems accidents to us, but they were planned or purposed. God uses coincidences to speak to us and confirm what He is doing in our lives to give direction and clarity of purpose.

I believe most Christians have probably experienced remarkable coincidences. You might have overheard several unrelated individuals refer to something specific in a short space of time when you were praying for God's confirmation. Or perhaps you kept noticing identical words in different places, from a book and to a billboard. Or maybe you crossed paths with a particular person in an unplanned place.

God speaks to us through these life events to connect us to a particular season, person, or place. A lot of apparent coincidences in my life were God leading me by His Holy Spirit to get me to a place to connect to a person to fulfill destiny. I love how things just pan out when we are not expecting them to. Oftentimes in our faith walk we don't have a road map to fulfill our God-given assignment and purpose, but the Holy Spirit can send someone to be the door to your next level.

The word *coincidence* is used only once in the New Testament, by Jesus Himself in the parable of the Good Samaritan. In Luke 10:31, Jesus said, *"And by a coincidence a certain priest was going down in that way, and having seen him, he passed over on the opposite side"* (YLT). The word is the Greek word *synkyrian*, which is a combination of two words—*sun* and *kurios*. *Sun* means "together with" and *kurious* means "supreme in authority." So a biblical definition of *coincidence* would be "what occurs together by God's providential arrangement of circumstances."

This is powerful biblical definition of the word coincidence. We can see that God directs and navigates our steps so that He becomes our bridge to connect us to our next season and those assigned to that particular season. Hearing the voice of God through coincidences is a blessing to know that God uses seemingly accidental occurrences for His purpose. I love Psalm 37:23, *"The Lord makes firm the steps of the one who delights in him,"* and Proverbs 16:9, *"In their hearts humans plan their course, but the Lord establishes their steps."*

The Lord is sovereign over our entire lives; nothing, strictly speaking, happens by chance. It is helpful to know He uses coincidences like these to speak to us. I am wholeheartedly persuaded and convinced by personal experiences that He does and that there are two mistakes that Christians often make in this area—one much more serious than the other. The first and less serious mistake is to deny that God speaks to His children through coincidences. There are many Christians who will testify that He has at times spoken to them in this way.

Keep in mind that God ordains every step we make, even when it seems like it was the wrong one. God will send divine detours and reroute us back on His path for our lives if we are obedient to His leading. God has predestined our steps to bring us to the place of fulfillment. What appears to us as random chance is in fact overseen by a sovereign God who knows the number of hairs on every head (Luke 12:7). Jesus said that not even a sparrow falls to the ground without our Father's notice (Matt. 10:29). In Isaiah 46:9-11, God states unequivocally that He is in charge of everything:

> *I am God, and there is none like me. I make known the end from the beginning, from ancient times, what is still to come. I say, "My purpose will stand, and I will do all that I please." From the east I summon a bird of prey; from a far-off land, a man to fulfill my purpose. What I have said, that I will bring about; what I have planned, that I will do.*

NOTE

1. *Merriam-Webster Dictionary*, s.v. "Coincidence," accessed April 22, 2019, https://www.merriam-webster.com/dictionary/coincidence.

60

CIRCUMSTANCES AND DIVINE APPOINTMENTS

We can make our plans, but the Lord determines our steps.
—**PROVERBS 16:9 NLT**

The Lord can communicate to us through unusual circumstances and divine appointments. These are meetings that God has set up for a purpose (Acts 8:27). A circumstance is the condition of your life. However, a divine appointment is often unplanned on our part. There are circumstances that create an event or situation in our lives that happens as a result of our decisions. God has unusual circumstances that He creates to move us in a direction so that things can pan out the way God has planned.

> *Not that I speak from want, for I have learned to be content in whatever circumstances I am* (Philippians 4:11 NASB).

Hearing the voice of God is imperative as we are on our spiritual journey. The enemy will set up circumstances against the believer to alter and forfeit what God has purposed. Divine appointments, on the other hand, are supernaturally navigated by God. It becomes like a divine scheduling. God will set a time, season, and place of destiny. In other words, the Lord sets your appointment and expects you to get there on time. The Holy Spirit will help direct your circumstances to get to the divine appointments that God has already set up.

Our decisions can bring us to unusual events and situations that may not be in our best interests. Resisting what God is trying to do in our lives will bring distress, hardship, and negative outcomes, but as we heed His commands God will hear us. He creates circumstances, situations, events, and divine appointments for you to fulfill the assignment of God on your life for your generation. There have been circumstances that the Lord created in my life to train my ear and heart to follow His direction.

We must not resist the signs and circumstances we are in because they are created by the Lord to get our attention. Oftentimes, circumstances don't make any sense, but God, as a loving Father, orchestrates and orders our steps on purpose to get us to our divine destination.

Jonah had to experience a divine appointment and change of circumstances by spending some time in the belly of a great fish (whale). God appointed the whale to create an unusual circumstance so that Jonah would make the decision to obey the plans and will of the Lord. The Lord had to break Jonah's will. After spending several days in an uncomfortable and unfortunate situation, Jonah prayed to the Lord: *"But I will sacrifice to You with the voice of thanksgiving; I will pay what I have vowed. Salvation is of the Lord"* (Jon. 2:9 NKJV). As soon as Jonah made a decision to finally fulfill his end of the bargain, God heard his cry, saw his distress, and responded to his heartfelt remorse. God caused the great fish to cough him up. God has a powerful way of convincing and persuading His people to submit to His purposes.

As he was coughed up, Jonah ended up where he was divinely appointed to be, and then the Lord did something interesting. As soon as Jonah submitted: *"Now the word of the Lord came to Jonah the second time, saying, 'Arise, go to Nineveh the great city and proclaim to it the proclamation which I am going to tell you.' So Jonah arose and went to Nineveh according to the word of the Lord"* (Jon. 3:1-3 NASB). Jonah's decision created a defining moment that catapulted him into his divine appointment and date with destiny to go to Nineveh. Jonah had to obey the plans and will of the Lord. When he did, he was at the right place, at the right time, doing the right thing for God. Then the men feared the Lord greatly, and they offered a sacrifice to the Lord and made vows to Him.

Divine appointments are out of our control, but the Holy Spirit can lead us to them as we are open to where the Spirit of God directs. It is not until during or afterward that we recognize our Father intended the meeting for a significant purpose. God can also speak to us through circumstances such as open and closed doors. As a traveling prophetic voice and minister of the Gospel, I can discern doors of opportunity that God has opened or closed.

We must hear God distinctively; doors that appear to be His may not be. As Spirit-filled believers we must hear the voice of God before accepting or declining opportunities. God's opportunities may not always be pleasant ones. Jonah was given an opportunity as a prophet sent to a dangerous city to prophesy the Word of the Lord. The call and assignment on your life will determine the doors God opens and closes.

I have encountered immature believers who claim to have heard the Lord through certain circumstances. As a precaution, I normally advise them to test their conclusions with other confirming evidence. The Lord can use "repeated cycles" to tell us that He doesn't want us to go in a specific direction. For example, you may be applying for a specific job and doors keep shutting, but when you apply for the one God is directing you to the door supernaturally opens. All of a sudden, you are hired on the spot, which I believe is a divine appointment. The continual closed doors were God speaking to you through circumstances. At times, believers blame every closed door on the devil, when it fact it could be the Lord Himself shutting the doors. Isaiah 22:22 declares: *"And I will place on his shoulder the key of the house of David. He shall open, and none shall shut; and he shall shut, and none shall open"* (ESV).

God is a sovereign and holy God, and He often uses circumstances to get our attention. However, the Lord will usually confirm what He is speaking through other methods. This happened to a married couple I once knew. When they were dating in college, they were both involved in what could have been a fatal accident. On an icy two-lane road, a speeding tractor trailer swerved uncontrollably toward their car head on. Her boyfriend, unsaved at the time, was on the side of the vehicle that was severely damaged by the truck's impact. She thought for sure her boyfriend would not survive.

Instead, they both escaped the accident with no severe injuries. Through that accident, this man felt the Lord had a divine purpose for his life. Did he literally hear God's voice speaking to him? No! However, through seeking God's Word, wisdom from other believers, fasting, and much prayer, he felt

God's confirmation on it. Several months later, he gave his life to Jesus Christ and is now in full-time ministry traveling the nation operating in the supernatural gifts of the Holy Spirit. This demonic circumstance was not directed by God, but what the devil meant for their demise, God used for His good. God got the glory out of this accident.

As Christians, we need to examine our circumstances and ask if we are hearing the voice of the Lord through them. Ask God what He is trying to reveal so that you will not make mistakes or repeat unnecessary cycles. Ask yourself these two questions:

1.   What's happening in my life currently?
2.   What is the Lord revealing to me through these circumstances?

61

Supernatural Visitation and Divine Appearances

There the angel of the Lord appeared to him
in flames of fire from within a bush.
—Exodus 3:2

God speaks through visitations and divine appearances. These types of prophetic encounters were the norm throughout the Bible. Visitations are supernatural encounters between heaven and earth, between the heavenly realm and man. Visitations are not to be categorized as spooky, new age, or mystical but supernatural and relational. We can see throughout the Bible that visitations are biblical. They are usually life-changing events. God can visit and appear to His people in any form He decides to.

In these powerful supernatural encounters, God reveals Himself to those He wills and chooses. Holy Spirit visitations and appearance were common in the Old Testament and still are today. God visited those with unprecedented mindsets who were "faith catalysts" or "vanguards of faith" in their generation. However, God also appeared to those who were antagonists of God. God revealed Himself to ungodly kings and even to His people who breached their covenant with God.

God speaks through visitations and through an audible voice. Daniel, the prophet in the Old Testament, experienced a supernatural visitation from the Lord and the audible voice of God: *"While I, Daniel, was watching the vision and trying to understand it, there before me stood one who looked like a man"* (Dan. 8:15). Samuel, the prophet-priest, had a visitation from the Lord when God spoke to him. It was God, but Samuel heard it audibly and literally and thought it was the voice of Eli. The Lord sometimes speaks in an audible outward voice as if someone is in the room speaking. The Lord Jesus revealed Himself to Paul on the road to Damascus and spoke to Paul regarding persecuting His church, which caused Paul's conversion:

> *Suddenly a light from heaven flashed around him. He fell to the ground and heard a voice say to him, "Saul, Saul, why do you persecute me?" "Who are you, Lord?" Saul asked. "I am Jesus, whom you are persecuting" he replied* (Acts 9:3-5).

Appearances were another way God supernaturally came to people in the Bible and spoke to them directly. Today, these types of appearances are not ruled out. In the New Covenant, Jesus appeared to Paul, several disciples, and others such as the women at His tomb after His resurrection. The Lord Jesus will appear in people's dreams, and angels will come today and speak to believers and through prophetic encounters such as trances, dreams, translations of the Spirit, etc. Here are some Old Testament examples of God appearances:

> *There the angel of the Lord appeared to him in flames of fire from within a bush. Moses saw that though the bush was on fire it did not burn up. So Moses thought, "I will go over and see this strange sight—why the bush does not burn up* (Exodus 3:2-3).
>
> *The Lord appeared to Isaac and said, "Do not go down to Egypt; live in the land where I tell you to live"* (Genesis 26:2).
>
> *Then God said to Jacob, "Go up to Bethel and settle there, and build an altar there to God, who appeared to you when you were fleeing from your brother Esau"* (Genesis 35:1).

He is sovereign and He is a Spirit. When the disciples wanted to know what the Father looked like, Jesus replied:

"If you had known Me, you would have known My Father also. From now on you do know Him and have seen Him." Philip said to Him, "Lord, show us the Father, and that is sufficient for us." Jesus said to him, "Have I been with you such a long time, and yet you have not known Me, Philip? He who has seen Me has seen the Father. So how can you say, 'Show us the Father'?" (John 14:7-9 MEV).

God doesn't limit how He visits or appears to someone. There are times He will come by way of an angel of the Lord. He revealed Himself to Moses through a burning bush. Moses saw the bush ablaze with fire, but it was not consumed! Balaam's donkey is a great example—when this unwavering prophet tuned out the voice and instruction of the Lord to do what he wanted, God spoke through the mouth of a donkey to get his attention (Num. 22:21-39). God visited John in Revelation 1:12 in a vision. Visitation from the Lord should never be classified in one way. Whenever God reveals Himself to you, it is a visitation.

62

ANOINTED SONGS, MUSIC, AND DANCE

When the Lord brought back the captivity of Zion, we were like those who dream. Then our mouth was filled with laughter, and our tongue with singing. Then they said among the nations, "The Lord has done great things for them." The Lord has done great things for us, and we are glad.
—PSALM 126:1-3 NKJV

God will speak through the song of the Lord, anointed instruments, and music. God will use godly music and songs to share His heart. Prophetic worship songs create a prophetic atmosphere for the voice of the Lord to be spoken through songs. David was used of the Lord to bring deliverance to Saul who was schizophrenic and jealous. David's prophetic worship soothed Saul's heart and brought peace to his mind.

I have prophesied the song of the Lord many times to individuals and corporately, which brought about mass healing and deliverance. When I have gone through tough times, the Lord plays a song in my heart. I can literally hear the song hummed in my spirit, and then I hear the words to the song. I just flow with what I hear, and moments later I am weeping.

Look at the below song that helped King Saul get delivered from evil spirits that were oppressing him:

Now, the Lord's Spirit had left Saul, and an evil spirit from the Lord tormented him. Saul's officials told him, "An evil spirit from God is tormenting you. Your Majesty, why don't you command us to look for a man who can play the lyre well? When the evil spirit from God comes to you, he'll strum a tune, and you'll feel better." Saul told his officials, "Please find me a man who can play well and bring him to me." One of the officials said, "I know one of Jesse's sons from Bethlehem who can play well. He's a courageous man and a warrior. He has a way with words, he is handsome, and the Lord is with him." Saul sent messengers to Jesse to say, "Send me your son David, who is with the sheep." Jesse took six bushels of bread, a full wineskin, and a young goat and sent them with his son David to Saul. David came to Saul and served him. Saul loved him very much and made David his armorbearer. Saul sent this message to Jesse, "Please let David stay with me because I have grown fond of him." Whenever God's spirit came to Saul, David took the lyre and strummed a tune. Saul got relief from his terror and felt better, and the evil spirit left him (1 Samuel 16:14-23 GW).

God speaks through anointed songs and music that is filled with God-inspired lyrics and sounds from heaven. There are many times I hear God through words that a singer, psalmist, or worship and praise leader will sing. It is powerful to hear my favorite worship song or music played; it brings me into a place of worship or weeping before the Lord. When I was working in banking, sitting in front of the computer for many hours on my headphones, I would have Gospel music playing and all of sudden I'd be in tears because something in the lyrics or in the song touched me deeply. The words greatly impacted my heart and moved me to tears.

Songs, music, and different genres of music are universal, not religious. Even God loves new songs sung, and there are songs in the Bible. God has anointed and called musicians to bring healing, deliverance, and prophetic songs of the Lord. God will rejoice over us with songs. Did you know that the Lord Himself can sing? He will sing over you and rejoice as well:

The Lord your God is with you, the Mighty Warrior who saves.
He will take great delight in you; in his love he will no longer
rebuke you, but will rejoice over you with singing (Zephaniah
3:17).

God loves prophetic songs that are released from a pure heart and sung to
bring Him glory. King David would sing and play many songs that released
the Word of the Lord. God is looking for true worshipers who will worship
Him in spirit and truth. God want to hear new songs, music, and prophetic
dances created by the Holy Spirit.

First Corinthians 14:15 says, *"So what shall I do? I will pray with my spirit,*
but I will also pray with my understanding; I will sing with my spirit, but I will also
sing with my understanding." There are times when I sing in the spirit and with
my understanding. We are admonished in Psalm 96:1 NLT to, *"Sing a new song*
to the Lord! Let the whole earth sing to the Lord!" There is nothing wrong with
old songs that have brought us through hardship and pain. But we must not
stay there. God wants us to release something creative, relevant, current, and
new that will bring Him glory but also bless others. That is why I love prophetic songs and anointed instrumentals that will stir up a culture of worship
and glory. David understood establishing a place of worship in the kingdom.

God wants to speak as we hear His voice through songs, music, and watching prophetic anointed dancers. He uses prophetic dance to demonstrate His
Word. There are modern-day churches and ministries that have embraced new
technologies in their presentation of worshiping God. We have monitors with
music lyrics to follow along with in praise and worship. Modern-day technology with lights, cameras, LED monitors, and state-of-the-art sound systems
has made worship accessible to enjoy. In addition, to see dancers with banners
will create an atmosphere that brings you into the presence of God.

Actually, seeing prophetic dancers with banners waving puts me in a place
where I feel like I am in the presence of God—heaven on earth. It's a visual
presentation that ushers me into God's presence. There is something profound
seeing prophetic dancers moving with the flow of the Spirit while praise and
worship is going forth. Many churches have dancers as part of their worship
team. Oftentimes, God will begin to choreograph a supernatural, spontaneous

dance, which is actually a prophetic act that the Lord is speaking to us through the dance.

> *Then young women will dance and be glad, young men and old as well. I will turn their mourning into gladness; I will give them comfort and joy instead of sorrow* (Jeremiah 31:13).

Prophetic songs release the voice of God. Often during worship, the Lord will give someone a spontaneous song that is from God to the people. It is common for God to give the prophetic singer the lyrics and the melody.

> *Let the message of Christ dwell among you richly as you teach and admonish one another with all wisdom through psalms, hymns, and songs from the Spirit, singing to God with gratitude in your hearts* (Colossians 3:16).

Prophetic worship will create a pulse of God's heartbeat and glory to come. I recall being in a meeting where the senior pastor, who is a prophet of God, recorded prophetic songs while in the service. They sang prophetically and God's healing, delivering song of the Lord blessed all in attendance. Furthermore, they would birth new songs every week in the service and they released the songs to the world for many to benefit from them. Anointed songs and music have the ability to minister to us in ways that we cannot understand. There is power in the words that are sung and keys or notes that are played.

We can hear God's voice through songs and music that triggers worship and the presence of God. I would play anointed songs and music at my job, in the shower, and of course remote places to soothe my mind and bring personal healing. Through anointed songs and music I have received personal deliverance and soul healing. God purges me and heals my broken heart through songs.

Music in itself is powerful; even secular songs carry spirits that are attached to them. We must be careful of the songs we listen to because they can influence or impact our moods and emotions and even incite some sexual or sensual appetites. Songs can bring us into an environment and setting that can emotionally, spiritually, psychologically, and physically impact us negatively or positively! Specific songs bring us into past memories, flashbacks, and thoughts of times, events, circumstances, and even people.

Music is universal, and the lyrics written and sung by artists create a portrait of the worldviews, trials, tribulations, victories, love, and vision they live, dream, cause, and advocate. Songs becomes a love language to the Lord and He loves to hear us worship Him through music, song, and dance.

63

PROPHETIC RECOGNITION, BODY CHECKS, AND ACTS

But you have received the Holy Spirit, and he lives within you, so you don't need anyone to teach you what is true. For the Spirit teaches you everything you need to know, and what he teaches is true—it is not a lie. So just as he has taught you, remain in fellowship with Christ.
—1 JOHN 2:27 NLT

Prophetic recognition, body checks, and acts are unique prophetic ways God will speak to you. First we are going to talk about prophetic body checks. This is a simple one that God uses to speak to any Spirit-filled believer, especially those called to healing and miracle ministries. God will use body checks to speak to me concerning an issue, problem, pain, or discomfort in a person's body.

Oftentimes, the Lord will communicate His desire to heal someone else's body by giving a pain or sensation in a certain part of the prophetic person's body. In other words, if God is trying to get my attention to bring healing breakthrough, He will cause a pain to happen in my actual physical body. The Lord decides to borrow our physical senses to address any pain that He wants to heal for someone.

I remember speaking on Jesus's healing ministry when all of a sudden I felt pain in my lower back. I thought my back was going to give out. The Lord was body checking me and speaking to me concerning someone in the meeting who had several back injuries caused by a car accident. I begin to share what I felt, and surprisingly half of those in attendance came up to the altar for healing. I jokingly asked if everyone was in the same vehicle. God has a sense of humor, but all were touched and healed that night instantly.

I often make sure I do a body check before I minister anywhere. The purpose for this is that I want the Holy Spirit to speak to me through my body. I make sure I am in good shape physically and that I have no prior pain or injuries before I minister in the prophetic healing.

God can use you in this type of prophetic body checking. You will be surprised how God will give you words of knowledge and even medical terms you are not familiar with to bring about healing and a miracle. If we receive this kind of information from the Holy Spirit, it is important that we are aware of what pain or discomfort is common to us. Without clarification, we could mistakenly confuse our own pain with a word of knowledge for healing.

The Holy Spirit can become your best friend. As you are in fellowship with Him, your impressions will become clearer. If we are not discerning and careful, we can at times confuse our own desires with our "inner witness" given by the Holy Spirit. We have to desire the voice of the Lord most. As we align with God's will for our lives, we become so intimate with Him that we know His heartbeat with assurance. Our heart begins to beat in unison with the Father. As we become established in His presence, we will experience much greater understanding and revelation.

God will also speak through what is called "prophetic recognition." There are times in the prophetic when you can look at someone and they remind you of someone else or you can see something about that person's characteristics and/or personality traits that is similar to someone you know. You recognize the person or know something supernaturally specific about them based on a prompting in your mind. This can be a prophetic recall. Though you may be meeting or encountering this person for the first time, it seems like you've known them all your life.

Once I was in a small Bible study gathering in the home of a pastor. While I was there, I glanced at a woman I didn't know who reminded me of my aunt, Lisa. Every time I looked at her I saw more things that were similar to my aunt. She didn't look, sound, or act like my aunt, but something about her spirit connected her to my aunt. Suddenly, I couldn't resist and asked her, "Who is Lisa?" Her eyes opened wide in amazement. She replied, "That's my name; I am Lisa!" That was the connection between her and my aunt. God revealed a prophetic recognition that connected the two women. I was able to prophesy and minister the Word of the Lord to her—she and my aunt both had evangelistic callings on their lives.

Government and police agencies use a system of facial recognition. A person's face will come up in the database and connect to their identity. We now have apps on our phones that will do facial recognition of the owner of the phone. Someone else will not have access to a person's phone and confidential information. It is the same with prophetic recognition—God knows each and every one of us individually and will give us words of knowledge, information, wisdom, and more concerning a person based off of similar characteristics, spirit, calling, etc. In prophetic recognition, the Lord is highlighting specific details about a person to you. This is a powerful way God speaks to us and you will be amazed how accurate it is when you operate in it by faith.

From my experience I define the prophetic as speaking something into existence that has not yet come into existence in the natural realm. What is a prophetic act? It's performing an act in the earthly realm guided by the Holy Spirit to release a powerful shift in the spirit realm. God uses prophetic acts to convey things He is saying and/or doing prophetically. He used the prophets many times in the Bible to demonstrate through action what He was saying and about to perform.

Oftentimes the Lord directs someone to do a prophetic act. God uses me to do prophetic acts to demonstrate what He is going to do in a person's life. Most prophetic people are dramatic under the leading of the Spirit of God. As an introvert in the natural, when God requires me to do something in a demonstration most people will know that it's God because I am usually more a reserved observer. God will take me out of my personal comfort zone to speak by acting out what He intends to do. I love prophetic action, when God becomes the director of the prophetic scene for someone He loves. God speaks through prophetic acts to reveal the severity or necessity of what He wants to express.

The Bible is full of small prophetic actions that had huge practical impacts. Perhaps nothing is better known than the hand of Moses against the Amalekites. In Exodus 17:11-13:

> *As long as Moses held up his hands, the Israelites were winning, but whenever he lowered his hands, the Amalekites were winning. When Moses' hands grew tired, they took a stone and put it under him and he sat on it. Aaron and Hur held his hands up—one on one side, one on the other—so that his hands remained steady till sunset. So Joshua overcame the Amalekite army with the sword.*

Prophetic acts were common practices in the Bible. Ezekiel set a brick in the middle of the city—a prophetic symbol of laying a siege wall against Israel. *"Now, son of man, take a block of clay, put it in front of you and draw the city of Jerusalem on it"* (Ezek. 4:1). Agabus the prophet tied a belt around himself to demonstrate Paul's fate:

> *After we had been there a number of days, a prophet named Agabus came down from Judea. Coming over to us, he took Paul's belt, tied his own hands and feet with it and said, "The Holy Spirit says, 'In this way the Jewish leaders in Jerusalem will bind the owner of this belt and will hand him over to the Gentiles.'" When we heard this, we and the people there pleaded with Paul not to go up to Jerusalem* (Acts 21:10-12).

This story takes us to a mysterious area of the prophetic. Why do certain actions release realities in the spiritual realm? I don't think anyone can give a definite answer about this area of the spiritual realm or how it functions, but there is no doubt that it does happen. Here is another example from the fiery prophet Elisha:

> *Elisha said, "Get a bow and some arrows," and he did so. "Take the bow in your hands," he said to the king of Israel. When he had taken it, Elisha put his hands on the king's hands. "Open the*

east window," he said, and he opened it. "Shoot!" Elisha said, and he shot. "The Lord's arrow of victory, the arrow of victory over Aram!" Elisha declared. "You will completely destroy the Arameans at Aphek." Then he said, "Take the arrows," and the king took them. Elisha told him, "Strike the ground." He struck it three times and stopped. The man of God was angry with him and said, "You should have struck the ground five or six times; then you would have defeated Aram and completely destroyed it. But now you will defeat it only three times (2 Kings 13:15-19).

This was a primary means of prophetic ministry for the Old Testament prophet Ezekiel. Many of Ezekiel's messages were conveyed through prophetic messages. Here is an example using Ezekiel's hair as part of a message from God.

Now, son of man, take a sharp sword and use it as a barber's razor to shave your head and your beard. Then take a set of scales and divide up the hair. When the days of your siege come to an end, burn a third of the hair inside the city. Take a third and strike it with the sword all around the city. And scatter a third to the wind. For I will pursue them with drawn sword. But take a few hairs and tuck them away in the folds of your garment. Again, take a few of these and throw them into the fire and burn them up. A fire will spread from there to all Israel (Ezekiel 5:1-4).

In the biblical examples we just read, some theologians call this "prophetic intercession." In this type of intercession, the will of God is released on the earth through the movements or actions of someone directed by God. The actions or movements of the earthly realm release a specific blessing or reality in the spirit realm.

God uses prophetic actions as His communication. God is not bound to our audible language. The prophetic can be powerfully communicated through acts and movements.

64

SANCTIFIED
IMAGINATION

Test me, Lord, and try me, examine my heart and my mind.
—PSALM 26:2

God speaks prophetically through our thoughts, mind, and heart. He uses our mind as a gateway or access point to disclose images, words, ideas, concepts, and inventive thoughts. The gateway to a renewed mind and a sanctified imagination begins with knowing the Word of God. In addition, possessing the Holy Spirit reveals the mind and will of the Lord. A sanctified imagination and a renewed mind happen when we as spiritual beings form holy thoughts through meditation and use our imaginations in the childlike way God intended.

Toxicity and perverse imagery can plague our minds and form unhealthy, ungodly, unholy, and demonic thoughts. Bob Jones told Naim and me that God uses our imagination as the headquarters to speak to His prophets and spiritual children. We were created in God's image and according to His likeness. In other words, we were created in the imagination of God. We were created through a divine idea, concept, and thought of the Lord. God spoke you into existence based on of what was in His imagination! You are a prophecy in existence!

God has created our imagination to tune into the realm of the spirit. Our imagination must be holy and pure in order for divine ideas and creative thoughts to occur. We are called to have a sanctified imagination so that we are able to see in the Spirit and move in the demonstration of the Spirit by understanding the language of God. God talks in many different ways, but the inward witness of God's Spirit tunes us into the heart of God in an invisible world all around us. We must understand the Kingdom of God within us from a spiritual perspective. God's Kingdom is eternal, spiritual, invisible, invincible, powerful, and not earthly or carnal.

Knowing the voice of God starts within us first. God started speaking to me as a young believer by speaking to my heart through my imagination. With a childlike heart at the age of seven years old I was able to hear the voice of the Lord as loud and clear as if someone called my name audibly. God was speaking to my untainted mind. God will speak to us as our minds are renewed daily in His presence by studying His Word. The concept of the Kingdom of God is inward to outward and depth to height. Romans 12 admonishes us to renew our minds so that we can prove what is the perfect will of God. Furthermore, in Ephesians 4:23 it says that we are *"to be made new in the attitude of your minds."*

In the prophetic we have to know the mind of God and keep a sanctified imagination through a renewed mind. God often speaks to me concerning His will and purpose for my life in prayer by downloading ideas into my imagination. As Christians start to use their minds for the purposes and love of God, they will be like Hebrews 5:14, which says, *"But solid food is for the mature, who by constant use have trained themselves to distinguish good from evil."* God wants us to train and recondition our imagination to align with perfect God's Word, will, and purpose.

Hearing the voice of God is not hard when our imagination is synchronized with the Lord's will through His Word. In prophetic activation we train prophetic people and prophets to use their imagination to hear, feel, sense, see, taste, smell, and wait on God's impression. As spiritual beings, we have the capacity and ability to tap into the realm of the spirit and gain insight, revelation, impartation, and detailed information from the Lord. God's will is His Word, but His will for everyone is not the same. He will speak a prophetic word that is supported through His written Word to convey His will for your life.

While here on earth, we can have encounters in heavenly places where God is. The Bible says that we are seated in heavenly places with Christ Jesus (Eph. 2:6). In prayer we can ascend to heavenly places with Christ while He is on our heart. It starts in the communication towers of our imagination. Just as a radio station picks up specific frequencies from the radio station headquarters to the towers around the world, God wants our imagination to be in tune to the frequencies of heaven through the Word of God. When we use all of our mind and spiritual senses, we grow and grow from glory to glory to know and demonstrate the Kingdom of God here and now on earth.

65

INSIGHT AND INSPIRATION

While I was speaking and praying, confessing my sin and the sin
of my people Israel and making my request to the Lord my God
for his holy hill —while I was still in prayer, Gabriel, the man
I had seen in the earlier vision, came to me in swift flight about
the time of the evening sacrifice. He instructed me and said to me,
"Daniel, I have now come to give you insight and understanding."
—DANIEL 9:20-22

One of the powerful ways God speaks prophetically to His people and especially those called to the prophetic is through divine insight and Holy Spirit inspiration. The Bible tells us that wisdom is the principal thing; if we get wisdom we receive understanding. In seminary, I took a study on the Book of Proverbs that defined wisdom as "thinking God's thoughts after Him." The definition sounded great but I never could figure out exactly what it meant. I've come to realize that having the wisdom of God is God's insight that comes with understanding.

When God gives us insight it is also connected to wisdom. God wants us to seek Him for insight concerning spiritual things such as truth in His Word. One of the most famous stories of wisdom-seeking in the Word of God is that of King Solomon. He was noted for asking for wisdom. In other words, he inquired of the Lord in a dream for divine insight in governing as a king. God speaks through divine insight when we ask Him for wisdom and understanding concerning anything in our lives.

First Kings 3 and 4 use the Hebrew word *chokmah*, meaning wisdom (Strong's #H2452); it's taken from the primary root *chakam*, which is "to be wise in mind, word or deed, to deal wisely, to make wiser" (Strong's #H2449). However, when we take a look verse 9—when Solomon asks the Lord specifically for a gift—that is not precisely what he asks for. What Solomon asks for in First Kings 3:9 is for the Lord to "*give Your servant an understanding heart to judge Your people to discern between good and evil. For who is able to judge this great people of Yours?*" (NASB). What Solomon actually requested from the Lord was an understanding heart—that is the Hebrew word *shama* (Strong's #H8085).

This is powerful to understand when it comes to the voice of the Lord, and as believers we can ask the Lord for a discerning heart as well. In other words, we can hear the voice of God daily to help us handle the most difficult situations in life. I believe we need divine insight and wisdom to address and tackle things that are not in our control. Having a discerning heart from God gives divine direction for your life in major and everyday decisions.

In addition, I believe hearing the voice of God with divine insight and having a discerning heart will allow you to discern where God is moving while partnering with Him to see the supernatural, healing, and breakthrough taking place in and through your life. We must seek the Lord and inquire of Him like King Solomon did by asking God for a discerning heart. What does that mean biblically? In Hebrew the word *shama* is a primary root that means "to hear." How powerful is that? King Solomon's request of the Lord was to hear the voice of the Lord. He needed the voice, wisdom, understanding, and insight of the Lord to carry out his kingly duties and responsibilities. God was so moved and impressed by his request to have a discerning heart—in other words, a listening ear to the voice of God. We all must ask the Lord for a heart like that. We need a discerning heart that is able to hear the voice of God daily.

God speaks to us and through us by the inspiration of the Holy Spirit. God's very own breath is in us and contains life itself. God speaks through His holy prophets to declare His will and word for those to whom He sends them. God spoke through the mouth of King David this way:

> *Lord, thou art God, which hast made heaven, and earth, and the sea, and all that in them is: who by the mouth of thy servant David hast said, Why did the heathen rage, and the people imagine vain things?* (Acts 4:24-25 KJV)

Paul describes the process of inspiration by the Holy Spirit in one of his Epistles:

> *But as it is written, Eye hath not seen, nor ear heard, neither have entered into the heart of man, the things which God hath prepared for them that love him. But God hath revealed them unto us by his Spirit. ...Now we have received, not the spirit of the world, but the spirit which is of God; that we might know the things that are freely given to us of God. Which things also we speak, not in the words which man's wisdom teacheth, but which the Holy Ghost teacheth; comparing spiritual things with spiritual* (1 Corinthians 2:9-13 KJV).

Most leaders don't ask for a heart to hear. Furthermore, there are intercessors and believers who don't pray for leaders to have a heart to hear. It's imperative for every believer and leader to possess the ability to hear! Hear what, exactly? The voice of God! The ability to hear and understand God is surely an aspect of wisdom. A wise person listens and sees others' point of view beyond their own. God will speak to anyone with a humble heart and openness to hear the voice of God and wise counsel from others. God wants to release divine wisdom, insight, and understanding when we are vulnerable before the Lord. He who has ears, let him hear. I wholeheartedly believe hearing is not the problem, but are we listening with our hearing heart?

This word *shama* is explained further in Second Chronicles: *"Now give wisdom and knowledge to me so that I might know how to go before this people, for who can judge this great people of Yours?"* (2 Chron. 1:10 MEV). Understanding, literally "hearing," comes by wisdom and knowledge. Furthermore, the hearing of the heart must refer to following the divine direction and promptings from within a believer. Therefore, knowledge and understanding are also aspects of having wisdom and insight from the Lord. We must know that a deep desire to know and understand always exists in the wise.

What does "insight" mean? To gain insight into a situation, you gain an accurate and deep understanding of it. I love words, and being a words type of person I get more insight when I research or dig for answers or understanding. That is the type of person I am by nature, and I believe it's part of my apostolic and prophetic calling. I wanted more clarity into the word *insight* so I looked up the synonyms—intuition, perception, awareness, discernment, understanding, comprehension, apprehension, appreciation, cognizance, penetration, and acuteness. God wants to give us a discerning heart and insight to hear God's voice in everything we do as we seek the Lord.

The first ten chapters of the Book of Proverbs describe wisdom and her characteristics in great poetic detail. Wisdom and divine insight involves some self-discipline, evaluation, and the ability to say no to one's self—the absence of entitlement—so perhaps a little humility is involved and needed.

> We are not provided with wisdom, we must discover it for ourselves, after a journey through the wilderness which no one else can take for us, and effort, which no one can spare us.
> —Marcel Proust, *In Search of Lost Time / Remembrance of Things Past, Vol II: Within a Budding Grove*

God releases divine inspiration by the Holy Spirit. The Lord will move upon your heart to do something or take action. You can feel His inspiration on you. For me it sometimes comes on me like a coat being placed on my shoulders or head. In addition, there are times I can feel the cool sensation or gushing of cold water flowing or springing up in my belly when there is a strong Holy Spirit inspiration for me to pray or prophesy to someone.

However, some Spirit-filled believers get a sudden flash of inspiration. In other words, they just have a knowing in their spirit. It's common for Spirit-filled believers to have these sudden inspirations. Oftentimes, people will say something like, "It strikes me…" or "It came to me…" or "Something said…." We must be able to know who that something is. That something is the Holy Spirit speaking to use. Many believers can't really explain or comprehend what's happening initially, but they just know that they know that they know it's the Lord.

Again, you should temper this with other tests—does it line up with biblical principles, does your spouse and/or church family bear witness, etc.— especially if you are making an important decision. But not everything is an important decision, and Holy Spirit is interested in helping you with even the small things in life. I've had sudden inspirations to get money out of an ATM for tolls and stop to fill up on gas when I was traveling to New York City and I ignored what I was hearing and sensing, only to discover later that I was in heavy New Jersey turnpike traffic, running out of gas, with no money to give to the toll.

Over time you will become accustomed to these flashes of inspiration and sudden inward promptings by the Holy Spirit. The inspiration is also connected to insight as well. The Lord will give us Holy Spirit inspiration to give us a listening heart to what is going on. When you get these flashes of inspiration, pay attention! God wants to save you time, energy, money, and unnecessary warfare and head and heartaches.

66

CONSCIENCE

Keeping faith and a good conscience, which some have
rejected and suffered shipwreck in regard to their faith.
—1 TIMOTHY 1:19 MEV

Holy Spirit speaks through our conscience—an inner feeling or voice, a guide to right and wrong. Our conscience sounds a lot like God because He speaks to our spirit and our spirit speaks to our conscience. In the early stages of my prophetic ministry, learning the voice of God was harder because I made it hard. I didn't realize that the Holy Spirit was already speaking but I just wasn't paying attention.

When God breathed the breath of life in the nostrils of Adam, he suddenly became a living being. Some translations call it a *living soul*. In addition to having a living soul and breathing the living-giving breath of God, man also became a thinking, decision-making, free-willed, emotional, sensitive, conscious individual. Adam and Eve were not sin-conscious. Eve was deceived by the serpent that caused them both to disobey the direct orders of God. They had no knowledge of good and evil until they ate the forbidden fruit.

Adam and Eve had a God-conscience, so to speak. They were created to hear and obey the voice of the Lord. They were not familiar with any strange or foreign voice except for God only. When they disobeyed God, they now were aware of their sin. What they had done caused them to be sin-conscious— guilty, ashamed, convicted, and embarrassed. When they ate the fruit of the forbidden tree, the Bible says in Genesis 3:7, *"Then the eyes of both of them were opened, and they realized they were naked; so they sewed fig leaves together and made coverings for themselves."*

When they sinned their eyes were opened, but it also revealed something they didn't understand yet and that was hearing their own conscience. They carried a guilty conscience and knew automatically that they had disobeyed the instructions of the Lord. God will speak to our conscience when we are wrong about something or guilty of an unrepented act of sin. God will speak to us continually through our conscience about unresolved issues that must be addressed. When we have a clear conscience, it is not that we are perfect or sin repellent but that we are in good standing with the Lord.

If a person, for example, commits murder, their guilty conscience confronts them. Even if the person is numb to what they have done, their conscience over time will get the best of them. Over time, unforgiveness, bitterness, and resentment can become insidious to our conscience if not dealt with early on. God speaks to our conscience to heal us, direct us, minster to us in deep or dark areas of our soul. If I have committed a wrongful act toward someone, God will deal with me through my thoughts and conscience until that issue is resolved. Never ignore or tune out the voice of the Holy Spirit through your conscience.

You may ask, "Well, how do I know if it's my conscience, my imagination, or God talking to me?" Consider this example: Have you ever met identical twins? At first, you can't tell them apart—but as you get to know them you will discover over time that they have their own distinctive, unique, and identifiable personalities. As you get to know them, you can tell the difference between the two. That's imperative to understand and recognize when hearing the voice of God and your own thoughts, imagination, or conscience, because your conscience is not God's. God's ways, thoughts, imaginations, and concepts are not ours either. We have to learn and align our will, desires, emotions, and thoughts to the Lord. It has to be redeemed, refreshed, revived, reconditioned, and sanctified through God's Word and the help of the Holy Spirit.

God will never lead anyone to kill someone or do evil or wicked things. God is a good Father, holy, just, and pure; He is Ruler, Judge, and Love just to name a few. Oftentimes, we as believers can reason ourselves out of God's will by following our conscience apart from the wisdom of the Father. God will use our conscience to speak to us and He does it by overriding what we think or believe. God does put thoughts in our heads and words in our mouths as we read, study, pray, fast, and commit to the Word of God and receive the Holy Spirit's baptism and infilling. God can speak to us if we allow Him to occupy those places in our heart and soul.

When God speaks to us through our conscience, it can almost be like dripping water from a faucet. You just keep coming back to that same truth. When you layer this with other ways God speaks, such as through His Word and through peace, you can be confident when it's God and when it's just you. As Spirit-filled believers and children of God we don't have to walk around with a sin-conscious mind, or if we sinned we can repent and get it right.

God doesn't want us to live guilty of something Christ died on the Cross of Calvary to pay for. We have been justified by faith in Christ. We should be God-conscious and walk morally, ethically, spiritually, and devotedly unto the Lord by faith. The Lord speaks to our conscience to keep us aligned to His will, purpose, and the prophetic destiny on our lives. Let's take a look at a few Scriptures about the conscience:

> *Paul, looking intently at the Council, said, "Brethren, I have lived my life with a perfectly good conscience before God up to this day"* (Acts 23:1 NASB).

> *But holding to the mystery of the faith with a clear conscience* (1 Timothy 3:9 NASB).

> *Let us draw near with a sincere heart in full assurance of faith, having our hearts sprinkled clean from an evil conscience and our bodies washed with pure water* (Hebrews 10:22 NASB).

> *However not all men have this knowledge; but some, being accustomed to the idol until now, eat food as if it were sacrificed to an idol; and their conscience being weak is defiled* (1 Corinthians 8:7 NASB).

> *By means of the hypocrisy of liars seared in their own conscience as with a branding iron* (1 Timothy 4:2 NASB).

> *For our proud confidence is this: the testimony of our conscience, that in holiness and godly sincerity, not in fleshly wisdom but in*

the grace of God, we have conducted ourselves in the world, and especially toward you (2 Corinthians 1:12 NASB).

Having a good conscience, so that, when you are slandered, those who revile your good behavior in Christ may be put to shame (1 Peter 3:16 ESV).

We can see how powerful the conscience can be when guilt gets the best of us. I am reminded of Judas, who betrayed Jesus and took his own life. He could have just repented and got it right as one of Jesus's chosen disciples and apostles. Allow the Holy Spirit to infuse your conscience with pure things, and when sin is present unaddressed please confront whatever it may be so that God can bless you and you will carry no unnecessary burden. God's voice can be activated when we activate our conscience.

God will awaken our ears morning by morning to His voice as we are consciously aware of His voice on the inside of us through a Holy Spirit-anointed conscience. There is hidden potential in us that God wants us to be conscious about as it pertains to our purpose and destiny in Him. God speaks to our conscience so that we are sensitive and aware of what He is doing in us and through us daily.

67

CREATION AND NATURE

Since what may be known about God is plain to them, because God has made it plain to them. For since the creation of the world God's invisible qualities—his eternal power and divine nature—have been clearly seen, being understood from what has been made, so that people are without excuse.
—ROMANS 1:19-20

Creation has a voice that declares the glory of God. God uses creation to speak of Himself: *"Let the rivers clap their hands; let the mountains sing together for joy"* (Ps. 98:8). It is clear that creation has the ability to reveal what God the Creator has spoken. Creation carries the voice of the Creator. When I look at the sky, stars, sun, and moon I am awestruck by the phenomenal creative ways of the Lord and His masterful creation. I love what Hebrews 11:3 declares: *"By faith we understand that the entire universe was formed at God's command, that what we now see did not come from anything that can be seen"* (NLT).

The voice of the Lord can be visibly seen through creation and nature. We understand that the entire universe was formed by God's command and the visible was created by the invisible. God's voice is demonstrated by what is spoken. In Genesis 1, God created everything by what was spoken. Furthermore, we can see that *"since the creation of the world God's invisible qualities—his eternal power and divine nature—have been clearly seen, being understood from what has been made, so that people are without excuse"* (Rom. 1:20).

God has the awesome power and ability to speak to His people by using nature in prophetic acts. In the Book of Numbers, God spoke through His creation, Balaam's donkey: *"Then the Lord opened the donkey's mouth, and it said to Balaam, 'What have I done to you to make you beat me these three times?'"* (Num. 22:28). God has created man in the highest order in the earth realm to become a speaking creation. Yes, we know that all that God created communicates, but not like mankind.

Creation and nature reveals the all-powerful nature and essence of what makes God, God. He is Alpha and Omega, the beginning and the ending. He is first and last at the same time. In the beginning was God and He is the beginning and has no end to Him. He is eternal, spiritual, and a loving Father. He created the earth realm for man. Psalm 24:1-2 declares, *"The earth is the Lord's, and everything in it, the world, and all who live in it; for he founded it on the seas and established it on the waters."*

What is nature, biblically speaking? We can see that nature is the silent shouting of God's creation, ordinary created objects showing His glory like a flower or a tree (Ps. 19:1-4). One of the astonishing things I have come to realize in my prophetic ministry and walk is that God speaks to me through creation and nature. What I mean by this is that when I am by the waterfront here in Wilmington, Delaware where I reside, I hear God speak to me in the flowing current of the waters. There is something soothing about hearing water running while trying to process things in my mind. God speaks to me clearly just by hearing streaming water, birds chirping in the morning, and the wind whistling.

I love hearing heavy raindrops and thundering. Sometime surrounded by creation can be a great way to hear from God. In Romans, Paul tells us that God's invisible qualities, His nature and power are revealed through creation. We can learn things about our Creator by what He has created. Pay attention to creation all around you and ask God to reveal Himself through what you experience. Go for a walk, enjoy a sunrise, or paddle in the sea. God can speak through natural manifestations. Romans 1:18-20 states clearly that God can make Himself known by nature.

We can know for sure that God does still talks today and even through creation His voice is evident by what is created. Furthermore, it is clear that through the intricate details and magnificent beauty of all that God has created, we are able to "hear" God's voice.

How? By simply observing the ant who stores up food all summer long, we learn about wisdom and industriousness. By studying the heavens, we understand more of God's powerful nature and greatness. And through planting and growing a beautiful garden or harvesting a field as a farmer we can hear God's voice in the reaping and blossoming of flowers and learn about the miracle of death and rebirth. God designed and spoke them all into existence.

God's voice in creation, nature, or the natural world means that when we look up at the stars or gaze at the breathtaking snow-capped mountains of Hawaii or the clear blue ocean of the Bahamas, we see the fingerprints of the Lord's creation. The more we fix our gaze on the wonder of God's creation, the more we must conclude that these things could not make themselves. Both the intricate design of creation and the way the entire universe and cosmos appears to be fine-tuned, handcrafted, and specifically designed for life declare that this couldn't happen by chance.

God doesn't just speak through the order and design we find in creation, but also through the jaw-dropping, eye-opening, awestruck, and breathtaking beauty that encompasses everything around us. From something as mundane as seeing and hearing the sound of a single hummingbird flying and feeding from a flower bed on a beautiful spring afternoon, to the spectacular views of nebulae in distant corners of the galaxy captured by the Hubble Space Telescope—creation doesn't just explains to us that a Creator exists, but that this Creator is an artist without peer.

The overwhelming feeling of awe that comes over us as we see the waves pounding against the rocks or a mother holding her newborn baby for the first time in her loving embrace is, in fact, God speaking to us through His masterpiece. Psalm 19:1-4 puts it this way:

> *The heavens declare the glory of God; the skies proclaim the work of his hands. Day after day they pour forth speech; night after night they reveal knowledge. They have no speech, they use no words; no sound is heard from them. Yet their voice goes out into all the earth, their words to the ends of the world.*

The above passage of Scripture is self-explanatory, but I love how Job 12:7-10 further explains nature and what it can teach us:

> *But ask the animals, and they will teach you, or the birds in the sky, and they will tell you; or speak to the earth, and it will teach you, or let the fish in the sea inform you. Which of all these does not know that the hand of the Lord has done this? In his hand is the life of every creature and the breath of all mankind.*

Furthermore, God speaks through creation and nature as the Bible also records God talking to many people in various locations, places, and unusual areas. Keep in mind that God can speak to you or anyone anywhere. However, there are people who believe that they can only hear the voice of God in a religious setting or place. This is far from the truth. God can speak to you in the bathroom, shower, car, workplace, business, grocery store, mall, or anywhere. God is everywhere and we can hear Him everywhere we may be.

God can talk to us anywhere, anytime He desires to. However, you are on to something when you ask about God speaking to people under trees and in nature. Here are some biblical examples of where and how God may speak to people just like you and me. Notice that some are inside and others outdoors:

- Jesus Christ speaks to us (Heb. 1:1-3) when we read our Bible (Ps. 119:105) wherever we might be.

- God talks to us when we are outside riding animals like a donkey (Num. 22:30).

- God talks to children when they are in the bed at night (1 Sam. 3:8-9).

- God talks to us when we are outdoors staring at the stars in the sky (Rom. 1:20).

- God talks to us in the church or assembly of other believers (Isa. 6:1-7).

- God talks when we are sitting beside bushes like He did to Moses (Exod. 3:1-4).

- God talks to us when we are sound asleep (Joel 2:28).

- God talks to us deep in our innermost human spirit (Jer. 29:12-13).

- God talks to us during storms, wind, earthquakes, and fire (1 Kings 19:11-13).

- God talks to us when we are sitting under trees (Jon. 4:6).

- God talk us to in nature when everything is silent and peaceful (1 Kings 19:13).

As you can see, God speaks in various ways and different places. However, there is a difference between God speaking and us hearing His voice. The method that works for me in hearing the voice of God speaking is to get alone and listen, especially in nature—basking in God's creation as long as it is quiet and peaceful. Throughout history the Christian mystics have championed this practice, and we as Spirit-filled, tongue-talking believers are missing a vital point. God is speaking daily, but are we listening and paying attention to His voice around us?

68

WEAKNESS, PAIN, AND SUFFERING

But he said to me, "My grace is sufficient for you, for my
power is made perfect in weakness." Therefore I will boast
all the more gladly about my weaknesses, so that Christ's
power may rest on me. That is why, for Christ's sake, I delight
in weaknesses, in insults, in hardships, in persecutions, in
difficulties. For when I am weak, then I am strong.
—2 CORINTHIANS 12:9-10

You may be looking at this particular chapter and wondering—how is weakness, pain, and suffering associated with hearing the voice of God? Well, God will use our weaknesses and pain to speak strength to us in times of need. When I was ill back to back with the flu in 2014 to 2015, I heard the Lord speak to me to take better care of my health. God wanted me to be in good health. In addition, I have found that pain, heartache, and heartbreak have given me wisdom. God doesn't like it when we are hurting. He uses those times to really come and minister to us personally.

When I would be very ill, my mother and grandmother would immediately come to my aid. There's nothing like a mother's and grandmother's love and concern toward you. God is the same way, and He comes to our aid when we need Him the most. When I am sick, my mother and grandmother give me wisdom and solutions to keep me from getting sick next time. You will be surprised by the prophetic way God speaks to us in pain, weakness, and suffering.

The word *pain* in some form occurs over 70 times throughout the Bible. The first mention of the word *pain* is in the origin of pain in childbirth: *"To the woman He said, 'I will greatly multiply your pain in childbirth, in pain you will bring forth children; yet your desire will be for your husband, and he will rule over you'"* (Gen. 3:16 NASB). The context here is that Adam and Eve had sinned and the pain of childbirth is one of the consequences of sin. Because of sin, the whole earth was cursed, and death entered in as a result (Rom. 5:12). So, it may be concluded that pain is one of the many results of original sin.

Medically, we know that pain is a gift even though this is not biblically stated. Without some level of pain in our physical bodies, how would we know if we needed medical attention? In fact, the absence of pain is one of the problems associated with leprosy. Children would never learn that touching a hot stove is not a good idea, nor would we be alerted to a dangerous medical condition without the pain indicators that are associated with it.

Spiritually speaking, the benefits of having pain, suffering, and trials are expressed by the apostle James: *"Consider it all joy, my brethren, when you encounter various trials, knowing that the testing of your faith produces endurance"* (James 1:2-3 NASB). According to James, when we as believers endure painful trials, we can take joy in knowing that God is at work in us to produce endurance and Christ-like character. This applies to mental, emotional, and spiritual pain as well as to physical pain.

Pain will birth purpose. Hannah need Peninnah to push her into prayer to conceive Samuel. Pain is not the end of a thing but the beginning of something new. Pain produces endurance and shapes our character to be like Christ. Oftentimes, I hear the Lord having a one-on-one dialogue with me when I go through life testing and trials. He speaks to me the most when I feel like I am at my lowest point. God knows this about us and that is why He sent the Holy Spirit to comfort us.

Pain, opposition, suffering, and persecution also provide an opportunity to experience the grace of God. Consider what Paul said: *"But he said to me, 'My grace is sufficient for you, for my power is made perfect in weakness.' Therefore I will boast all the more gladly about my weaknesses, so that Christ's power may rest on me"*

(2 Cor. 12:9). What a powerful passage of Scripture—the apostle Paul stating that power is perfected in our weakness and His grace is sufficient for us. I have met some of the most anointed individuals who have encountered some of the most traumatic and humbling experiences. They become glory carriers and have exceptional characters because of the pain that they endured in life. If you want more anointing and power in your life, get broken so that God can heal you and use you for His glory.

Pain produces power! Paul in the above text in Second Corinthians was speaking of a thorn in his flesh that was troubling him. We don't know specifically what the thorn was, but it seemed to have been painful enough that Paul asked the Lord to remove it three times. God didn't remove it but kept it there to buffet and to humble Paul. There are things we are praying for God to remove in our lives and God won't. The thorn in our flesh comes as a reminder not to get puffed up or above ourselves. God will use us for His glory and not for our own glory.

We cannot ask God to remove something He is using to keep us humbled. The apostle recognized that God's grace was being given to him so he could endure. God will give His children the grace to bear pain. Pain will make some people or break them. God will not put on us more than we can bear. Pain, weakness, and suffering bring the glory and power of God out of us.

However, with pain, rejection, setbacks, opposition, suffering, and in our weakness we have to look at the brighter side of it all. The really good news is that Jesus Christ suffered too and died in our place for our sins: *"For Christ also suffered once for sins, the righteous for the unrighteous, to bring you to God. He was put to death in the body but made alive in the Spirit"* (1 Pet. 3:18). There is no pain that could approach the horrific events of Jesus's crucifixion, and He suffered that pain willingly to redeem us and glorify His Father.

Therefore, in believing in Jesus Christ, God grants the believer eternal life and all the blessings that are included. One of those great incentives as a newborn believer in Christ is, *"He will wipe every tear from their eyes. There will be no more death' or mourning or crying or pain, for the old order of things has passed away"* (Rev. 21:4). It is hard to grasp that the pain we often experience as a natural part of living in a fallen, sin-cursed world will be a thing of the past for those who, through faith in Christ, spend eternity in Heaven with Him.

I believe that physical suffering is God's megaphone to gain our attention or teach some life lesson to overcome. God will provide strength for us to fulfill our purpose, calling, and mandate in the earth.

> *Fear not, for I am with you; be not dismayed, for I am your God; I will strengthen you, I will help you, I will uphold you with my righteous right hand* (Isaiah 41:10 ESV).

> *I can do all things through him who strengthens me* (Philippians 4:13 ESV).

My mother and grandmother are strong and they are examples of strength to me when I feel like I am unable to make it. Looking at their courage and strength, God speaks to me through them. He will give us strength when we are weak; soothe our pain when we hurting physically, emotionally, or mentally; and give us courage when we are fearful or uncertain.

> *Be strong, and let your heart take courage, all you who wait for the Lord!* (Psalm 31:24 ESV)

> *He gives power to the faint, and to him who has no might he increases strength* (Isaiah 40:29 ESV).

Our physical bodies speak to us through the pain that we feel. God also speaks through what we may be feeling or experiencing physically to tell us to go to the doctor and not to ignore what is going on in our bodies. I recall a time when I was putting off getting my teeth checked. I was getting constant headaches. I had a bad toothache that cause headaches, sore throat, neck pain, and swelling of the jaw. I ended up going to the emergency room and the orthodontist stated if I didn't come in I would have ended up with a heart attack and stroke because my blood pressure was stroke level. God was speaking to me the whole time for months to go to the dentist to get checked out. We must always pay attention to the warning signs in our bodies. God knows what's going on even though we may not have foreknowledge of something.

There have been unhealthy relationships I was part of that caused emotional pain and suffering. God was speaking to me prophetically to get out of that toxic relationship and be free emotionally. Relationships that are toxic or unhealthy can plague our spirituality and relationship with God. God uses also our weakness to allow us to solely depend on the strength and power of God. Life is a great teacher, but also through pain we will be able to make better decisions to protect and guard ourselves.

In modern times, one of the most difficult topics is explaining the problem of suffering, which is challenging among Christians. There are those who struggle with the concept of how a loving God could allow suffering to continue in the world that He created. For many who have endured personal persecution and suffering, we know that it's a deep-seated personal and emotional issue, not a philosophical issue.

Briefly, how does the Bible address suffering? Does the Word of God reveal any examples of people who have suffered and supply any solutions? The Word of God is realistic when it comes to the problem of endured suffering. One of the fruits of the Holy Spirit that I had to cultivate in my own life was longsuffering. There is nothing like having to wait it out. Interestingly, the Word of God dedicates an entire book to the problem of suffering.

Many of us have heard the story of Job. It begins with a scene in heaven that discloses to the reader some background of Job's suffering. Satan goes before God and God mentions Job and allows satan to cause him to suffer. Furthermore, this dialogue between God and satan was never revealed to Job or any of his friends. Therefore, their ignorance is not surprising, until Job finally rests in nothing but the faithfulness of the Lord and the hope of God's redemption.

Job and his friends couldn't wrap their minds about the purpose of his suffering and loss. Job's wife had another mindset that Job didn't agree with nor concede to. In fact, when the Lord confronts Job and gives him a history lesson on creation and God's overall will, Job is found silent. Job's silent response does not in any way trivialize the intense pain and loss he had endured through longsuffering. Rather, it underscores the necessity of total reliance on and confidence in God's purposes even in the midst of personal suffering, persecution, and rejection, even when we are clueless of His purposes.

God will use our suffering, pain, and weaknesses to speak to us to bring clarity and understanding to His purpose for our lives. He uses what we are enduring as birthing pains to conceive God's prophetic purpose to bring Him glory out of our lives. He reveals that we are weak and He is strong. Suffering, like all other human experiences, is directed by the sovereign wisdom of God. In the end, we learn that we may never know the specific reason for our suffering, but we must trust in our sovereign God. That is the real answer to suffering.

> *He will wipe away every tear from their eyes, and death shall be no more, neither shall there be mourning, nor crying, nor pain anymore, for the former things have passed away* (Revelation 21:4 ESV).

> *For I consider that the sufferings of this present time are not worth comparing with the glory that is to be revealed to us* (Romans 8:18 ESV).

69

GIFT OF SERVICE

Employ it in serving one another as good
stewards of the manifold grace of God.
—1 PETER 4:10 NASB

A believer can hear the voice of God speaking through the gift of serving others. The Lord has equipped people with gifts that are perfect for the purpose He has for them in this life. We must understand that your entire personality—our motivations and tendencies—bears the imprint of your gift and your purpose. Those with the gift of service see and meet practical needs in people's lives. These individuals will hear God move upon their heart when they can identify a need and accomplish the task at hand.

In others, a person with the gift of service will be the first person in a group to notice the needs of others and to step forward to meet those needs as the Lord has directed them. God speaks through them by meeting a specific or unique need. This is a gift that automatically turns on when needs are not met. God gives a special sensitivity to these believers, and oftentimes they will think of another person and feel the desire to serve them in some way. Paul writes that since our gifts vary, we should use them appropriately (Rom. 12:6-8).

We need this type of gift operative in the life and culture of the believer. While there are groups of people who would rather be served than serve, God is raising up people who will learn how to serve others—that will be their gratification. I love serving others in my prophetic ministry and gift. I love to see people delivered, set free, healed, and blessed by the Lord through my gift. God speaks to people and demonstrates His love through their actions and gifts.

Those with the gift of service free others to achieve. Their special joy comes in being a part of someone else's achievement. They are blessed when others are blessed. In turn, God supernaturally provides for them because of their selflessness. These men and women have no hidden agenda or motive for attention. They discover an awesome spiritual principle—when we give of ourselves freely to help other people succeed, God turns the blessing in our direction.

Jesus lived out this principle in all His days on earth. Those with the gift of service have no regard for weariness. These servants work almost ceaselessly, beyond the point at which others grow weary. They delight in accomplishing the task and fulfilling someone else's need, and that joy drives them onward. Those with the gift of service are the last to rest.

70

GIFT OF HOSPITALITY

Don't just pretend to love others. Really love them. Hate what is wrong. Hold tightly to what is good. Love each other with genuine affection, and take delight in honoring each other. Never be lazy, but work hard and serve the Lord enthusiastically. Rejoice in our confident hope. Be patient in trouble, and keep on praying. When God's people are in need, be ready to help them. Always be eager to practice hospitality.
—ROMANS 12:9-13 NLT

God speaks to those who have the gift of hospitality. There is a blessing in being able and willing to put your plans to the side for a moment and bless others. I remember when I was hospitalized and in recovery from surgery. I was tremendously blessed by the overwhelming text message, emails, phone calls, visits, and social media responses. Just the thoughtfulness and prayers of others caused me to recover fast from surgery. There is a power in love from people who are selfless and give themselves sacrificially to others.

People who possess the gift of hospitality oftentimes are taken advantage of by those who only seek to hurt others. It can be easy to feel so comfortable that we forget to be grateful or we ignore the kindness inherent in this gift. Yet the most amazing part of this gift is that it is offered without any need for reciprocity. I recall a time when God spoke to me in prayer concerning someone who was in need. Later, on their social media post, I discovered they were in need of help and assistance. I went ahead and extended my helping hand. I thought it was one thing that they was in need of, but God spoke to me and challenged me do more for them within my resources.

After helping and being led of the Lord, the person wanted to return the favor. I declined and they were brought to tears. I said I wanted to obey God but God didn't tell me to do more for the person. It was a decision I made that ultimately blessed the person tremendously and I was told that I was an angel sent by God. You never know whose life you will impact by just being generous and showing a sign of hospitality. Being thoughtful about others has opened tremendous doors for me. There is nothing wrong with being nice, kind, respectful, and courteous to others. A person with this gift loves to share his or her home or space without any need for you to do the same.

> *But those who won't care for their relatives, especially those in their own household, have denied the true faith. Such people are worse than unbelievers* (1 Timothy 5:8 NLT).

> *Do not forsake your friend or a friend of your family, and do not go to your relative's house when disaster strikes you—better a neighbor nearby than a relative far away* (Proverbs 27:10).

71

GIFT OF EXHORTATION

*Preach the word; be ready in season and out of season; reprove,
rebuke, and exhort, with complete patience and teaching.*
—2 TIMOTHY 4:2 ESV

One of the prophetic ways that God speaks to us is through those who possess the gift of exhortation. We must understand that exhortation functions prophetically but exhortation is not solely prophecy. We are able to hear the voice of the Lord through this special gift. Are you a person who is concerned about adjusting error wherever and whenever you hear or see it? Are you deeply concerned with helping others avoid mistakes? Or if someone has already fallen due to a mistake, do you desire to see them repent of their ways and return to a walk of righteousness before God?

If you are that type of person, you may possess the motivational gift of exhortation. The apostle Paul was one of those key biblical figures who exemplified the gift of exhortation in his preaching. Here is the heart of Paul's purpose for apostolic ministry: *"Him we preach, warning every man and teaching every man in all wisdom, that we may present every man perfect in Christ Jesus. To this end I also labor, striving according to His working which works in me mightily"* (Col. 1:28-29 NKJV).

Moreover, in this above passage of Scripture the word warning is also translated as *exhorting* or *admonishing*. Even in the prophetic gift, when a prophet exhorts they are actually bringing precaution and adjustment to the one they are ministering to. It's bringing alignment to bring out the best results. For example, when a car needs a wheel alignment, the mechanic will tighten or replace what is damaged, corroded, or broken. Once the alignment is fixed the wheel is stronger, tighter, and works effectively for maximum performance. The gift of exhortation always has an element of caution and concern about it. The person who is exhorting is ultimately trying to see every Christian stay on track and take the narrow road in their Christian walk that leads to both heavenly and earthly reward.

Primarily, an individual who possess the gift of exhortation wants to see others mature in their faith. The exhorter desires to see that others are growing in their spiritual lives. Exhorters are people-oriented, discipleship-oriented, growth-oriented, and maturity-oriented. The exhorter is quick to inquire, "Where are you in your spiritual life? Are you growing? In what ways?" God will use people who see the best in you to follow up to make sure you are doing what God has purposed for you to do. An exhorter would be described like a life coach. They will tweak you until you are adjusted correctly.

72

GIFT OF GIVING

*Give, and it will be given to you. Good measure, pressed down,
shaken together, running over, will be put into your lap. For
with the measure you use it will be measured back to you.*
—LUKE 6:38 ESV

The Bible says that we are more blessed to give than to receive. I cannot tell you how many people I have come across in my Christian walk who hear the Lord say to them to sow financially in my life. These individuals are definitely sent by the Lord. But more importantly, they possess a motivational gift of giving. Generally speaking, these people possess a keen ability to make wise investments and purchases in order to have more money to give. These people are not stingy or selfish people. They are very generous, but with wisdom. God has gifted them with the ability to see and meet the financial needs of others. They become great financial donors, contributors, investors, sponsors, and business partners. They have been graced to make power moves that will bring projects to their completion.

Those who possess this gift of giving are great at budgeting and saving. They are not concerned about quantity but quality. Many people are bargain hunters and wise investors. The person with the gift of giving, however, seeks to save and to invest in order to have more to give. Many bargain hunters desire to save money so they can spend the savings on themselves; the person who is a giver desires to spend the savings on advancing the King and His Kingdom.

They are ones who will hear God and sow seeds to meet major projects such as mission trips, building project funds, land purchases, and commissioning of leaders or new church plants. They love and are moved with passion to get involved financially. Do you respond immediately to a need by saying, "What can I do? How can I help solve this need?" You may have the gift of giving. God will speak to someone to sow a significant amount of seed for others. We need those who possess this gift to hear God and obey. As the person hears the Lord specifically on what to give, God in turn supernaturally replenishes and restores back to them 30-, 60-, 90-, or even 1,000-fold. The people with this gift sow without expecting anything in return.

In addition, a person with this particular gift has the ability to motivate others to give by being accountable to a common cause. As a giver and person who possess this particular gift, I often can stir up others to sign on to what God wants to do. Someone with this gift normally gives discreetly or quietly, not drawing attention to themselves. God is going to use kingdom funders who are anointed and gifted to give. We need believers who possess this gift of giving to mark places that need the capital and funding. However, it's not just the responsibility of those with the gift of giving to sow, but every believer is called to give what they can.

People who have this gift are not concerned about personal accolades or praises of men. They hear God and sow accordingly to receive a heavenly reward and blessing from God. Those who possess the gift of giving understand that God will make room for them and bring them favor with men. In fact, their total emphasis is on meeting the need, not on having others acknowledge that they have met the need. Those with this gift often do not respond to great pressure to give or to ardent appeals by professional fundraisers. They want to give out of their own inner motivation, not from outward forced pressure.

God is looking for cheerful givers and I will go so far as to say even faithful sowers. The person with the gift of giving rejoices when they perceive that their financial seed is a financial miracle and answer to someone else's prayer. I am grateful for all the people who hear God and sow seeds into my life financially, and they in return see tremendous miracles, breakthrough, and favor.

Finally, those with the gift of giving are those who cheerfully love sharing what they have with others, whether it is financial, material, or the giving of personal time and attention. The giver is concerned for the needs of others and seeks opportunities to share goods, money, and time with them as needs arise.

73

GIFT OF RULING AND ORGANIZATION

Those who have the gift of leadership....
—1 CORINTHIANS 12:28 NLT

We know that everyone is not called to leadership positions. However, all can learn the life principle of being teachable, trained, and called to follow. I believe we are all leaders called of God in a specific area but we must find that place and work it faithfully. God uses those with the gift of leadership to organize, coordinate, direct, and rule. God speaks through those who are called to rule and organize His agenda and purposes. Those in leadership positions are not perfect but should be able to help by perfecting, leading, training, and serving others. The greatest among us should be the greatest servant.

Are you uncomfortable in a "leaderless" group? Do you feel restless or godly frustration if things seem to be out of order? You may be a person who possesses the motivational gift of organization. Those with this gift discern quickly what is out of order and needs to be done to bring proper adjustment to bring about a flow. This gift of leadership or organization can be often called the gift of leading, ruling, or the gift of administration.

The Greek word literally means "the one who stands out front." The person who has the gift of organization is frequently misunderstood. Often, this gift is looked at as not being very spiritual, or it is perceived as being a matter of solely human ambition to serve in that capacity. In man there is an innate ability and desire for power, authority, and to rule. I believe we should never lose sight that the Creator God created the universe, including mankind, with a strong sense and desire for order. God created everything strategically, purposefully, and in a very precise, sequential, and organized manner.

The church was designed by God as well to function with order, with all gifts of the Holy Spirit exercised in an orderly way. God is not the author of confusion. God has a system that must flow according to how He has established it. There needs to be those who will lead and are called to leadership. God will speak to us through leadership as long as the leadership has ears to hear the voice of God. I love what Hebrews 13:17 says: *"Have confidence in your leaders and submit to their authority, because they keep watch over you as those who must give an account. Do this so that their work will be a joy, not a burden, for that would be of no benefit to you."*

Those who are gifted with the gift of leadership/organization will be individuals who have an ability to see the "big picture" in a vision, project, and mission. These types of leaders carry a winning attitude to see the solution, outcome, and positive results over the problem. They possess the capacity to dream big and to believe that God desires to do something major. Those with the gift of organization are very positive that God-given goals can be accomplished with a goal-driven attitude. In addition, those with this gift possess the power to motivate others to action. They can see a problem and turn it into an answer.

Those with the gift of organization have an ability to methodically dissect and analyze large projects into bite-sized pieces. They are able to break down long-term objectives into a sequence of short-term goals and objectives. People gifted in leadership are self-starters and natural born leaders. Again, I must repeat that leaders are not perfect, just as there is no perfect follower. Leaders are gifted with the ability to oversee, govern, problem-solve, and take appropriate steps to see things through with excellence and professionalism.

I want to say that there is a difference between a leader and a manager. The difference is that leaders have people who are willing to follow them while a manager has people working for them. Just because someone is in management doesn't mean they are gifted and called to be a leader. However, every good leader knows how to lead and manage by first learning the art of following and being managed. God is raising up leaders who will lead by example. They are highly motivated to accomplish the goals that are before them. They take great joy in seeing the pieces of the larger puzzle fall into place one by one.

God will use and speak through godly leadership. They are gifted to rule, preside over, and manage other people in the church. The word literally means to "guide" and carries the idea of one who steers a ship. One with the gift of leadership rules with wisdom, grace, and exhibits the fruit of the Spirit in their own life as they lead by example. Leaders should be models of change and not exceptions to the rules.

74

GIFT OF MERCY

Blessed are the merciful, for they shall obtain mercy.
—MATTHEW 5:7 MEV

The Bible shares with us that we are blessed when we are merciful toward others. When we give mercy to others, we will obtain mercy. From a character standpoint it takes real compassion and wisdom to extend mercy to others. We can hear the voice of God through the Holy Spirit when it comes to giving mercy to the most complicated, unreasonable, and unjust people. Demonstrating mercy is not for just those who have the gift of mercy, but this is to admonish every disciple of Christ.

Do you have a real passion and love for people? Do you feel tenderness toward others? Are you concerned with finding ways of showing kindness? One of the flaws that I often encounter in some churches I visit to speak is that there is a lack of mercy if someone falls short. There is a critical and judgmental spirit that is released rather than the mercy of God toward the fallen. In addition, I have personally encountered other believers who express a double standard when it comes to sin.

We must show mercy and loving kindness to others even if they disagree with our theology. God desires to use people in the realm of mercy and release the love of God. If you are a person who often sees injustice and feels compelled to take action to defend others, I believe you may have the gift of mercy.

In the New Testament, the apostle John was one of those leaders who best exemplifies the gift of mercy. One of the foremost characteristics and signs of an individual gifted with mercy is love, and of all the apostles John is the one who wrote the most concerning the topic of love. He would expressively and emphatically write about the love of God, recite the Lord Jesus's admonishment to love one another, and encourage the early believers about love. John was considered Jesus's beloved and John would often refer to himself as "the one whom Jesus loved." To have been loved by Jesus was the highest commendation and the most meaningful mark of identification that John felt he could claim for himself.

Those with the gift of mercy have a great ability to feel empathy for a person, church, or a group of people. They have an "I understand," "feel your pain," and "sense your heart" in a matter. These people are moved with compassion and display the mercy of God in any situation. They are relatable people. I have experienced and witnessed this level of the mercy of God demonstrated when I was prophesying over a couple and sharing God's goodness. Most people in attendance knew personally what this couple just went through. I was able to speak the heart and mind of God and it was like everyone in the room was weeping in joy and celebrating. It was as if I was prophesying corporately because of the radical response. The mercy of God can bring the joy of the Lord and the love of God at the same time. The whole church was able to feel empathy for this couple and share in the prophetic word.

Have you heard someone getting blessed with a prophetic word or be given money for a personal need and you were moved to tears? Well that's what mercy filled with love looks like. Those who have the gift of mercy will feel your pain and will rejoice with you in gladness. Furthermore, those who possess this gift often have a heightened sense of discernment regarding the emotions of others. They rarely have to ask, "How are you doing?" They intuitively sense how others are feeling. This often is prophetic as well because most prophets, intercessors, and those who operate in some capacity of healing carry this type of gift or feel the mercy of God through the Holy Spirit. Those with a gift of mercy desire to see those who are hurting alleviated of their hurt. Those with a gift of mercy are able to identify with others and to vicariously experience what others are going through.

God speaks to someone and they reach out to me and feel what I am experiencing in my heart. When that happens they are able to minster effectively because they sense what's going on and can minister to me the way they would like to be ministered to. Hearing the voice of God through the lens of mercy will cause us to be kindhearted. I have personally witnessed the mercy of God blanket a whole congregation where deliverance, healing, and miracles broke out because of the love of God and His lovingkindness that draws us closer to Abba-Father.

75

GIFT OF HELPS

Those who can help others....
—1 CORINTHIANS 12:28 NLT

The Lord will always use and send people who will help and bless others. There are kind people in the world who will not sit back and let an elderly woman carry heavy bags. In addition, there are what I call "heroes" who go around doing good for others. As believers we should always keep in mind being there for others. God will speak to someone willing to make themselves available to be a blessing to someone else. There are people gifted with the ability to serve regardless of the duties. They will find it a joy and honor to serve His people in the house of God. I believe that leaders on the frontline should be gifted with the gift of helps. It comes with the territory, in my opinion.

Leaders are commissioned by God to help, serve, and bless others with their gifts unto the glory of God. Moreover, we can see that the spiritual gift of helps is one of the spiritual gifts in the Bible. The Greek word translated "helps" in First Corinthians 12:28 is found only there in the New Testament; therefore, the exact meaning of the gift of helps is somewhat obscure. The word translated "helps" means literally "to relieve, succor, participate in, and/ or support." Those with the gift of helps can aid or render assistance to others in the church with compassion and grace.

This gift has a broad range of applications, from helping individuals with daily chores to assisting in the administration of the affairs of the church. God will speak to and use people prophetically to assist others. Hearing the voice of God is imperative when it comes to helping and lending assistance to others, not just those you know personally. God speaks to me a lot in helping others and being a model of love like Jesus.

Jesus was in the help-others business. Jesus understood why He was sent to the earth to help the helpless. There is a laboring anointing upon those who are willing to give themselves to the work of God. God will speak to them and they will discreetly get things done. They are not looking for attention or praises at all. They love working behind the scenes and God will reward them, often publicly.

Helping in the Body of Christ can take a variety of forms. Some see the gift of helps as given to those who are willing to "lend a helping hand" and do even the most mundane and disagreeable tasks with a spirit of humility and grace. God will raise up helpers who will sacrifice and volunteer to work regularly around church buildings, properties, and grounds, often laboring in obscurity. These people are those who possess a keen sense of knowing what to do and when to do it. They are not title driven but servant driven. These people gifted with the gift of helps will serve in many different capacities in the church. They do their job with honor, excellence, and love.

76

GIFT OF GOVERNMENTS AND ADMINISTRATIONS

But be sure that everything is done properly and in order.
—1 CORINTHIANS 14:40 NLT

One of the prophetic ways that God speaks will be through those who are gifted in the area of administration. With any gift we have to understand that the Lord will use and equip someone who has His heart. God needs people who are able to hear His voice and by faith obey. There is a difference between someone with the gift of leadership, organization, and ruling than someone with the gift of administration or government. The ones with the gift of leadership will have those with the gift of administration working alongside to help bring organization and systematic flow.

God will speak to people with the gift of government to come alongside a leader in the church or Body of Christ to carry the heavy load. Depending on the size of a person's ministry or church they will need more than one individual who possess the gift of administration. This is a vital and most needed gift in the church today. If you are a leader or lead in some capacity you must hear the voice of God and be led in those you call to work with you. Everyone is not gifted in the area of administration or government. God will send those who are gifted and qualified to get the task done with less supervision.

Are you one who can handle multiple tasks and fulfill them effectively? Are you a team player but also doesn't require a lot of hand-holding? Do you have an ability to coordinate, manage, delegate responsibilities, and carry them out proficiently? Are you one who is creative in coming up with instant solutions and cannot handle disorder, confusion, and chaos? Then you may be one gifted with the gift of administration.

The spiritual gift of administration may not be one you thought you would have as a teen, but you'd probably recognize it more if we called it the spiritual gift of organization. This person will manage projects and is very efficient in what they do. People with this gift help save the church time and money by being able to see how things can be done better.

People with this gift are able to really see the details clearly. They are good problem solvers, and they keep their eyes on achieving a specific goal and are not distracted. They have an ability to organize information, money, individuals, projects, and more with little oversight. People with the spiritual gift of administration have a tendency to get so involved in how things should be done they forget about the people who are doing things. This insensitivity can lead to bullying or becoming closed-minded.

Also, individuals with this type of gift of government/administration can sometimes take on way too many projects at one time because their heart is to carry the load. The Lord might get pushed out of the picture because they are focused on the workload and forget the grace needed to do the job. With any gift we have to hear God so that we are not consumed, distracted, and forget that it is God who gifted us and not we ourselves. It's important for people with this gift to pray, fast, study the Word of God, and receive constant encouragement from their leaders.

People with the gift of administration tend to have a do-it-all mentality and will run the risk of being drained or burned out. They need other outlets to relax, regroup, and refocus. In addition, they must hear God so that they are not so focused on the work that their own personal dreams, visions, and prophetic words are not fulfilled. There must be a balance and God will speak to those with this gift to take a vacation, rest, and receive ministry as well.

People with this gift of administration are prone to focusing on the tasks at hand rather than meeting their own spiritual needs, objectives, goals, and prophetic promises of God. In addition, leaders must hear God and be sensitive to minister to those on their team, staff, or administration. Retreats and small meetings of appreciation are needed and should be considered for those are working diligently and faithfully behind the scenes. They are the real engine that makes the dream work with the help and direction of the Holy Spirit.

77

Anointed Minstrels, Musicians, and Worship Leaders

"Let our lord now command your servants who are before
you. Let them seek a man who is a skillful player on the
harp; and it shall come about when the evil spirit from God
is on you, that he shall play the harp with his hand, and you
will be well." So Saul said to his servants, "Provide for me
now a man who can play well and bring him to me."
—1 Samuel 16:15-17 NASB

Music can communicate without words and penetrate the hearts of men. God will speak through and use worship leaders such as in the days of David. Asaph, a Levite, was a skillful prophetic worship leader, one of the leaders of David's choir (1 Chron. 6:39). Psalms 50 and 73 to 83 are attributed to him. He is mentioned along with David as skilled in music and a "seer" (2 Chron. 29:30).

God is raising up anointed minstrels and worship leaders who release the sound of heaven. They have an ear to hear what the Lord is singing and saying prophetically. We need worship leaders and minstrels who understand their gift and bring glory to the name of the Lord through it. The spirit of prophecy is the testimony of Jesus initiated through worship.

At this I fell at his feet to worship him. But he said to me, "Don't do that! I am a fellow servant with you and with your brothers and sisters who hold to the testimony of Jesus. Worship God! For it is the Spirit of prophecy who bears testimony to Jesus (Revelation 19:10).

I have heard the song of the Lord through anointed minstrels playing keys, notes, and chords that unlock the prophetic well on the inside of me. Prophets have the ability to hear something in the spirit and release it through song. Often as I am praying over a service or in a meeting, the music played by someone skillful causes the prophetic anointing to come on me to prophesy. God is using anointed and skillful minstrels and worship leaders to become prophetic.

Minstrels and worship and praise leaders carry a great responsibility to set the atmosphere for the glory of the Lord to come. They are called to go before us to pave the way for God to come. An anointed minstrel or in other words a Spirit-filled musician can create an invitation. In addition, there is an *asaph* anointing that is coming upon worship leaders who are passionately and madly in love with Jesus to usher people into that place of intense worship.

Prophetic worship leaders have an ear to release not only a sound but prophetic action in the words they sing. Like intercessors, anointed worship leaders have a powerful responsibility to discern the atmosphere to usher people into victory mode or warfare mode through songs. They prophesy through songs and coordinate by directing the minstrels to go in a different direction as the Lord leads them.

They have a powerful gifting to cause the heavens to open over a service or region. There is a sound of freedom released that rallies the people to get in one accord. I have been in settings where the worship leaders, background singers, and band, in one accord, created a culture of glory and breakthrough. Before the pastor or senior leader got up to speak the atmosphere had already been tilled and cultivated to receive the message. God is raising up worship leaders who are prophetic psalmists who will flow with the Spirit of God and not be bound to programmatic or systematic songs that are out dated.

The *asaph* anointing is prophetic worship that brings about change instantaneously. The "sons of Asaph," mentioned in First Chronicles 20:14 and Ezra 2:41, were his descendants, or more probably a class of poets or singers who recognized him as their master. We must have anointed and skillful musicians, worship and praise leaders with a heart to play and sing prophetically. Prophets love these types of minstrels who can create an environment for the presence of God and prophetic utterance.

Minstrels, anointed musicians, and worship and praise leaders are called to hear the voice of God as well. We as believers can hear the voice of God through anointed vessels of the worship while appreciating their ministry to the Body of Christ. Oftentimes, minstrels, musicians, and worship and praise leaders are not respected and honored in the church as they should be. I have personally made it my business to prophesy and minister to musicians, worship and praise leaders, dancers, ushers, and whomever. We should never overlook people because they seem to not be primarily in the forefront. We need anointed music, minstrels, and those able to play under the anointing and power of God.

78

ORDINARY PEOPLE, BELIEVERS, AND STRANGERS

This is one interesting prophetic way God speaks because anyone can be used by the Lord. There are ordinary people, strangers, and other Christians who will come with the Word of the Lord. We can hear God speaking through just about anybody. I believe we have to be open to tune in and pay close attention; then we have the ability to receive. I cannot tell you how many times the Lord will speak through people I don't know to bring confirmation of something I have been praying for.

God using someone who is not a believer or prophetic to confirm something I been praying for is mind-blowing. We cannot limit who and how God wants to get something across to us. This prophetic way God speaks is one of my favorites because whenever I pray I expect God to send me the most unusual people. He tends to keep a good track record regarding this. God has use ordinary people at a bus stop or at the city library to encourage, bless, or pray for me. I believe we block our blessings because we have our own religious lens and preconceived thoughts on who the Lord will use.

God can be sending us an angel in disguise to release the Word of the Lord. Throughout my life and Christian walk I have met some great believers who have offered me tremendous wisdom, godly advice, information, and even an occasional prayer, prophetic word, and a word of knowledge that was spot on. In addition, I have come across random people in unusual places in unusual circumstances who come with answers to what I have been praying and fasting about, and oddly these people are not believers. However, through casual conversation they would all of a sudden talk about something specific I may be dealing with personally or something I needed affirmation about. I would be standing there with tears coming down my face because they would be talking and the love of God would be speaking through them. I don't look at the outward appearance; I look and hear the Father speaking and using them for that moment.

Honestly, it is my prayer that God always use me in this way when I come across not just fellow believers in Christ but anyone. I want to be a voice of the Lord for someone. I enjoy being in covenant relationships with others radical believers who are lovers of Christ, studying His Word with them, and being transparent enough to admit I don't have it all figured in my own personal life all the time. Connecting with other believers will fine-tune your ability to hear God.

When I was in my sophomore year in college attending Marshall University in Huntington, West Virginia, I surrounded myself with other believers who were sensitive enough to hear God and minister to me. They looked to me as a leader and I always had a prophetic word of encouragement for each of them, but when I was down they would in turn minister the Word of God to me. There is nothing wrong with people who love you and release the love of the Father to you in your most vulnerable seasons.

Not everyone we cross paths with will be sent, but there are times we will meet people by coincidence who will connect us to our purpose. Most individuals we encounter in our daily lives are going to share their ideas, thoughts, opinions, and experience, with us at some point. Those thoughts and experience, will have the ability to impact us or influence us. In conservation there may be something you hear that sparks an interest or opens up a further dialogue, whether it's on beliefs, theology, current events, politics, family, or life itself. You may hear something a person said on a phone call with someone else or they might have commented out loud on a social media post they read and sparked a conversation with you. No matter who the person is, God may have a greater purpose in mind for casual conversations, so we must be open and ready to listen.

Prophetically speaking I have come across many people whom I have different views with but ended up agreeing one way or another throughout the conversation. Differences shouldn't divide us, just as doctrines shouldn't. Healthy dialogues and conversations should be welcomed because when we converse with others we may or may not realize when someone is being utilized by the Lord to communicate His truth to us. There may be an instant connection between what someone is revealing to you and what God is showing you, but it could also take some time to understand. God can be using someone to stretch your faith or challenge your theology to seek more understanding and draw closer to God.

God will use strangers to speak words of life and comfort when you least expect it. I have had children, the elderly, the less fortunate, and people from different cultural backgrounds speak life to me. The voice of the Lord is not locked into our own geographical, theological, and psychological grid. God uses and speaks through whomever, whenever, and anywhere. God used a donkey to talk, so what's wrong with those different from us? We have to ask ourselves, does everyone we encounter have to be a Christian to share truth, wisdom, and understanding? No! There is a saying that we are not to judge a book by its cover. I agree—the content carries the true reality of a person's life and message.

We shouldn't ignore anyone who crosses our path in life. They may be God-sent. However, we must take precautions and discern what we hear from others and discard anything that isn't of God. If anyone brings a message or a prophetic word that causes you to think, take it to God and ask for Him for further clarity. Ask the Father to confirm whether the person is speaking on His behalf and if this is a confirmation sent by Him. Or use your spiritual discernment to distinguish what source, spirit, and agenda it is coming from.

There will be times in your life when God will be using you to speak to others on His behalf. You must be open and willing to speak at any time. The Bible says to be ready in season and out of season. There are times I don't feel like ministering to anyone prophetically and God will create unusual circumstances and have me meet people I don't know. The Word of the Lord will be strong on me when I am conversing with a stranger. God will use ordinary people to speak messages, wisdom, and revelation to us. God wants to use ordinary people to do extraordinary things.

Hearing the voice of God is always an exciting part of our Christian walk. You may experience a nudge or feeling of being pushed to share a story, give a piece of your own testimony of faith, or even share hard truth from the Bible. It will likely seem awkward or difficult, but when this happens, pay attention. Your words might not be your own! Throughout the Bible God used ordinary people to bring His message to His people. He's still doing it today—and not just through pastors in the pulpit but apostles, prophets, evangelists, teachers, strangers, children, elderly, coworkers, and other believers in Christ.

When you are in touch with God's Word, the Holy Spirit's promptings become clearer. We never know who we will come in contact with who will transform our lives. Likewise, you may be able to take part in transforming the lives of others by being obedient to the voice of the Lord to speak when asked or led to do so. Sometimes you are just speaking and it's as though the words are flowing from your lips before you ever think them as thoughts. They are so brilliantly wise and on point that they just couldn't be your own. That's the Holy Spirit talking. But remember to always be vigilant with your words. It is imperative that we carefully examine our motives to be sure we aren't misconstruing our own messages as His. This takes intention, self-control in the moment, and patience to wait and pray before speaking something that can't be taken back. Ordinary people and strangers will bring a word that will help you in your journey with Jesus.

79

CHILDREN

*From the mouth of infants and nursing babes You
have established strength because of Your adversaries,
to make the enemy and the revengeful cease.*
—PSALM 8:2 NASB

God can speak not just through adults but through children and use their precious gifts to bless us and bring Him glory. Babies and children are pure, innocent, inquisitive, explorative, and sensitive. God can speak through children often to get our undivided attention or make us inquire what they actually said. My niece Jasmin Collins would see things and tell me what they looked like. I knew she was able to see into the spiritual realm. She would describe angels that looked like men and would often see demon spirits and describe it like the face of Elmo, the Sesame Street character. She didn't think that Elmo creature was pleasant and she would scream and say, "Elmo is looking at me."

Children and babies are sensitive to the spiritual realm and don't even know it. They are able to have vivid dreams, prophetic encounters, and share what they experience unfiltered. I recall a powerful prophetic text message that I received from a married couple about their four-year-old daughter named Hannah, who heard the voice of the Lord. This is the text message from Hannah's mother Nadine that brought tears to my eyes:

> So when I was pregnant with Hannah, God revealed to me a ton of things about her. Since she's been able to talk Hannah has revealed

things to us and they have come to pass. So today, just a regular Monday, Julian prayed with the girls before dinner and when they were finished Hannah said, "He (referring to God) will talk back?" And Julian said, "Yes, if you sit down, be quiet, and listen, He'll talk back to you." We continued with what we were doing while starting a new conversation, when suddenly Hannah walked up to us and said, "We have to be quiet so we can hear what God is saying!" She was so serious about hearing from God after prayer that Julian replied, "Okay, we'll be quiet." However, something surprising happened— she got up again and said to us intently that we must be quiet so she can hear what God is saying. Again we took her request seriously as the house got silent and we replied okay. Minutes later Hannah came over to us and said, "I heard Him! He spoke to me!" My husband and I asked her, "What did He say?" And she said that God says thank you for saying all those nice things about me in prayer!

God not only speaks to and through children and babes but He will speak through born-again believers and newbies in Christ. God will speak to His children who may not be chronologically young but spiritually young. God's children can hear his voice even though they may not be young in age. God wants to speak to us, but are we listening? God wants us to come before Him with a childlike faith and He will speak to us if we are willing to listen and obey. The children of God all throughout the Old Testament were in direct covenant and communication with the Lord.

80

SPIRITUALLY SEASONED MEN AND WOMEN OF GOD

Teach the older men to be temperate, worthy of respect, self-controlled, and sound in faith, in love and in endurance.
—TITUS 2:2

God speaks through men and women who are seasoned enough to realize their errors and can prevent you from repeating any problems or issues. God use seniors and seasoned men and women who possess wisdom to help protect your from unnecessary attacks. Seasoned men are to bring discipline to the young men in the faith and the older women to train the young women how to conduct themselves in their daily affairs. The season men and women are to be good teachers. God uses them as great models and examples of life but most importantly in the faith. I have benefited greatly in my Christian walk by having older women and men of God in the faith to be accountable to.

> *Do not rebuke an older man harshly, but exhort him as if he were your father. Treat younger men as brothers* (1 Timothy 5:1).

The Bibles says in Proverbs 29:18, *"Where there is no prophetic vision the people cast off restraint, but blessed is he who keeps the law"* (ESV). In other words, where there is no prophetic vision, revelation, divine guidance, and prophecy the people are unaccountable. God will use men and women who carry vision for others to commit to.

God speaks through spiritual leaders whom we may relate with. Spiritual fathers, mothers, mentors, coaches, and counselors will keep us accountable. The voice of the Lord will be released through people who have your best interests at heart. There is safety in a multitude of advisors. God has sent me spiritual leaders to whom I am able to reach out to keep me humble, sharper, and relevant.

> *He who goes about as a talebearer reveals secrets, but he who is trustworthy conceals a matter. Where there is no guidance the people fall, but in abundance of counselors there is victory. He who is guarantor for a stranger will surely suffer for it, but he who hates being a guarantor is secure* (Proverbs 11:13-15 NASB).

God will send you people who are wise, smart, and loving who will tell you the truth. My prayer is not that God sends me people who will give me sugar but people who will keep me seasoned with salt. The Bible says that we are the salt of the earth and light of the world. The Lord will use people in your life to keep you current, relevant, and up to date. Just as we are given natural parents and guardians in our lives, we should have spiritual fathers and mothers to cultivate us.

I realized that the most important wisdom I received didn't come from reading the Book of Proverbs but through the prophetic revelation, divine guidance, prophecy, and vision given by those I am in covenant relationship with. There is something amazing about hearing the voice of God and seeing the love of the Father through spiritual leaders. Samuel heard the voice of the Lord through a familiar voice in Eli. Samuel ministered unto the Lord before he ever encountered God personally. He had to learn how to serve the Lord first and later came the encounter. He was dedicated back to the Lord by his mother Hannah. He was dedicated to serve the Lord in the priesthood.

Later, God called him to the prophetic ministry as well. He learned to serve under a spiritual leader until God Himself revealed and called him personally. First Samuel 3:1 says, *"The boy Samuel ministered before the Lord under Eli. In those days the word of the Lord was rare; there were not many visions."* In those days there was no prophetic vision due to the closed spiritual climate. Eli was responsible for the spiritual environment as a high priest. He was to steward and keep the priesthood sacred. He allowed his own sons to do whatever without holding them accountable. The prophetic revelation, direction, vision, and frequency were scarce. The heavens were closed because of Eli's lack of spiritual vision.

God use the young prophet Samuel to bring back holiness and the order that God required out of Eli's leadership. Samuel later was sent to anoint King David and the prophetic voice was established through the school of the prophets.

God calls the young because they are strong and He calls the seasoned because they know the way. There is a balance in this and there will be a merging of generations respecting each other's differences, especially in age. God is doing a new thing, but He hasn't removed or done way with the foundational things. I believe the young need the old and the old need the young. We are not to be an island to ourselves. Everybody needs someone in their life to help them along the way. Regardless how old we become we are not done with learning something.

We are living in a lone-ranger Christianity and society where there are those who refuse to listen to wise spiritual advisors. Some believe they don't have to submit and run spiritual things by those in authority. I believe that God's plan for the Spirit-filled believer in this hour is submission to the local church. There is nothing wrong with conferences, seminars, webinars, and workshops by other spiritual leaders that provide extra training, education, equipping, and impartation. But we should also be connected to a local pastor and network of other believers.

As I travel the nations I have those whom I hear the wisdom of God from who keep me grounded in my faith. These individuals I trust with my spiritual condition and soul. Whenever there is a dark area in my soul, these covenant leaders and peers are able to pick me up and minister to me. In addition, I have submitted to not just one alignment but several people who can correct, adjust, assess, and hold me accountable for the doctrine I share.

As a public figure and prophetic leader in the Body of Christ my submission to other apostolic and prophetic leaders keeps me protected, guarded, and aligned. Every Spirit-filled believer should be a part of a local church but also voluntarily put themselves under the accountability of that local leadership to serve that church in their spiritual gifts. I have several vertical and horizontal spiritual alignments. I have a primary spiritual covering and secondary, third, and fourth accountabilities.

Having a mentor, coach, and spiritual father and mother is great, but make sure you also have a pastor and church to get fed from as well. I believe you should have more than one true voice speaking in your life. God will send people in your life who will be experts in areas your pastor is not called to. Find people who know the voice of God and have your best interests in mind. Now, for millennials this may be a tough pill to swallow. The word *submission* to some is *control* in their mindset.

God is not using vagabonds, renegades, and lone rangers. Some young people may ask, "Why should I let a pastor or anybody control my life?" However, the truth of the matter is this—the Word of God talks consistently of the importance and the value of wisdom. Submission and having a spiritual covering is not control but wisdom. Wisdom is the ability to make good, spiritual, God-honoring decisions. However, there are some young people who lack the wisdom of God.

This is why I believe it is so necessary among millennials that we learn the principle of sitting at the feet of spiritual leaders such as pastors, parents, mentors, advisors, and seasoned men and women of God. Every major decision I have ever made in my life I have done with the approval and consent of my pastor. Why? I trust my pastor. He's a man whom God has sovereignly put into my life to assist in my spiritual walk. Pastors are given a great responsibility to become watchmen over our souls, and we are in their care or under their covering.

> *Obey them that have the rule over you, and submit yourselves: for they watch for your souls, as they that must give account, that they may do it with joy, and not with grief: for that is unprofitable for you* (Hebrews 13:17 KJV).

You know what? I've been tremendously blessed every time I made the personal decision to submit myself under good leadership. I have people who speak into my life during the most crucial seasons and they help me get delivered, healed, and whole again. It's a mutual submission as the Bible says that we are to submit one to another in Christ (Eph. 5:21).

81

God's Correction and Judgment

From infancy you have known the Holy Scriptures, which are able to make you wise for salvation through faith in Christ Jesus. All Scripture is God-breathed and is useful for teaching, rebuking, correcting and training in righteousness, so that the servant of God may be thoroughly equipped for every good work.
—2 Timothy 3:15-17

God is a Father and He speaks by correcting us as His children. God only disciplines those He loves. As children of God we will experience the Father's love and even chastening that brings alignment, adjustment, and correction to our spiritual walk and relationship with Daddy-God. Growing in the prophetic and learning the voice of God, I have learned to recognize His voice as a Father who addresses, speaks, and deals with His children. Job 5:17 declares, *"Blessed is the one whom God corrects; so do not despise the discipline of the Almighty."* We are blessed when we allow God to reprove us and do not despise His discipline:

> *Discipline me, Lord, but only in due measure—not in your anger, or you will reduce me to nothing* (Jeremiah 10:24).

> *Because the Lord disciplines those he loves, as a father the son he delights in* (Proverbs 3:12).

God corrects those He loves, and through that correction we are saved from hell's grip. Oftentimes, we don't like to be corrected or judged but sometimes it is needed to bring understanding. The children of Israel disobeyed the instructions of God. They broke the covenant that He established with them. There were conditions to the covenant that the Lord had given them. Those covenants were not hard ones to follow, but His people constantly broke them. When they broke them, it would break the Lord's heart. His children whom He loved were at one point wanting to be like other nations to have a king over them.

The Lord was their King. This attitude of His people desiring a king to be like pagan nations angered the Lord. He gave them what they wanted to prove that earthly kings will let them down. God also wanted godly kings that He chose. They also broke His covenant. God brought national judgment and correction to His people and turned them over to their lusts to cause His people to turn their hearts and love back to Him. God wanted to be in direct relationship and fellowship with His people.

They were not like other nations. They were set apart and a chosen nation. God wanted them to know who they were and the power they possessed. He ultimately kept His covenant promise that was fulfilled through His Son Jesus Christ. God speaks through judgment and correction to allow His people to repent and come back to Him. We have the Holy Spirit now to reveal things concerning the Father's will for our lives but also convict us of sin. Hearing the voice of God is not just for good things but we should be open for reproach, correction, alignment, and the Lord's chastening.

82

PEACE OF GOD

*And let the peace of God rule in your hearts, to the which
also ye are called in one body; and be ye thankful.*
—Colossians 3:15 KJV

When God speaks to our hearts, He gives us a deep sense of internal peace to confirm the message is truly from Him. Jesus said, *"Peace I leave with you; my peace I give you. I do not give to you as the world gives. Do not let your hearts be troubled and do not be afraid"* (John 14:27). When confusion, chaos, and disorder is all around us there is nothing like having the peace of God. The peace of God is something that I have come to learn to understand. I have learned how to tap into the inner peace of God that surpasses my own understanding. I know how to close myself in and hear the voice of God.

The peace of God will calm every inner storm that arises. I remember when there was a fire several doors from my home and everyone on the block was panicking because they didn't want the fire to reach their homes. One neighbor asked me why I was so calm. I responded that I was happy that I was still alive and made it out safe and no one was hurt or killed. That is the peace of God. God spoke to me right then to respond to my neighbor.

I didn't have much of an answer, but I heard the Lord bring to my mind, "Hakeem, you are alive, and you can build another home, but I cannot build another you." God speaks to us even in the midst of disarray and turmoil. I have learned how to mute the noise and get focused on what the Lord desires to reveal to me. We as believers must not allow the enemy to distract us. You have the power to take control of the situation and not panic but release the peace of God.

When the devil comes to speak to us, he cannot give us peace in our hearts. We might experience peace emotionally, but emotional peace won't last. Only spiritual peace of the Lord will endure to the end. If we attempt to solve things with our own reasoning, power, and understanding, we cannot experience lasting internal peace. The mind of the flesh (which is sense and reason without the Holy Spirit) is death (death that comprises all the miseries arising from sin, both here and hereafter). But the mind of the Holy Spirit is life and peace (both now and forever) according Romans 8:6.

When this happens we need to go to prayer; sometimes we need to ask, and other times just to be still and listen. When we do and we hear from God and we know we are doing His will, we will have peace. There will be an uneasiness or check in our spirit when we are not to do something. If we have conflict within ourselves God tells us how to resolve it. *"Thou wilt keep him in perfect peace, whose mind is stayed on thee: because he trusteth in thee"* (Isa. 26:3).

Therefore, we must keep our mind on the Lord and trust Him and we will have that inner perfect peace in our lives because we trusted totally in God in all things. Maybe it will take a little time to build up that trust. When we permit this peace of God to rule and reign in our hearts, our lives can be directed by the Lord through the recognition of His peace. If there is inner peace we can proceed. If our inner peace is gone there is a problem and we need to look to God. Ask the Lord to speak to your heart and download His peace.

I remember a time when I lost several close family members back to back and I felt so overwhelmed emotionally. I felt targeted by the enemy. When I started to pray, God supernaturally brought peace to my heart out of nowhere; I felt unnecessary burdens and stress lift off my heart. God's peace overwhelmed my heart. God's peace resolved any fears, paranoia, and depressions. God's word breaks the power and stronghold of the enemy over our mind.

83

Journaling, Writing, and Scribing

My heart overflows with a pleasing theme; I address my verses
to the king; my tongue is like the pen of a ready scribe.
—Psalm 45:1 ESV

There is something powerful about journaling and writing what God is saying. We know the Bible was written by men who were inspired by God.
The Logos is the written Word of God. Jesus said man shall not live by bread
alone but every word that proceeds out of the mouth of God. God will speak
through you by what you write. After prayer I oftentimes will sit quiet and
then write what I hear the Lord says to me personally. It becomes a prophetic
word for me for the day.

My book *Heaven Declares: Prophetic Decrees to Start Your Day* was a book
that I wrote as a 90-day devotional where God spoke to me daily. If you don't
have that book, I would suggest you get it to see what I am saying concerning
prophetic writings. There is something powerful about journaling and recording what you hear the Lord say. I started out in the prophetic with writing the
words of prophecies. I would start or activate in it by writing this, for example:

The Word of the Lord came to me, saying, _____
_____ _____

Starting out like this will start the conversation to hear God and write
what I believe He is saying to my spirit. I would write blogs, articles for major

publications, and prophecies that would bless people. Most of my daily journaling after prayer or studying the Word of God would become book chapters, preaching or teaching messages, or prophetic words. I would also journal revelation that I get from the Lord or dreams or visions that I receive. Prophetic people must be people who record by journaling what they hear from the Lord.

In addition writing your ministry, church, business, or life vision, goals and objectives can be inspired by God. *"And the Lord answered me: 'Write the vision; make it plain on tablets, so he may run who reads it'"* (Hab. 2:2 ESV). Moses wrote the Ten Commandments on the tablets of stones. *"It came about, when Moses finished writing the words of this law in a book until they were complete"* (Deut. 31:24 NASB). God will cause us to journal and write down what He says prophetically.

What is a scribe? *Easton's Bible Dictionary* defines scribes as:

> Anciently held various important offices in the public affairs of the nation. The Hebrew word so rendered (sopher) is first used to designate the holder of some military office (Judg. 5:14; A.V., "pen of the writer;" RSV, "the marshal's staff;" marg., "the staff of the scribe"). The scribes acted as secretaries of state, whose business it was to prepare and issue decrees in the name of the king (2 Sam. 8:17; 20:25; 1 Chron. 18:16; 24:6; 1 Kings 4:3; 2 Kings 12:9-11; 18:18-37, etc.). They discharged various other important public duties as men of high authority and influence in the affairs of state. There was also a subordinate class of scribes, most of whom were Levites. They were engaged in various ways as writers. Such, for example, was Baruch, who *"wrote from the mouth of Jeremiah all the words of the Lord"* (Jer. 36:4; 32).[1]

God will use prophetic scribes who will write prophetic words to leaders and even scribe what was prophesied by a prophet. God is raising up anointed authors who will write content and messages that will equip, train, educate, and impart into people. God will use the pen of the ready writer to release the oracles of God for their generation. We can hear God through anointed books, articles, blogs, social media posts, memes, memoirs, etc. God is going to speak to us in times of prayer, fasting, and devotion unto Him to write what's on

God's heart according to God's Word. You will learn how profound, accurate, and easy it is to hear the voice of God when you write or journal your thoughts.

The Scriptures are clear that God has spoken. He's deliberately chosen to reveal specific aspects of Himself and His character to us. He's interacted with certain men and women from the beginning of history. But while God has revealed Himself perfectly and accurately, how can we trust that the prophets and apostles have accurately passed on this information and message to us? More importantly, how could God Himself trust the prophets and apostles to accurately remember and convey everything He told them? How could God be assured they'd make no mistakes as they transmitted His message to others?

The answer is inspiration. When the spokesman was in the process of passing the message along either by writing it down or by speaking it, God exerted a power, an influence upon that person in a way that guaranteed what this person said would be what God wanted him to say or write. This influence is what we call inspiration. It enabled them to communicate without error or omission those truths, received through revelation or otherwise, which God deemed necessary for our salvation and service. Inspiration is one of the prophetic ways God speaks through the Holy Spirit. When it comes to writing a book, letter, poem, song, composing music, prayers, journaling, and so much more, everything we do in God should be under the inspiration of the Holy Spirit. I am not saying that we should be anointed 24 hours a day, 7 days a week. But what we do for God should be lead and done by the Holy Spirit's inspiration and influence.

NOTE

1. *Easton's Bible Dictionary*, s.v. "scribe," accessed April 24, 2019, https://www.blueletterbible.org/search/Dictionary/viewTopic.cfm ?topic=ET0003241.

84

TIMES AND SEASONS

Preach the word! Be ready in season and out of season. Convince,
rebuke, exhort, with all longsuffering and teaching.
—2 TIMOTHY 4:2 NKJV

God speaks in seasons of our lives. There are times when the Lord will be silent and times when He will speak more than ever before. When the Lord is silent, that doesn't mean He is upset with us or we did anything wrong. God loves to be pursued. In addition, I have come to find out that the Lord may be silent because you are already doing what you have been called to do. He will speak at times to give direction and guidance when we have reached the close of a season.

> *To everything there is a season, a time for every purpose under heaven* (Ecclesiastes 3:1 NKJV).

The Bible gives us a better understanding of what times and seasons are purposed for:

> *To every thing there is a season, and a time to every purpose under the heaven* (Ecclesiastes 3:1 KJV).

> *The eyes of all look expectantly to You, and You give them their food in due season* (Psalm 145:15 NKJV).

> *A word spoken in due season, how good is it!* (Proverbs 15:23 KJV)

And let us not be weary in well doing: for in due season we shall reap, if we faint not (Galatians 6:9 KJV).

The word translated "time" means "a point in time." Within any given season, there is a point in time in which God has ordained everything to happen. Within the season of our older youth, my brother Naim and I decided to attend college after spending two years working after graduating. We were in the season of our early 20s, but the time for enrollment was on August 21st for the fall semester at Delaware State University in Dover, Delaware. So we can see that season means a period of time and time means a point in time. There was a point in time that we made a decision to further our education during the season of our youth.

This somewhat explains Solomon's thesis—every activity of mankind has a proper time and a predetermined duration. However, our lives will be stress free if we recognize that the omniscient hand of God has appointed a time when things are to be done, and He has a predetermined duration for those things to last. The voice of God is imperative in our daily walk so that God can give us direction and encouragement on our journey to fulfill His prophetic purpose. God is not blinded or taken by surprise when sudden things occur in our lives. I look at things as ordained by God. We must seize the times and seasons that we are in. Maximize the time given to you.

Solomon revealed seasons and times in Ecclesiastes 3:1 and then demonstrated how this process of time fitting into a season takes place. For example, in verse 2 he declares, *"A time to be born and a time to die, a time to plant and a time to uproot."* This is now speaking of the cycle of time. The text exclaims that nature has a season of growth, but within that season there is a time to plant and a time to harvest. The life cycle has a season of birthing, but within that season there is also a time to die. So with any seed, it must be planted and the seed dies, but the real purpose will emerge or live. Life is like sowing seeds—you sow first, then, after a duration of time, you harvest. How often we allow the tyranny of time to rob us of the patience of seasons. There's also the process of constructing and destroying or tearing down.

Time is limited to man. We live in a physical world with its dimensions of length, width, height (or depth), and time. However, God dwells in a different dimension—the spirit realm—beyond the perception of our physical senses.

It's not that God isn't real; it's a matter of His not being limited by the physical laws and dimensions that govern our world (see Isa. 57:15).

In Psalm 90:4, Moses the prophet used a simple yet profound analogy in describing the timelessness of God: *"A thousand years in your sight are like a day that has just gone by, or like a watch in the night."* The eternity of God is contrasted with the temporality of man. Our lives are short and frail, but God does not weaken or fail with the passage of time. A thousand years in God's eyes are like one day that has passed in the realm of man. The number *one thousand* speaks of and represents eternity. It's a symbolic number of the eternal nature of God that cannot be figured out.

God does not count time as man does, but God understands time because He has given it to man. We must know that God is above and outside of the sphere of time. God sees all of eternity past and eternity future in one moment. The time that passes on earth is of no consequence from God's timeless perspective and paradigm. A second is no different from an eon; a billion years pass like seconds to the eternal God. In a sense, the marking of time is irrelevant to God because He transcends it. The apostle Peter, in 2 Peter 3:8, warned those present that they shouldn't allow this one critical fact escape their notice—that the Lord's view on time is far different and greater than mankind's perspective (see Ps. 102:12,24-27).

As believers it's hard to fathom or comprehend this idea of eternity or the timelessness of God; we in our finite minds try to confine an infinite God to our time schedule. Those who foolishly demand that God operate according to their time frame ignore the fact that He is the *"high and exalted One...who lives forever"* (Isa. 57:15). Our destiny was planned *"before the beginning of time"* (2 Tim. 1:9; Tit. 1:2) and *"before the creation of the world"* (Eph. 1:4; 1 Pet. 1:20). *"By faith we understand that the universe was formed at God's command, so that what is seen was not made out of what was visible"* (Heb. 11:3). In other words, the physical universe we see, hear, feel, and experience was created not from existing matter but from a source independent of the physical dimensions we can perceive.

"God is spirit" (John 4:24), and, correspondingly, God is timeless rather than being eternally in time or being beyond time. I believe that time was simply created by the Lord as a limited part of His creation for accommodating

the workings of His purpose in His disposable universe (2 Pet. 3:10-12). Time and seasons are for mankind to fulfill what they were created to fulfill in the time and season that they were born in. You were not an accident. God created you on purpose for a purpose to fulfill your God-ordained destiny. You were a prophecy spoken out of eternity past to come forth as a fulfilled seed to bring about change to the present and, possibly, future!

85

HOLY SPIRIT LEADS,
CHECKS, AND PROMPTS

For those who are led by the Spirit of God are the children of God.
—ROMANS 8:14

The Holy Spirit will give us indicators in our spirits that will alarm or alert us. God uses Holy Spirit leadings and spiritual checkers in our spirit to get our attention. These are the most common ways that God speaks to His people. We are not to ignore these inner red flags, gut feelings, and markers. There are times you cannot miss them because they become stronger than other times.

I recall a time when I was driving to work one morning and I got a strong gut feeling that there was going to be an accident. I was concerned because I didn't get a feeling that it was me personally, per se, but I sensed something was going to happen. In other words, there was a check in my spirit by the Spirit of God to make a decision. The Holy Spirit was speaking to me through an impression in my stomach that cautioned me. The Holy Spirit was leading me to take an alternate path to work. The more I tried to ignore what I was sensing and feeling by the Spirit of God, the more intense the check got.

In my mind, I was like, "That way will make me late to work." God repeated what He said, "Go another way!" Finally, I obeyed what the Lord was doing within me and I went another direction to work. When I got to work suddenly we got news that there was a fatal accident on the highway heading into the city of Wilmington, Delaware. It was exactly at the time and place where I made the decision to get off of that particular road. There was a multiple car pileup that took the lives of several people. It was very tragic and heartbreaking. My colleagues were calling in late for work because of the accident. They were stuck in a two-hour traffic jam. God spared my life and maneuvered me out of the devil's grips. I was so grateful that I heard the Lord speak to me through the check in my spirit.

The Holy Spirit's churning and checks in our spirit are God's warning signals. In addition, those inner impressions can also tell us that God is not pleased with our conduct, ways, etc. God was speaking to me but it was my decision to respond. The Lord is always speaking to us and our first thought can be the Lord dropping something on us to make a life decision. The Father does not want to see harm done to His people.

We cannot allow our own program, stubbornness, and routine to make us miss what God wants to do in and through our lives. He saved my life because that same truck was in front of me before I made that final decision to change plans. I was so concerned about being late to work, but God was concerned about my life and wellbeing. God will speak to us this way more often than we think. We have to trust our instinct and go with it. He will speak through our natural instincts when we are yielded to the Holy Spirit's impressions on the inside of us.

Can you imagine if I didn't obey the leading of the Holy Spirit and ignored those checks in my spirit? I wouldn't be here to tell you how important it is to be led of the Holy Spirit. I don't question what I sense in my gut feeling. I don't ignore any repetitive checks and nudging in my spirit. I am not looking for any outward sign or impression, but those Holy Spirit checks always seems to bless me one way or another.

God will lead us to do something remarkable for someone or lead us to do something uncomfortable that feels like it's not God but it is. God's ways of doing things will oftentimes feel uncomfortable. That is why faith is required and He is pleased when we act in faith. Holy Spirit's communication will challenge us to do and say things that we wouldn't normally say or do. In addition to communicating a direct message to you, the Holy Spirit can also give you "leadings" on what to do and what not to do. It is the job of the Holy Spirit to lead us in this life. Jesus Himself was also willing to be led by the Holy Spirit when He was walking down here on our earth in the flesh.

> *For those who are led by the Spirit of God are the children of God* (Romans 8:14).
>
> *Then Jesus was led by the Spirit into the wilderness to be tempted by the devil* (Matthew 4:1).

God does not just want us to hear His voice for ourselves but also be led by His Spirit. If God is telling us that we are to be led by His Holy Spirit and then He reveals it to us by the example of His own Son Jesus who had to be led by the Holy Spirit, there can be no other conclusion but that the Lord desires all of His people to learn how follow the leading of the Holy Spirit in this life.

When it comes to these basic leadings, some people have different terms and expressions to describe the way the Holy Spirit comes in on them. I have met people who would say they had a "leading" from the Holy Spirit to accept that job opportunity. Other people will often say that they felt or sensed an unction or prompting from the Holy Spirit to do something specific. These Holy Spirit leadings can be anything from a very gentle nudging, pulling, and burden to something that could be much stronger like a knot in the stomach or nauseated feeling.

There are times when I have felt a strong leading from the Lord, more like an uncomfortable feeling of urgency. It can get so strong to do something specific it will feel like the Lord has His large hand on the small part of your back pushing you forward. It feels like the wind at your back to move and navigate you into a specific or certain direction. Oftentimes, a person will feel or sense a very strong unction, a very strong prompting by the Lord to move in that direction without full understanding. However, if the Lord prohibits you to move in that certain direction, then you will sense or feel no leading or thrusting at all from the Spirit of God. When you think of moving in that direction, you will get a real flat witness from the Holy Spirit. There will be no inner witness to move forward.

Listening to the leading, prompting, or nudging of the Holy Spirit is clearly a powerful arsenal in the believer's life. Hearing the voice of God through these various ways is easy but unique in your own way. How God speaks to you may be different from how He speaks to someone else. The myriad ways He speaks to all of His people are similar but expressed differently depending on the spiritual maturity level of the believer.

Importantly, as Spirit-filled believers we must be sensitive to the Holy Spirit's warning signs and promptings. I believe we must be one with the Holy Spirit who has been sent to help us draw closer to the Father. The Holy Spirit is like a navigational system to help us to our final destination, reroute us if we make the wrong decisions in life, and allow us to avoid dangers up ahead. Being able to discern and pick up these types of leadings from the Holy Spirit is something that we can and will learn through a process of trial and error with Him. God wants to develop and train our Holy Spirit senses to adapt to the many ways God speaks and gets our attention.

God uses checks in our spirit to talk directly to us to prevent abductions, scandals, assaults, scams, financial losses, car accidents, plane crashes, train collisions, accepting wrong jobs opportunities, marrying the wrong spouse, connecting with the unhealthy, unproductive, and toxic relationships in this life, etc. As you can see, there can be an infinite number of situations where the Holy Spirit will tell you not to keep going in that specific direction. Here is a very good verse from the Bible where the Holy Spirit did exactly that for the apostles:

> *Paul and his companions traveled throughout the region of Phrygia and Galatia, having been kept by the Holy Spirit from preaching the word in the province of Asia. When they came to the border of Mysia, they tried to enter Bithynia, but the Spirit of Jesus would not allow them to* (Acts 16:6-7).

The Holy Spirit lets us know what's on the mind of God and communicates to us as well. At times, through our physical body He will let us know what God is telling us to do. Learning the voice of God will make our spiritual journey pleasant and fulfilled. After you have received a few of these leadings from the Holy Spirit, you can then become quite adept at being able to tell when a leading is coming in directly from Him or when it is coming in from your own natural desires and emotions.

86

OPPORTUNITIES

Be not deceived; God is not mocked: for whatsoever a man soweth, that shall he also reap. For he that soweth to his flesh shall of the flesh reap corruption; but he that soweth to the Spirit shall of the Spirit reap life everlasting. And let us not be weary in well doing: for in due season we shall reap, if we faint not. As we have therefore opportunity, let us do good unto all men, especially unto them who are of the household of faith.
—GALATIANS 6:7-10 KJV

One of the things that I know about the Lord is that He can open doors for us that no one can shut and shut doors that no one can open. God can advertise and promote someone better than we can ourselves or man could. An opportunity is a set of circumstances that makes it possible for someone to accomplish something. God is all about giving His people opportunities to do what He has called them to do. God creates opportunities for His people to fulfill His plan, will, and purpose for their lives. God speaks by opening doors and creating circumstances that give you a way to become and do all that you were born to do.

Hearing the voice of God is easy when something you've been praying for opens up suddenly. On the other hand, the opportunity can allow us to hear God to wait or proceed. Hearing the voice of God when in an opportunity can often be confusing depending on if an opportunity is something God opened or the enemy or yourself. We have to be cautious of certain open doors that are not in the plan and will of God. Having discernment is key to knowing what doors to walk through and which ones are not from Him.

Keep in mind that a good opportunity doesn't mean it's a God opportunity. I recall when I was applying for several different colleges after high school and I prayed and asked God to open the opportunity for the one that He wanted me to go to. I applied to six colleges and four rejected me and two accepted me. It was Marshall University in West Virginia and Delaware State University in Dover, Delaware. I attended first Delaware State University as a freshmen and transferred to Marshall University my sophomore year. Both universities were great for me, but I felt that God didn't want me to transfer but to stay local at Delaware State University.

After being at Marshall University for two years I heard the Lord say to transfer back home and withdraw. I was very upset because I loved Marshall. I wanted to play collegiate football—I had walked on the field and made it on the roster. However, it wasn't the will of God for me to play football but to graduate college at Delaware State University. God opened both opportunities, but I was supposed to hear God tell me specifically which out of the two was best for me. We have to pray and seek the Lord for wisdom when opportunities open up. The Lord is a good Father and knows what's best for us.

Even concerning employment, I applied for dozens of jobs after college to find out later that I was considered over-qualified. I was out of work for three years and needed income desperately. Nothing seemed to open up, and I went on a three-day fast. When I broke my fast on the third day suddenly a hiring manager called me. I didn't recall which job it was because I applied for so many; I couldn't remember the position either. They wanted to hire me for a part-time customer service position but I applied for full time. God spoke to me to go for the interview and He would do the rest.

I went in for the interview and after the interview was concluded they stated that they would call me in a few days. They also mentioned that they were looking to hire three people for the part-time position. In other words, they were going to take one full-time position and hire three people and make it part-time instead of hiring one person for a full-time position. I didn't want part-time but I needed something so I obeyed God. I didn't hear from the hiring manager at all as days and weeks passed by.

I suddenly heard the Lord say, "Go on a one-day fast," and I obeyed. I went on the fast and 24 hours later the same hiring manager called me apologizing for the delay and stated that they wanted to hire me for a full-time position instead of part-time because I was the best candidate out of hundreds of applicants. You see, God opened up an opportunity for me to work in banking when I had no prior experience in the industry. God opened the opportunity that man couldn't close. Hearing God's instruction to fast cause me to break through.

Working for that bank for eight years taught me a lot about how to discipline myself and be financially stable. God opportunities are not just a blessing for ourselves but for others as well. It was that job that gave me the able to turn my 525 bad credit score to a 748 great credit score. It was that job that took me from catching the public transportation to owning and paying off my car. It was that God opportunity that caused me to tithe, sow, and give to ministries and my own church to advance the Kingdom of God. God opportunities make way for other opportunities. Remember that Ecclesiastes 3:1 declares, *"To everything there is a season"* (NKJV). To everything there is a season that God will use to open up a divine opportunity for you. Have you ever heard the saying "It's someone's season"? This is what I call a divine opportunity of favor that God creates for a person who is obedient, faithful, and diligent to their calling, assignment, and purpose.

If you endure through the process and stick it out, your season will come. When your season comes, perpetual doors will begin to swing open effortlessly. Everything will begin to yield to you and you must take full advantage of the season of opportunity. God uses seasons in our lives to speak to us to prepare us ultimately for what is next. To prepare us for greater opportunity and harvesting seasons God must cultivate, groom, and polish us for the exposure He is bringing us into.

God has to test us and teach us in seasons of isolation, obscurity, and hiding before we are made visible, open, and exposed. Not every opportunity that presents itself is a God opportunity. The devil will lure people into opportunities of compromise, deceit, greed, perversion, sin, destruction, lack, temptation, and much more. God opportunities will impact and change the lives of others.

87

THE WORD OF GOD—BIBLE

Man does not live on bread alone but on every word
that comes from the mouth of the Lord.
—DEUTERONOMY 8:3

God communicates to His people through His Word. The Word of God is the only source of knowing the will of God. For someone who wants to know what's on God's heart and mind the Bible is the only reliable source of reference. Before I was able to hear the voice of the Lord prophetically through the Holy Spirit it was reading and studying the Holy Scriptures that caused me to understand God's ways, will, and plan for my life. It was the Word of God that allowed me to relate to many of the biblical characters just like you and me.

What is the Bible? The English word *bible* comes from *bíblia* in Latin and *bíblos* in Greek. The term means book or books, and may have originated from the ancient Egyptian port of Byblos (in modern-day Lebanon), where papyrus used for making books and scrolls was exported to Greece. Other terms for the Bible are the Holy Scriptures, Holy Writ, Cannon, Scripture, or the Scriptures, which really are called the sacred writings.

The Bible is compiled of 66 books and letters written by more than 40 authors during a period of approximately 1,500 years. The authors were prophets and apostles of the Old and New Testaments. Its original text was communicated in just three languages. The Old Testament was written for the most part in Hebrew, with a small percentage in Aramaic. The New Testament was written in *Koine* Greek.

Going beyond its two main sections, the Old and New Testament, the Bible contains several more divisions—the Pentateuch, the historical books, the poetry and wisdom books, the books of prophecy, the Gospels, and the Epistles. Even though the Scriptures were written in three different languages in the past, today the Bible is the best-selling book of all time, with billions of copies distributed throughout the world in more than 2,400 languages.

Believers hold their Christian faith, core values, and disciplines based on the Bible. A key doctrine in Christianity is the inerrancy of Scripture, meaning the Bible in its original, handwritten state is without error. The Bible itself claims to be the inspired Word of God, or "God-breathed" (2 Tim. 3:16; 2 Pet. 1:21). The Bible unfolds as a divine love story between the Creator God and the object of His divine love, which is man. Throughout the pages of the Bible we will discover and learn of God's interaction with mankind, His will, purpose, and plans from the beginning of time and throughout history.

The centralized theme surrounding the Word God is the ultimate plan of salvation, which is God's way of providing deliverance and an escape plan from sin and spiritual death through repentance and faith. In the Old Testament, the concept of salvation is rooted in Israel's freedom from Egyptian strongholds in the book of Exodus. The New Testament reveals the source of salvation through His begotten Son—Jesus Christ. Having faith in Jesus, unbelievers become believers and are saved from God's judgment of sin and its consequence, which is eternal death.

I believe to hear the voice of God through the Word of God you must first know who the Bible is all about. In the Bible, God reveals Himself to us. We discover His nature and character, His love, His justice, His forgiveness, and His truth. Many have called the Bible a guidebook for living the Christian faith. Psalm 119:105 says, *"Your word is a lamp for my feet, a light on my path."*

On so many levels, the Bible is an extraordinary book, from its diverse content and literary styles to its miraculous preservation down through the ages. While the Bible is certainly not the oldest book in history, it is the only ancient text with existing manuscripts that number in the thousands. In addition, this book is loaded with themes and supernatural stories that cannot be denied. Today, we have many different interpretations of Scripture by fallible men. It will take a spiritual-minded individual to interpret God's will. We need both the written, inspired Word of God, the *Logos*, and the specific prophetic Word of God that is the *rhema*. The Lord will speak to us daily as we read the Bible. We can experience both the Logos and the *rhema* word as we read the Word of God.

1. **Logos:** the entire written 31,173 verses of the Bible inspired by God given to man. We can see according to Second Timothy 3:16-17 that:

    All Scripture is God-breathed and is useful for teaching, rebuking, correcting and training in righteousness, so that the servant of God may be thoroughly equipped for every good work.

2. **Rhema** is a specific, right-now word from the Lord. It also a prophetic word released from the Holy Spirit, which can be a creative word or a single promise or phrase that has a special anointing for you for a specific time, purpose, and season. We can see that the word of God should be spoken so that:

    Man shall not live on bread alone, but on every word that comes from the mouth of God (Matthew 4:4).

The rhema (inspired word) of God is like a specific verse from the *Logos* (written Word) that the Holy Spirit has breathed upon just for us to take a look at. The verse or phase seems to become highlighted and jumps off the pages to speak to us specifically as a witness. When the Holy Spirit quickens a verse, we should stop and mediate on it, even speaking the verse aloud until it is made alive within us. We can hear the voice of God through reading and studying His Word. In addition, I believe there is power released in the rhema word of God when decreed, declared, spoken, and prophesied. God does communicate to us by speaking directly to you in both ways. The Bible is one of God's provisions to equip us to do His will (see 2 Tim. 3:16-17).

There are five simple and powerful ways of hearing the voice of God and learning how God communicates to us through His Word:

1. Read the Word of God.

2. Memorize the Word of God.

3. Meditate on the Word of God.

4. Speak the Word of God.

5. Live out the Word of God.

God's Word is alive; it is active in our lives. We are given revelation concerning God's will for our lives as we are in relationship with that revelation God unfolds to us. We must understand that the Word of God is an absolutely essential part of our Christian walk with the Father. We should never neglect or ignore His Word. It is one way that He speaks to us personally, powerfully—today (see 1 Thess. 1:5; 2:13).

88

CONCORDANCE
DEFINITIONS

I have found one interesting way God communicates is through concordance definitions. In studying or preparing a message to minister, I always use my Bible concordance to further my understanding of the subject. Hearing the voice of God through biblical resources is key to growing in your spiritual walk and relationship with God. A Bible concordance can be a helpful tool for studying the Word of God.

You may ask, "What is a concordance?" A concordance contains an alphabetical index of words used in the Bible and the main Bible references where the word occurs. A Bible concordance is useful in locating passages in the Bible. If you can remember just one word in a verse, you can often find what you're looking for. If I am preparing a message on the subject of love, I will not just rely on a Bible verse speaking on love; I will look at the index in the back of my Bible to find the word *love* to getting a better understanding. There are also Bible concordances that you can find online or in bookstores to purchase.

Through this method, God leads and teaches us to utilize tools for enhancing our relationship and understanding of His original concept. We must keep in mind when studying the Word of God that Bible concordance definitions are translation-specific; that is, different concordances are based on different translations of the Bible. A concordance for the NASB will not help you find much in the ESV, simply because those two translations use different English words. A parallel Bible, such as the KJV/NIV, will usually have two concordances in the back—one for the KJV and one for the NIV.

A good concordance will also help a believer with learning and becoming acquainted with the original language. As I study the Word of God and use *Strong's Concordance*, for example, each English word is assigned a number that corresponds to the original Greek or Hebrew word. The Old Testament (Hebrew) words are numbered 0001 through 8674; the New Testament (Greek) words are numbered 0001 through 5624. Strong's includes Hebrew and Greek dictionaries at the back of the concordance, allowing you to easily look up the meaning of every original word in the Bible.

Why use a concordance?

- A Bible concordance is a helpful tool when doing a word study. Using an exhaustive concordance like Strong's, you can locate every occurrence of the word in the Bible and gain helpful insight into what it means.

- A Bible concordance will assist you in learning various definitions of Greek, Hebrew, or Aramaic words.

- A Bible concordance is helpful when trying to locate a Bible verse, but you can't remember the chapter and verse.

How does a Bible concordance work? Perhaps you remember a verse about Noah finding grace in the eyes of the Lord, but you can't remember where it is found. You can look up *grace* in a concordance in order to discover the reference. Here is an excerpt from the entry for grace:

- Genesis 6:8: *But Noah found grace in the eyes of the...* (H2580).

- Genesis 19:19: *Behold now, thy servant hath found grace* (H2580).

- Genesis 32:5: *...my lord, that I may find grace in thy sight* (H2580).

- James 1:11: *For the sun is no sooner risen with a burning heat, but it withereth the grass, and the flower thereof falleth, and the grace...* (G2143).

When you look up the word *grace* in the Old Testament Hebrew in the concordance you will see H2580 חֵן chen. That means "grace, favor, gracious, pleasant, precious, well-favored." When you look up the word grace in the *New Testament Greek* in the concordance you will see G2143 εὐπρέπεια euprepeia—that means "grace."

God will speak to you with regard to what grace means and how to apply it in your life. We can use the example in the life of Noah as we hear God through the eyes of grace in the sight of God. There are times when I study the Word of God and God speaks to me through one highlighted word that blesses me. It further blesses me when I see that specific word in the concordance and the meaning and Scripture references are provided. So when it comes to the word *grace* we notice the verse you're looking for is Genesis 6:8, the one that mentions Noah. While you're at it, you can look up other instances of the same Hebrew word translated "grace." Notice that Genesis 19:19 and Genesis 32:5 have the same reference number in the right column. Those two verses use the same Hebrew word (H2580).

If I'm studying the word *grace*, I would look up the definition of the Hebrew word translated "grace" by using the reference number. At the back of the concordance, you will find this entry for H2580: "H2580 *chēn* from H2603 *chanan*; graciousness, i.e. subjective (kindness, favor) or objective (beauty): favor, grace(-ious), pleasant, precious, (well-)favored." Same with the Greek word translated "grace" by using the reference number G2143, *euprepeia*: "goodly appearance, shapeliness, beauty, and comeliness."

A Bible concordance, whether online or in print, is a valuable resource for any student of the Bible. It is a basic tool and is often one of the most used in Bible study. I am amazed at the guidance God gives us. By learning from God's wisdom and insight, we can live free from many problems that others experience simply because they don't know His Word. It is through the Bible that we learn who God is, what He values, how to trust Him. I have found a remarkable way to listen to the voice of God through the Bible.

89

BIBLE DICTIONARIES

G od will communicate through Bible dictionaries. There are times study-ing the Word of God that when I put in the extra time to find the true meaning of a word God would speak through the meaning. There is nothing like hearing the voice of God just by looking up a simple word for its original meaning. Oftentimes, we barely have time to just read our Bible, but a little time investment to look up a biblical meaning will bring divine revelation. Bible dictionaries bring clarity to what God is really saying in that time and culture.

When studying the Word of God there's no guarantee that acquiring more knowledge will translate to greater insights or to spiritual transformation—it takes a work of the Spirit God to accomplish that. But as Spirit-filled believ-ers we can position ourselves to be more open to spiritual growth and maturity. That's one reason I love Bible dictionaries because of the deeper search for truth and understanding of God's precepts and concepts. With a small invest-ment of time, you can reap major benefits.

What is a Bible dictionary? Bible dictionaries are concise reference tools that, at a minimum, provide a short definition of an English word. However, they can also give definitions of the original Hebrew or Greek words. Some provide added scriptural references, pronunciation guides, parts of speech, word derivations, synonyms, and brief contexts with supporting biblical references. There are also dictionaries for Bible names, subjects, places, backgrounds, his-torical charts, and themes.

Two of my personal favorite Bible dictionaries are the *Strong's Concise Concordance* and *Vine's Concise Dictionary* of the Bible and the *Holman Illustrated Bible Dictionary*—truly amazing resources for studying and going deeper in the Word of God. While there may be a few Bible dictionaries that are written specifically for Bible scholars, the most popular ones are easily understood by those with no formal theological experience and seminary training.

Some well-established dictionaries include *Strong's Bible Dictionary*, *Smith's Bible Dictionary*, *The Complete Word Study Dictionary*, *Vine's Expository Dictionary*, and *Thayer's Greek-English Lexicon*. Many dictionaries are free online from a direct site (ex: *Easton's Bible Dictionary*) or embedded in broader Bible study sites (such as Bible Gateway or Bible Study Tools). God will communicate through Bible dictionaries as we get in the habit of using them and utilizing the extra time to do the research.

While a dictionary won't provide an all-encompassing study and won't give you much context (other resources are available for that), it is a great starting point and is often all the extra information you need. Understanding God's message more clearly can help you see God Himself more clearly. The more you see, the more you'll love and want to share His love with others. So the next time you see an interesting word in your Bible reading, I encourage you to go look it up. See what new treasures you will find to build your faith to ultimately honor the Father

90

BIBLE VERSIONS AND TRANSLATIONS

God communicates to His people using different versions and translations of the Word of God for greater insight. Hearing the voice of God is not just hearing Him in prayer, fasting, and in worship but also in studying, reading, and researching biblical truth. Today, the Bible is available in about 600 languages worldwide, with thousands more copies of the Word of God in different translations or versions.

I used to ask, "Why are there several different English translations?" I have found it wise to have a more personal method in determining which Bible translation is more accurate or close to the original text. I personally use the English Standard Version, which is close to the King James Version. You want to use a Bible version and translation that is close to the original Bible manuscript and a translation and version that speaks to you personally. I like a the English Standard Version, *The Message*, and the New King James Version that makes more sense than the "thee, thou, and art" language. In my time of studying I would go to several different versions and Bible translations to get a more specific answer. Even writing books I always provide several cross references and different versions of Scriptures for the reader to understand my point, topic, or subject. There is nothing like hearing a sermon, reading a book, or studying the Word of God with biblical support in other translations.

Most people I mentor, cover spiritually, and relate to in covenant ask me as an itinerant prophetic leader and minister what version I would recommend to them. I share with them to use the one that make sense and is easy for them personally to understand. Some translations are harder than others to understand. I don't believe using only one version is good.

Here are a few Bible versions below provided by Mel Laurenz in his blog on BibleGateway for you to go and take a look at and find what best fits your personal study needs:

1. *New International Version* (NIV)—a standard translation using universally used English (thus, "International")

2. *King James Version* (KJV)—the classic 1611 translation that is a landmark in English literature, but far removed from contemporary English

3. *New King James Version* (NKJV)—a very literal translation, updating the language of the King James Version

4. *English Standard Version* (ESV)—an "essentially literal" update of the widely used Revised Standard Version

5. *Common English Bible* (CEB)—a new translation blending word-for-word and thought-for-thought approaches

6. *New American Standard Bible* (NASB)—widely seen as the most literal translation produced in the twentieth century

7. *The Message* (MSG)—a free paraphrase by Eugene Peterson using everyday modern English, idea for idea

8. *New Living Translation* (NLT)—an easy-to-read thought-by-thought translation from Hebrew and Greek[1]

God will use whatever version and translation speaks to you personally. The Lord will speak to you in your time of studying and reading His Word. There are a lot of different versions and translations today. However, there are some that take away a lot of the original manuscript of the Word of God. Be careful when purchasing a Bible.

NOTE

1. Mel Laurenz, "What About Bible Translations?" https://www .biblegateway.com/blog/2014/11/what-about-bible-translations.

91

CROSS REFERENCES

God can speak to us through cross referencing when you are studying the Word of God. The Word of God must be supported with other related Scriptures. When I speak a prophetic word to someone, God will give me several Scripture cross references to validate and establish His word. When I use multiple biblical sources when speaking a word to someone it raises their faith.

God wants us to go deeper in His Word, and like a treasure hunt we are to find pearls that are valuable for spiritual enrichment. How can a believer utilize the tool of a cross reference when they're studying the Bible? How can this assist them in hearing the voice of God and does this help in their spiritual growth?

Most Bibles have cross references in Scripture passages so that a person can look at the other Bible passages that relate to the one that had a cross reference on it. For example, the apostle Paul wrote in Romans 1:17, *"For in the gospel the righteousness of God is revealed—a righteousness that is by faith from first to last, just as it is written: 'The righteous will live by faith.'"* My Bible has a cross reference on Romans 1:17 to Habakkuk 2:4 and Galatians 3:11. Paul quotes Habakkuk 2:4, which declares, *"Behold, the enemy is puffed up; his desires are not upright—but the righteous person will live by his faithfulness,"* and repeats in in Galatians 3:11. The cross reference allows me to read other verses that mention the same thing.

Cross referencing is critical in building your case and bringing biblical balance. Moreover, I make it a habit to make sure that any and every topic I am studying is backed up and supported in the Old and New Testament. Cross references can add meaning to a Bible verse because we can also see where other authors have written the exact same thing or a similar passage. In the Gospels, when you study the Book of Matthew you can find cross references to Mark and Luke.

Different cross references shed more light or insight on a specific verse or topic. For example, the phrase *"the just shall live by faith"* (KJV) or *"the righteous shall live by faith"* (ESV) is found throughout the Bible in both the Old Testament and the New Testament. These multiple mentions in Scripture also show the importance of certain teachings because God often repeats important statements in His Word. When He does, we know that God is stressing the importance of certain passages. God repeats Himself by emphasizing something specific through cross references. Using cross references makes hearing the voice of God simple.

We must know that Scripture interprets Scripture. Martin Luther once wrote that "Scripture is its own expositor" and he was right. The authors of the Westminster Confession wrote that "The infallible rule of interpretation of Scripture is the Scripture itself: and therefore, when there is a question about the true and full sense of any Scripture...it must be searched and known by other places that speak more clearly." This speaks of the great value that Bibles with cross references have.

A good set of cross references, when used diligently and with intelligence, will make much commentary unnecessary. Some study Bibles base their notes upon cross references. They see the verse and compare it with similar verses that can explain difficult passages, which I often use when I am not clear on something. They are indispensable tools that the reader can use to broaden the meaning of verses that might be more difficult to understand if read alone. We are admonished by the apostle Peter to *"grow in the grace and knowledge of our Lord and Savior Jesus Christ. To him be glory both now and forever! Amen"* (2 Pet. 3:18).

Peter's conclusion is mine—to Him be all the glory, right now and for all time. *"His divine power has given us everything we need for a godly life through our knowledge of him who called us by his own glory and goodness"* (2 Pet. 1:3). That should be the divine objective when we are studying the Word of God—to learn how to hear the voice of the Lord in our everyday affairs. That is a worthy goal and one that fits graciously with the plan and purpose of God.

92

BIBLE HEADERS AND MARGINS

As a devoted Bible reader, I have come to realize that God will communicate through Bible headers and margins—in other words, the subtitles found in each chapter of the Bible. There is something prophetic when you are in need of the Lord's direction and suddenly open up your Bible and the page lands on a header that says "The Lord Your Shepherd" in Psalm 23. Have you ever wondered where the bolded section headings in the Bible come from? With the exception of the titles in Psalms, the Bible's authors didn't write their books of Bible with chapters or section headings in mind.

Bible headers were inserted later by translators in order to help organize, coordinate, and divide the chapters into easy to locate and digest pieces. There is something powerful about these section headings because the context of the chapter reveals the story and revelation that God wants us to know. In addition, headers, subtitles, and margins are given for us to reflect, meditate, and pause on what we just read.

The Bible headers are also used to bring a smooth flow and highlight specific parts related to the context or chapter. They are used for breaks and transitions to show when a topic has started or ended. Many great books use subtitles, headers, and transitional words to keep your focus, attention, and concentration.

You can see headings in most English translations of the Bible, though they do vary across different translations. For example, Genesis 1 starts out with a heading that says "The Beginning" in the New International Version and "The Account of Creation" in the New Living Translation. However, if you take a look in the King James Version you will notice that there's no header at all. A side-by-side comparison of Genesis 1 in five translations easily highlights the differences in section headings. In other words, the headers will say something slightly different.

These different types of headers or subtitles can bless you when you are personally going through something; writing a book, song, play, movie, or research paper; or preparing a sermon or message. I use headers to write inspiring devotionals and prayer starters. God will speak to us through them to make sense of the chapter and the substance provided. As you study and read the Word of God, start searching the bold chapter headers or subtitles and watch them minister to you. It will create an appetite to read that particular chapter. God will speak to you and you can use the margin footnotes to write down points drawn from Scriptures.

93

BIBLICAL TYPES AND SYMBOLISM

God will oftentimes uses types, shadows, symbols, examples, metaphors, allegories, and parables to communicate to His people. God speak to us symbolically through types and scenarios in the lives of biblical characters we can relate to. God will use their lives and events to get His point across. There are many symbols and examples in the Bible through which I have personally received answers to what was going on in my life at the time. Hearing God is easier than you think when you allow the Holy Spirit to illuminate the complex things and make them simple enough for a child to understand.

Typology is a special kind of symbolism. (A symbol is something that represents something else.) We can define a *type* as a "prophetic symbol" because all types are representations of something yet future. More specifically, a type in Scripture is a person or thing in the Old Testament that foreshadows a person or thing in the New Testament. For example, the flood of Noah's day (Gen. 6-7) is used as a type of baptism in First Peter 3:20-21. The word for *type* that Peter uses is *figure*.

When we say that someone is a type of Christ, we are saying that a person in the Old Testament behaves in a way that corresponds to Jesus's character or actions in the New Testament. When we say that something is "typical" of Christ, we are saying that an object or event in the Old Testament can be viewed as representative of some quality of Jesus. Jesus was the greater David, Moses, and Elijah in the New Testament.

His ministry was the fulfillment of the type of ministry, administration, and mantle David, Moses, and Elijah had in the Old Testament. God is raising up different types of Jesus's ministry today in every generation. We are mandated to fulfill the Great Commission and be the extension of the type of ministry in our generation like Jesus had when He was on the earth.

God has placed symbols in the Bible to help the reader to receive a fuller and deeper understanding and meaning. The Lord uses word pictures to give an illustration of what He is saying. God uses symbols to paint a word picture of the true meaning of His message. He will speak to us through symbols prophetically. There are seer prophets who speak symbolically often to share a message that God is showing them.

For example, I may share a word that God is going to use an individual as a key to open doors. The Scripture God gives me is Isaiah 22:22, which speaks of the keys to the house of David to open and shut doors. The person is not a key per se, but the key is a symbolic object used to communicate what God desires to do in that person's life. If you have studied the Bible, symbols are used often whether you are familiar with them or not.

94

BIBLICAL ALLEGORIES

But Jesus answered, "I tell you, if these become
silent, the stones will cry out!"
—LUKE 19:40 NASB

God communicate through allegories that reveal something specific to the reader that they can relate to. Hearing the voice of God through the life of a biblical character or leader is refreshing because they are human just like you. God uses allegories to paint and tell a beautiful story with a real message to bring about real results.

One may ask, "Well, what is an allegory?" *Baker's Evangelical Dictionary of Biblical Theology* defines *allegory* as "a popular form of literature in which a story points to a hidden or symbolic parallel meaning. Certain elements, such as people, things, and happenings in the story, point to corresponding elements in another realm or level of meaning."

An allegory can be used to deliver a broader message about real-world social issues and occurrences. Allegories have occurred widely throughout history and are expressed in all forms of art. They are used widely because they can readily convey complex ideas in ways that are comprehensible and appealing to readers. God uses them as His artistic way of explaining spiritual matters in an easily understood manner. Throughout the Word of God we can notice that allegories assist His people in understanding difficult ideas. God speaks to us this way for us to gain a deeper appreciation of the mysteries of God.

Galatians 4:21-31 gives an example of what an allegory looks like in Scripture. We see the apostle Paul uses the story of the children of Sarah (Isaac) and Hagar (Ishmael) and the images of the city of Jerusalem and Mount Sinai as a double allegory of two different covenants—one covenant of freedom (Isaac) and the other covenant of slavery (Ishmael).

God will use the allegories found in the Word of God compare or contrast points. Isaac was a son of covenant and Ishmael was not; his mother, Hagar, was not married to Abraham. With this double allegory Paul makes a contrast between those who are free in Christ when they are saved and those who are not in covenant and are still in bondage. Allegories and figures of speech are powerful when applied within the context of Scripture and Holy Spirit understanding.

95

BIBLICAL COLORS
AND NUMBERS

*They put a purple robe on him, then twisted
together a crown of thorns and set it on him.*
—MARK 15:17

*"Then Jesus was led by the Spirit into the wilderness to be tempted by
the devil. After fasting forty days and forty nights, he was hungry."*
—MATTHEW 4:1-2

God is a colorful God. He communicates to us through different colors. While colors have various meanings depending on the culture one lives in, I believe it's imperative to understand what the Bible speaks about them. There are biblical meanings that will help us comprehend what God is speaking through different colors. God's creation is immersed in a beautiful array of colors.

The rainbow is a sign of His covenant with man never to flood the earth again and depicts the diversity of God (see Gen. 9:13). Hearing the voice of God through colors and their meaning will open up your mind to the awesomeness of God's creation and language. Colors play a major and oftentimes unnoticed role in our lives. Colors can influence the way a person feels and thinks.

For example, I have a friend who laughs at my jokes and turns red in the face. Or at times when he isn't feeling good he appears to be pale looking or even yellowish. Interior decorators use a different array of colors to create an environment that is peaceful, serene, calm, and comfortable. When I was working in banking they would use the three colors on the bank's logo—blue, gray, and white. My office was very calm because of the blue and gray colors everywhere. I enjoyed coming in to work even when there was a hostile, high-stress environment. The colors around me would speak to me and bring calmness in spite of what was going on.

Colors can speak one way to one person and something totally different to another depending on ethnicity, culture, and background. For example, the color blue may bring solidarity to me but to another person it may bring excitement. In other words, a color that stirs up faith may trigger fear in someone else. God speaks to us in our own language, culture, and environment that we are familiar with and accustomed to. God is not color blind! He sees through our own cultural lenses as well. We shouldn't be color blinded when it comes to the many ways God desires to speak to us through other races, people, and cultures. God can and will speak through an array of things like the rainbow to express His love, mercy, grace, and heart toward His people.

The Hebrew word translated in the King James Version as "color" is *ayin* (Strong's #H5869), meaning "an eye" either figuratively or literally speaking. The powerful thing about this Hebrew meaning of the word *color* is that there are people who have different eye colors. I have seen green, blue, hazel, black, and other eye colors depending on race. According to the 1913 Jewish Encyclopedia and several Bible commentaries, ancient Hebrew had no specific term to describe the property of light we call colors. Although the King James Version lists various colors (bay, black, blue, brown, crimson, green, gray, hoar, purple, red, scarlet, sorrel, vermilion, white, and yellow), a precise translation of the underlying original language word(s) is difficult.

Below is a list by Jacob Olesen in his article called "Biblical Meanings of God"[1] where he provides a brief summary of the primary and secondary Bible colors:

1. **Amber**—Glory of God, judgment upon sin, endurance, and perseverance.

2. **Orange**—Fire of God, deliverance, passionate praise.

3. **Pink/Fuchsia**—Right relationship, divine connection, union, and equality.

4. **Scarlet**—Royalty, fine linen for tabernacle and sacrifice.

5. **Red**—Blood of Jesus, love of God, blood of lamb, atonement, salvation and sign of the times, oath and covenant agreement.

6. **Blue**—Heaven, Holy Spirit, authority, Covering, supernatural, dimensions, prophetic/prophecy, deep, depth, and spiritual realm.

7. **Purple**—Priesthood, kingship, royalty, mediator, wealth, and prosperity.

8. **Gold**—Glory, divinity, Kingship, eternal deity, foundation, altar, beauty, precious, holiness, majesty, righteousness.

9. **Wine**—New birth, multiply, overflow.

10. **Sapphire**—Law, commandments, grace, Holy Spirit, divine revelation.

11. **Turquoise**—River of God, sanctification, healing, New Jerusalem.

12. **Green**—Praise, growth, prosperity, new beginning, flourishing, restoration, life, fertility, good fruit, and rest.

13. **Silver**—Word of God, purity, divinity, salvation, truth, atonement, redemption.

14. **White**—Bride of Christ, surrender, harvest, light, righteousness, conquest, victory, blessedness, joy, angels, saints, peace, completion, purity, and triumph.

15. **Brown**—End of season, rags/filthy, people, flesh, carnal, pride, weary, and faint.

16. **Yellow**—Faith and Glory of God, anointing, joy or disease (negative side).

17. **Black**—Darkness, sin, Earth, affliction, humiliation, calamity, death, mourning, and mysteries.

Another powerful way that God communicates is through biblical numerology. Numerology is the study of numbers from a biblical base or standpoint. We must avoid the New Age approach to numerology like the plague. God is a God who knows how to count and uses numbers to get His point, message, and precept across. We know there is a book in the Bible called the Book of Numbers. He uses numbers for consensus, data, blessings, and other divine purpose that speaks of His vastness and infallible nature.

We try to figure God out but most of us cannot figure out basic Algebra, calculus, trigonometry, statistics, geometry, topology, logics, number theory, mathematical physics, computation, and the lists goes on and on. However, God doesn't want us to understand all of Him *per se* but to believe Him and that He is God. God is not requiring us to know everything about Him; it would be impossible to try to figure Him out, but we are required to be in love, fellowship, and covenant to believe and have faith in Him. God will use numbers to speak prophetic revelation to us.

I remember when I turned 22 years old the Lord spoke to me out of Isaiah 22:22: *"Then I will set on his shoulder the key of the house of David; when he opens no one will shut, when he shuts no one will open"* (AMP). In other words, God spoke a *rhema* (inspired word) through the *Logos* (written Word of God) in my current season. He used the number 22, my age, and Isaiah 22:22 as reference Scripture of encouragement. Later that year I went to college where other doors of opportunity that were shut before began to open because of the prophetic Word of God.

God is a God of numbers just as He is a God of colors. Students of the Word of God will use biblical numbers to reveal God's concepts, intents, and mind. Oftentimes, numbers have both a symbolic and theological meaning according to Scripture, and numbers we see in visions, dreams, and prophecy could reveal what God is speaking or planning to accomplish in the life of someone or even in a society, region, or the world.

Furthermore, numbers can have various meanings in Scripture. This is not a study of numbers but a summary of what biblical numbers briefly can convey to those who are children of God and Spirit filled. The objective of this section is not to offer you a complex study guide on numerology. The premise here is to shine light on what numbers mean biblically and give you a primer on biblical numerology so you can see how the Lord can and does communicate prophetically through numbers in the Bible to people just like you and me.

There are some prophetic books in the Bible like Daniel and Revelation that show a complex interrelated numerology system that provides a definite sequence or pattern. Most Bible scholars traditionally agree that the follow numbers below have either a literal or symbolic significance:

Number One (1): Scriptural significance: *"Hear, O Israel: The Lord our God, the Lord is one"* (Deut. 6:4 ESV).

Number Two (2): Scriptural significance: *"Two are better than one because they have a good reward for their toil"* (Eccles. 4:9 ESV).

Number Three (3): Scriptural significance: *"Jonah spent three days and three nights in the belly of the fish"* (Matt. 12:40).

Number Four (4): Scriptural significance: *"He will raise a signal for the nations and will assemble the banished of Israel, and gather the dispersed of Judah from the four corners of the earth"* (Isa. 11:12 ESV).

Number Five (5): Scriptural significance: *"And he directed the people to sit down on the grass. Taking the five loaves and the two fish and looking up to heaven, he gave thanks and broke the loaves"* (Matt. 14:19).

We can see from the brief list above that numbers can speak to us. God can speak to us through colors and numbers that are relevant to our time, culture, calling, and personality. Most of you have a favorite color or colors. What makes that particular color important to you? It's probably because that particular color stands out and it speaks to you personally. Numbers can speak and mean something to us as well. God speaks to us about colors and numbers that are biblically relevant and gives us a fuller meaning of them when we share them with others.

NOTE

1. Jacob Olesen, "Biblical Meanings of God," https://www.color-meanings .com/biblical-meaning-colors.

96

PARABLES

He said, "To you it has been given to know the secrets of the
kingdom of God, but for others they are in parables, so that seeing
they may not see, and hearing they may not understand."
—LUKE 8:10 ESV

God will communicate through parables in the Word of God to get a hidden truth across. Hearing the voice of God through a parable is revealed to those of the Kingdom of God. The mysteries of the Kingdom are given to those who are Spirit-filled and born-again believers. God uses parables to pitch a truth so that the truth is revealed or discovered. Keep in mind that both allegories and parables are symbolic messages that actually speak something else. God can and will use parables to relay a message symbolically to address something else more specific in its meaning.

In the Word of God Jesus's parables are some of the best examples of how the Lord conceals His treasures from the proud, arrogant, and conceited. Jesus told parables to demonstrate spiritual principles with natural illustrations. However, Jesus made it clear that He told parables so that people would not understand truth and become powerful. God does not want the prideful to be the powerful. Parables were told not to reveal truth, but to hide it. Jesus would hide the truth from the arrogant and give clues to the humble and meek.

What is a parable? A parable is a simple story in the Bible that illustrates or depicts a spiritual or moral lesson. It is recorded that there are about 35 recorded parables used by Jesus in the Gospels. Jesus spoke in parables often.

Why did He used parables when speaking? He would use them in order to share a hidden truth by illustrating that truth. They were teaching aids to His disciples. He would speak in parables to cause them to search out the meaning and specific truth found in them. Parables were like inspired comparisons or analogies.

In other words, Jesus would share an earthly story or scenario, providing a spiritual meaning. In the earlier part of Jesus's ministry He didn't use a lot of parables. Later, the disciples of Jesus asked Him why He used them:

> *His disciples came and asked him, "Why do you use parables when you talk to the people?" He replied, "You are permitted to understand the secrets of the Kingdom of Heaven, but others are not. To those who listen to my teaching, more understanding will be given, and they will have an abundance of knowledge. But for those who are not listening, even what little understanding they have will be taken away from them. That is why I use these parables, for they look, but they don't really see. They hear, but they don't really listen or understand"* (Matthew 13:10-13 NLT).

Jesus spoke in parables to those who would understand the mysteries of the Kingdom. In addition, we must know that a parable has a two-fold purpose:

1. To disclose a truth to those who desire to know.
2. To conceal a truth from those who are indifferent.

When I read a parable in the Synoptic Gospels spoken by Jesus, something awakens on the inside me to discover the truth in the parable. Understand that parables are presented to give spiritually minded people a spiritual nugget, key, or life lesson to implement. God speaks through parables to get His point of truth across to us. Parables in my opinion become like gold in a treasure box on the deep floor of the ocean. We must dive into the Word of God with the Holy Spirit's assistance to find the gold like a scuba diver.

As Christian believers we must not read a parable and think it's just a story; there is a supernatural truth and deposit that God wants to share with those who have spiritual ears to hear what the Spirit of God is saying (Mark 4:9,23). There are other analogies and parabolic language throughout Old Testament as well. There are prophets and prophetic people who speak parabolically in their prophecies. That is why with any prophecy and vision it must be discerned, backed, and judged by the Word of God. He who has an ear must hear what the Spirit is speaking through parables or analogies in the Bible.

> *But blessed are your eyes because they see, and your ears because they hear. For truly I tell you, many prophets and righteous people longed to see what you see but did not see it, and to hear what you hear but did not hear it* (Matthew 13:16-17).

Those who are hungry will search out the treasures that God has hidden for them. The Greek word for "hidden" is *kroop-tō* (Strong's #G2928), which means "that which is hidden; concealed, keep secret."

Here is an example of a parable and its truth hidden in the story. In Proverbs 20:2 it says, *"A king's wrath strikes terror like the roar of a lion."* The essence of parabolic language is to compare the roaring of a lion and a king's wrath that brings terror to the hearts of men. One of my favorite parables of Jesus is the five talents in Matthew 25:15-21:

> *To one he gave five bags of gold, to another two bags, and to another one bag, each according to his ability. Then he went on his journey. The man who had received five bags of gold went at once and put his money to work and gained five bags more. So also, the one with two bags of gold gained two more. But the man who had received one bag went off, dug a hole in the ground and hid his master's money. After a long time the master of those servants returned and settled accounts with them. The man who had received five bags of gold brought the other five. "Master," he said, "you entrusted me with five bags of gold. See, I have gained five more." His master replied, "Well done, good and faithful servant! You have been faithful with a few things; I will put you in charge of many things. Come and share your master's happiness!"*

The spiritual truth in this passage of Scripture is that we are to invest and reproduce ourselves. The talents distributed by the master to three individuals were to receive interest or to be used to bring in a profit. The talents were compared to money or currency. The two servants were able to multiply their talents; however, the other one did nothing and hid what was given to him. He was later judged for not profiting his earnings. In addition, he was labeled as wicked and lazy.

In the Kingdom of God we are commanded to reproduce, maximize, and make great use of what God has entrusted into our care. The moral lesson and spiritual principle in this parable is that that the faithful will be given more. And the lazy and unprofitable servant's gifts will be repossessed. God spoke to me through this particular parable, saying, "Hakeem, I have given you special abilities, giftings, and a call to bring impact and people unto Me." The gifts and call on our lives are to bless and win others to Christ.

97

THE INNER WITNESS

I speak the truth in Christ—I am not lying, my
conscience confirms it through the Holy Spirit.
—ROMANS 9:1

There is an inside voice that speaks to us through the Holy Spirit, which is profound. God communicates to His people through an *inner witness or inner knower.* This is another prophetic way God speaks that we can hear His voice. I remember speaking on the phone to a ministry friend and I was so into the conversation and forgot where I was that someone asked me to use my inside voice. To use my inside voice is to use different tone and volume. There is an inside voice through the Holy Spirit that bears witness with our spirit as children of God.

> *The Spirit himself testifies with our spirit that we are God's chil-*
> *dren* (Romans 8:16).

Romans 8:16 tells us that the Holy Spirit Himself bears witness in our human spirit that we are children of God. An inner knower is like a gut feeling or inner witness to something specific God is highlighting. The Spirit of God will bear witness with our spirit if something is of Him or not. Therefore, we must be sensitive to the inner triggers and "bells and whistles" that are going off in our spirit. Whenever the Lord wants to speak to me concerning a prophetic word that I just received or a Bible verse I just heard, the Holy Spirit's inner witness will give me a physical impression in my stomach.

There are times God will alert me about something He doesn't want me to do or places to go—I have this nauseated feeling. Hearing the voice of God through the inner knower or witness is easy to discern. God uses our physical body, normally our stomach, to draw us in to His heartbeat. With an inner witness or knower God will use our thoughts. Thoughts will just come to you out of nowhere through the Holy Spirit. A true Holy Spirit inner witness will come out of our spirit and not our imagination or carnal thoughts.

Keep in mind that thoughts can come from other sources. Go to the written Word of God to judge if it's God or another source. The inner witness is not usually a voice you hear but a peace, hunch, intuition, idea, or impression. The inner witness is used at times when things are weighting heavy on your heart. God will use your thoughts to speak to you through an inner witness. Romans 2:15 says, *"They demonstrate that God's law is written in their hearts, for their own conscience and thoughts either accuse them or tell them they are doing right"* (NLT).

Don't ignore what you feel in your gut or stomach concerning things you are asking the Lord about. Have you heard of gut feelings? Most people that have these gut feelings or gut knowings but don't realize that they may be the Holy Spirit's inner witness getting their attention. Usually, when I know that something doesn't feel right I have these strange gut feelings that tell me "proceed with caution" or "no!" In addition, God will also speak to you when you least expect it to bear witness to what He is doing in you and through you. Trust your inner witness by the Holy Spirit He is never wrong and will not lead you in the path of danger.

98

MOVIES, COMMERCIALS, AND ADVERTISEMENTS

Have you ever watched a movie, commercial, or theater play that touched you deeply that brought you to tears, joy, anger, excitement, or peace? There is something powerful in the message that the movie, commercial, or billboard advertisement conveyed to us. God can use and speak to us prophetically through these simple but profound methods.

I remember watching a show on *60 Minutes* of a man named Nick Vujicic born in Australia with no arms and legs. I watched this show of a person who didn't allow his disability to stop him from doing normal things that we so take for granted. He was able to cook, clean, swim, read, and so many things. Nick defeated the tremendous odds and proved many wrong. Watching the show brought tears to my eyes and I heard the Lord speak to me through Nick's life. His story inspired me not to give up and to break any laziness, complacency, and contentment.

God spoke to me through this show that I could overcome any odds set against me if I believe in myself and work hard to achieve what I want. I didn't need an Archangel Gabriel to come speak to me. I did not need God to give me a dream, vision, and speak audibly to get my attention. God used this show that revolutionized the way I see myself and shifted my way of thinking. If a man born with no legs or arms can live a normal human life with his physical disabilities, then what is my excuse?

I remember watching a one-minute "feed the children" commercial and I was moved by the Spirit of God to do something about it. I heard the Lord impress upon my heart to donate to the cause and it wasn't even a week later I received a release of a financial settlement of $20,000. The money was held up for three years in a litigation civil case, and as soon as I saw this commercial and gave my settlement payment was released.

God will speak to us when we are paying attention to the signs. I am not talking about supernatural signs in this chapter but signs like a billboard ad. I saw an advertisement on the highway that really ministered to me every day while on my way to work and it is interesting to me that God will speak through movies, commercials, and advertisements that we watch on television or hear on the radio. Most prophetic people reading this understand what I am talking about.

Oftentimes, God will give me a prophetic word of confirmation or revelation in a scene from a movie or a word that I hear in a commercial. There are times I receive my sermon messages after praying for God to confirm and lo and behold I would see something that stood out to me from a movie name, scene, commercial, or billboard advertisement.

There have been times when God would speak a word to me prophetically by a billboard advertisement. I recall a time I was looking for God to confirm for me to start a ministry but was uncertain of the timing. Next thing I saw while driving from state to state were different billboards saying, "Write the vision," or "The time is now to start your dream," or "Don't hesitate to start." God was allowing me to see those billboards that made sense to me in that particular season. The funny thing about it is that I would ride past those signs all the time but it meant something to me in that moment.

Those words on the billboards or movie theme can speak to us prophetically and personally to allow me to obey God's instructions. I will say that not all movies will speak to us by revelation or prophetic insight because there are movies that are clearly demonic. However, certain things in movies, commercials, or advertisements will mean something to us personally that we can relate to culturally, spiritually, economically, socially, and mentally.

Movies can move us emotionally to take a stand for something or make life-altering changes depending on the topic or subject. I love Marvel comic movies and the superheroes always stir me up to do good and fight against evil spiritually speaking. With anything like movies we must still discern and distinguish if it's God speaking to confirm or our own impulsive desires, needs, and cravings.

License plates, traffic signs, billboards, text messages, blogs, paintings, advertising mottos, slogans, logos, pitch phrases, websites, digital marketing, book trailers, etc. are unique ways that God will communicate to us prophetically by revelation through someone else. God takes the meaning of these things and applies them to our own situations. God uses these simple but practical things that we use daily to speak to us.

There was a time I was praying to the Lord concerning what I should do with regard to a particular job. All of a sudden I would see advertisement signs out of nowhere about banking positions "now hiring" or "apply today." I would be watching television and see all the commercials of banking jobs that were hiring. I would at times get on the Internet and see the same banking job postings saying *apply today*. God was confirming what I was requesting from Him in prayer. Finally, receiving the many obvious signs from the Lord, I finally applied at this bank in Wilmington, Delaware called The Bancorp Bank, which several weeks later hired me as a customer service representative with no banking experience.

God has a sense of humor and will use modern-day technology to speak to us directly. He will use what is holding our attention like our cell phones, social media, sports, etc. to intervene to talk to us. The power of multimedia and social media is a major marketing engine that just about anybody can share what's on their heart and mind. We are living in a progressive generation and time when God is speaking so clearly. The Gospel is preached around the globe from right in front of a computer without ever having to leave your home. The modern-day technology is reaching multitudes of people for Christ.

I remember praying about a particular state I wanted to minister in and had never been to before and I was praying for God to confirm what's next for me. Suddenly, throughout that whole week I kept running into vehicles that had Florida license plates. I reside in Delaware and everyone I talked to that week was from Florida. Later, I was invited to a prophetic conference in Orlando, Florida and throughout that same year I went to Tampa, Clearwater, Gainesville, and Jacksonville, Florida.

God can and will speak a revelation, insight, warning, and prophetic word through multimedia and modern-day technology. Movies, music, and other things can influence and impact us emotionally, spiritually, and mentally. Make sure that you use the power of discernment and quickening influence of the Holy Spirit to reveal to you what is and not from the Lord.

99

ANIMALS

*Then the Lord gave the donkey the ability to
speak. "What have I done to you that deserves your
beating me three times?" it asked Balaam.*
—NUMBERS 22:28 NLT

In the Word of God we see one instance of God using an animal to speak.
God opened the mouth of a donkey to speak to a stubborn prophet. The
interesting part about the donkey speaking to Balaam was that Balaam held a
whole conversation with an animal. I am sure many of us today would be very
afraid, surprised, awestruck, and amazed if our pet spoke to us in our native
language. If the Bible says that God used the mouth of a donkey to speak then
it must be taken literally. I know it is very hard to comprehend this because we
have never heard an animal speak. Just because we haven't experienced, witnessed, or heard it personally doesn't mean it's a myth.

I am not saying that you are to look for our dog, cat, or guinea pig to hold a
conversation with you. However, I wanted to point out for the premise of this
book that God can and has used an animal biblically to speak just as we see
the devil using a serpent to speak and deceive Eve (Gen. 3:13). I want to highlight that God will communicate to us today through animal's personalities,
character, abilities, function, and ways. He can speak to us to get a prophetic
revelation through the animal or your favorite pet.

Why did the devil use what God created, a serpent, to deceive Eve? The
enemy used the serpent because its cunning ability suited the devil's evil

purpose. Animals' characters and personalities can speak to us and give clarity to something. For example, when God was teaching and sharpening my gift of discerning of spirits, I would see a particular manifestation in an individual that was serpentine or snake-like. In operating in deliverance ministry I have seen people slither on the floor like a snake or have stubborn ways, rebellious like a mule or even a bull.

God uses animals to speak to us about characteristics and personalities. God might reveal to me that there are people who have a gossiping spirit like a dog that carries a bone or digs up dirt like someone digging up someone's past. An animal or reptile is not actually speaking but God will use their nature to speak to us to get an understanding. There is some allegorical, symbolic, and metaphorical insight that God will use to speak to us. However, we are not to ignore the natural ways of an animal.

I had a beautiful black cocker spaniel dog that was very protective and assertive. She would communicate to me in unique ways and I was able to understand her by her actions. In other words, I was able to know when she needed to go out, if she was hungry, sad, sick, etc. She was able to effectively speak to me through her actions.

One revelation I have learned through having a dog is that they are truly man's best friend—faithful, loyal, and committed. Once, I had an allergic reaction to something I put on my skin thinking it was lotion and my face blew up like a blowfish. I was very embarrassed and needed to take steroids pre-scribed by my doctor to get the swelling and inflammation down. Meanwhile, I wasn't feeling my best and I thought my dog would be frightened by my appearance. She came over and licked my face and was jumping up and down wagging her tail happy to see me.

The medication made me drowsy, but when I woke up my dog was lying right under me. She didn't see my flaws but knew my scent and that I was her owner. God spoke to me through this dog's unconditional love that He loves us unconditionally when we mess up and don't feel like we are His children. God used my dog to speak to me prophetically to receive insight to the heart of God. God will and can communicate to us through strange and unusual ways through animals and especially our pets.

Numbers 22 shares the famous story of the talking donkey. The pagan prophet Balaam practiced divination, among other things contrary to God's ways, and led Israel into a season of apostasy and was regarded as a greedy individual by Peter and Jude (2 Pet. 2:15-16; Jude 1:11). Moab's king Balak was afraid of the approaching army of Israel so he sent for Balaam by cursing God's own people. The Lord spoke to Balaam not to go to Balak, although God relented under the condition that Balaam would only prophesy what God had spoken. Meanwhile, Balaam disobeyed God's direct orders and got on his donkey and went with the princes of Moab back to King Balak.

The Lord's anger kindled against Balaam because God already knew his heart, intentions, motives, and rebelliousness. God sent an angel with a drawn sword to block Balaam's way. In the realm of the spirit the angel was present, but Balaam could not see him. However, his donkey could see the angel, and she tried to discontinue the journey by going off the path, crushing Balaam's foot against the wall and lying down on the path.

Angered by her abrupt behavior, Balaam started to chasten her with his staff three times. We read in Numbers 22:28, "*Then the Lord opened the donkey's mouth, and it said to Balaam, 'What have I done to you to make you beat me these three times?'*" Then Balaam and the donkey proceeded to hold a unique dialogue about the situation, with Balaam angrily berating the donkey, after which the Lord opened Balaam's spiritual eyes to see the angel with the sword and he suddenly understood why his journey was stopped. We can see clearly that there is no doubt that Balaam's donkey was able to speak. God caused her to speak and Balaam evidently understood what she said by his response to her after berating her.

Right after that Balaam's eyes were opened, the angel proceeded to ask identical questions to those that came from the mouth of the donkey—further evidence that God, not the donkey, was actually speaking both times. This is reiterated by Peter, who identifies the donkey as "*an animal without speech*" and who "*spoke with a human voice*" (2 Pet. 2:16). Whatever the method, the donkey was able to talk by a miraculous working of God's power.

I find it odd that Balaam didn't flinch about a talking donkey. He didn't hesitate about responding to her questions. Under normal circumstances the obvious reaction would have been for him to at least ask how she came to be speaking. The Word of God doesn't reveal to us why he didn't find it strange or awkward to be addressed by a donkey, but we do know something about his state of mind. First, he was in rebellion against the instruction of the Lord to not return to Balak. His own agenda caused him to go to Balak for his own purposes and not the purposes of God. He was once a genuine prophet of God now turned into a pagan false prophet of man.

Second, he lost the ability to think clearly and his anger caused him to beat her because of her refusal to continue down the path he set out. Anger has a way of curtailing rational thought, and perhaps Balaam was intent on exerting his dominance over the animal. He felt that she was rebellious by mocking him that made a fool of him. It's funny how he wanted her to do something she didn't want to do and God intervened, prohibiting them. But Balaam was rebellious and God gave him a taste of his own medicine.

A rebellious prophet became upset by a rebellious donkey. It wasn't until the angel opened Balaam's eyes to see reality that he relented in his anger against the donkey, listened to the angel, and repented. Numbers 22:38 discloses to us that Balaam went to Balak and told the king, *"I must speak only what God puts in my mouth,"* which just goes to show that the Lord can use anyone, even a talking donkey and a rebellious prophet, to do His will and speak His truth. Balaam heard the voice of God through a donkey. God will miraculously speak through whomever or whatever He chooses.

100

ARTS AND CRAFTSMANSHIP

God is the Master Designer and used His craftsmanship to create you and me and the whole universe. The Lord does speak through the arts and the power of His design speaks of His glory (Ps. 91:1). God is a Creator, Designer, Builder, and Father. He wears many hats, so to speak. As believers and children of God He has given us delegated authority in the earth over the works of His hands. What God created in Genesis was approved with a declaration that it was "very good." God signed off on what He had created and needed no one to approve, verify, and confirm.

Hearing the voice of God through artistry is remarkable in itself. God uses the pen of His Word to create such life, which is beautiful and supernatural. In Exodus 31, God was very particular about who He wanted to be His interior decorator. He chosen Bezalel and Aholiab to be skillful, anointed, and wise artisans who knows how to create things by hand. God speaks through arts and crafts. When you create or design something it takes skill. God is the Master Artisan because He created and formed us by His word and gave us charge over the works of His hand. The Lord will give skill to the skillful. In Exodus 31:6 NASB, The Lord said, *"In the hearts of all who are skillful I have put skill."* We can see that it is God who gives people the ability to do something well and gives them a skill set that is unique.

God loves beautiful things that represent His purity, holiness, and creativity. He desires that those who are gifted in this area express it through the arts. God speaks through the arts to bring glory to His name and deliver a message.

I have seen amazing murals on city walls, statues, and even graffiti done that is unique to see. God will speak through the arts and what He builds. When I go to large cities, the many different types of skyscrapers are breathtaking. I wonder how they are masterfully engineered and built by man. God has gifted us with these powerful gifts and abilities. But to see them in full manifestation is a wonder of God.

Look at Exodus 31 again: *"See, I have chosen Bezalel son of Uri, the son of Hur, of the tribe of Judah, and I have filled him with the Spirit of God, with wisdom, with understanding, with knowledge and with all kinds of skills"* (Exod. 31:2-3). Bezalel was chosen by God to oversee the work of the Tabernacle. He was the chief superintendent over the whole project that God employed him for. God knew who He wanted and put special abilities and skills within him to do the work. God filled him with His Spirit, skill, wisdom, knowledge, and understanding in all the workmanship. In addition, Bezalel was innovative, creative, genius, and master in the artisan field. God anointed him for the job and he needed to hear the voice of God to build what God wanted. Moreover, Bezalel and Aholiab both were used to design and build the ark and mercy seat in the tabernacle among other things (Exod. 31:1-11). Their creativity spoke of what God wanted to see as it pertains to every detail of articles of furniture and items in the tent of meetings.

Hearing the voice of God is through what you create, paint, write, sing, sculpt, and act. When God tells me to write a book He knows that I have the ability to finish and to become an author. Through the creative arts God will communicate what we see through the lens of it. Whenever I see a portrait, painting, statue, or building it conveys a message to the eyes of the beholder. God will inspire us through the Spirit of God to write, sing, build, etc. God is the one who allows gifts and skills to be placed upon those He will use. Furthermore, He will use the means of arts and craftsmanship to build and showcase His beauty, holiness, message, and love.

Without skillful builders, artists, and craftsmanship we wouldn't have homes to live in and clothes to wear. In addition, music is a form of art, and King David was a skillful musician himself to establish the order of worship. *"David also commanded the chiefs of the Levites to appoint their brothers as the singers who should play loudly on musical instruments, on harps and lyres and cymbals, to raise sounds of joy*" (1 Chron. 15:16 ESV). There is nothing like the Spirit of God upon you when you draw, paint, build, sing, play, and create something from concept to reality.

In First Kings 6, we see Solomon creating a temple for the Lord. In verse 4, "artistic frames" were made for the house. We can see that God is not just concerned about the house being established but the beauty of it as well. He is a master interior decorator just as He is a master architect. The Lord likes to be surrounded by beauty, glory, and power. God is glorified by beauty! I can only imagine what Heaven looks like because it's full of glory and His presence.

101

BOOKS AND TEACHING RESOURCES

One of the most powerful ways to hear and learn the voice of God is through impartation from equipping and training materials from leaders. Powerful books, teaching resources, and even furthering your education in the area that God called you to will enhance your ability to serve your generation. God will use preaching, teaching, and training products to assist us in our spiritual development.

There have been times when I have found myself in a dark place mentally and spiritually and I would put on faith-inspiring teaching from men and women like Joel Osteen, Joyce Myer, Myles Munroe, or Bishop T.D Jakes just to name a few. Their teaching would stir me and ignite a passion that was once burned out. Their teachings, among others, would awaken something on the inside of me that God was speaking through them. Through digital mass media we have access to a plethora of messages, ebooks, and resources to grow in our Christian walk. Interestingly, when I am led by the Holy Spirit to go to the archives of old messages taught by some of today's most influential Christian leaders, their messages always seem to speak to me when I am in my most challenging or faith-testing seasons.

I will be weeping, laughing, and rejoicing because through the message I hear God speak. Through the messages and demonstrations performed through A.A Allen, Smith Wigglesworth, Kenneth Hagin, William Brannem, John G. Lake, William Seymor, Bill Hamon, Leif Hetland, Bill Johnson, Bob Jones, Randy Clark, Guillermo Maldonado, and other generals of the faith the supernatural would be activated on the inside of me. There is something unique about the power of impartation that comes through books, CDs, DVDs, mp3s, audiobooks, videos, social media, and live streaming services. The world of technology is increasing and the access that we have to powerful information is remarkable.

God uses men and women in every generation to share insight into what God is doing. Furthermore, the Lord wants us to not just receive information but divine impartation and revelation by the Holy Spirit. In my arsenal I have hundreds of books by leaders on various different subjects, topics, and genres. I believe leaders are readers! We should be ever growing and learning. We must have a teachable and receptive heart toward the things of God.

Reading Spirit-filled books and gaining more understanding will further increase your knowledge and comprehension. There is a saying that "knowledge is power." I believe that statement is true when the knowledge is applied. God wants us not just knowing the truth but living by the truth. We must be in relationship with the revelation we receive from the Lord. I have seen how my prophetic anointing has increased when my vocabulary and knowledge increase in the Word of God.

Ezekiel had to eat the whole Word before he could ever prophesy the heart and will of God to a rebellious nation. As believers we should always want to grow in the knowledge of Christ and learn of Him. Oftentimes, I play teaching series from different types of leaders of my interest to broaden my spiritual capacity. I grow when I am submitted to learning from others. I am an author, speaker, business owner, and public speaker and I must sharpen my understanding daily to stay relevant, current, and innovative. Hearing the voice of God is easy when we are always at the feet of Jesus learning more and gaining wisdom.

Jesus was 12 years old in the synagogue with the Jewish teachers. They were astonished by Him and His ability to understand. The Lord is not raising up ignorant leaders and believers. He is not concerned if you are the smartest, brightest one in the room. The Lord is concerned about the hungriest, humblest, and most teachable in the room. God is looking for sons and students.

In other words, He is in need of sons and disciples who will reproduce Him to impact and change their generation for Him. Learning the voice of God is easy when we apply the Word of God to our own lives and make it a habit to walk in it by faith. We should study and learn often, which will increase influence, access, and favor our life.

ABOUT
DR. HAKEEM COLLINS

Dr. Hakeem Collins is an empowerment specialist, respected emerging prophetic voice, governmental minister, life coach, and sought-after conference speaker. He is known for his keen accurate prophetic gifting and supernatural ministry. He is the founder of Champions International, The Prophetic Academy, and Revolution Network based in Wilmington, Delaware, where he resides. He is the author of several books including *Heaven Declares, Prophetic Breakthrough,* and *Command Your Healing.* He has been featured on many television and radio programs including *Sid Roth's It's Supernatural, The Word Network, Cornerstone TV, The Atlanta Live, Elijah Streams TV, and GOD TV.* He is a regular contributing article writer for *Charisma* magazine and The Elijah List.